Assessment Sourcebook

THE UNIVERSITY OF CHICAGO SCHOOL MATHEMATICS PROJECT

PRECALCULUS AND DISCRETE MATHEMATICS

INTEGRATED MATHEMATICS

About Assessment
Assessment Forms
Chapter Quizzes
Chapter Tests, Forms A, B, C, and D
Chapter Tests, Cumulative Form
Comprehensive Tests
Answers
Evaluation Guides

Scott Foresman
Addison Wesley

Editorial Offices: Glenview, Illinois • Menlo Park, California
Sales Offices: Reading, Massachusetts • Atlanta, Georgia
Glenview, Illinois • Carrollton, Texas • Menlo Park, California

Contents

ISBN: 0-673-45921-7

123456—ML— 01009998

Pages	*Contents*

Tests

Pages	*Contents*

Answers
Quizzes; Tests, Forms A and B, Cumulative Forms; Comprehensive Tests

Evaluation Guides
Tests, Forms C and D

Assessing Student Performance in Mathematics

The Changing Face of Mathematics Instruction and Assessment

In the past decade, the National Council of Teachers of Mathematics and other mathematics education organizations and professionals have examined the methods teachers use to instruct students in mathematics and have recommended ways to improve this instruction. Their recommendations stress the importance of providing more diverse methods of instruction including activities, open-ended investigations, and long-term projects, many of which utilize cooperative learning. They challenge us to make the goal of mathematics the acquisition of the dynamic processes of critical thinking and problem solving, rather than merely the mastery of a static body of facts and procedures.

Instruction and assessment are closely linked. As instructional methods change, the methods of evaluation need to change. New forms of assessment being proposed provide a more authentic way of evaluating the depth of our students' knowledge of mathematics rather than their ability to memorize facts and procedures. These alternative methods of assessment offer students the opportunity to display how they approach problem situations, collect and organize information, formulate and test conjectures, and communicate their mathematical insights.

An authentic assessment program contains tasks that are appropriate to the topics the students are learning and that provide outcomes that are valuable to the students. Such an assessment program allows for such highly individual factors as a school's curriculum objectives, a teacher's style of instruction, and a student's maturity level and preferred learning style. Each individual teacher determines the assessment program best suited to the needs of his or her students.

In an instructional environment that demands a deeper understanding of mathematics, testing instruments that call for only identification of single correct responses no longer suffice. Instead, our instruments must reflect the scope and intent of our instructional program to have students solve problems, reason, and communicate.

NCTM Standards

To help a teacher select the most appropriate evaluation tools for his or her classroom, this *Assessment Sourcebook* provides the following materials. (See pre-chapter pages in UCSMP *Precalculus and Discrete Mathematics* Teacher's Edition for correlation of test items to chapter objectives.)

Assessment Forms

- student-completed forms
- teacher-completed forms for individual, group, and class activities

Assessment Instruments

- **Chapter Quizzes,** two per chapter, which cover three or four lessons and which contain mostly free-response items
- **Chapter Tests, Forms A and B,** which are alternate versions of each other and which test every chapter objective in primarily free-response format
- **Chapter Tests, Form C,** which consist of 4 to 6 performance-based, open-ended items, many of which assess several chapter objectives
- **Chapter Tests, Form D,** which are performance based and which often assess 5 or more chapter objectives as applied to a single larger task
- **Chapter Tests, Cumulative Form,** which contain mostly free-response items
- **Comprehensive Tests,** every three or four chapters, which are cumulative in nature and consist primarily of multiple-choice items

Precalculus and Discrete Mathematics © Scott Foresman Addison Wesley

To assess development of a student's mathematical power, a teacher needs to use a mixture of means: essays, homework, projects, short answers, quizzes, blackboard work, journals, oral interviews, and group projects.

Everybody Counts:
A Report to the Nation on the Future
of Mathematics Education

Guidelines for Developing an Authentic Assessment Program

Developing an authentic program of assessment is an ongoing process. Some assessment instruments will seem perfectly suited to the teacher and his or her students from the start. Others may be effective only after the teacher has had a chance to experiment, and refine them. Still others may be inappropriate for a given class or instructional situation. The following are some guidelines that may be helpful when choosing the types of assessment for a particular program.

Assessment serves many purposes.

- For the teacher, assessment yields feedback on the appropriateness of instructional methods and offers some clues as to how the content or pace of instruction could be modified.

- For the students, assessment should not only identify areas for improvement, but it should also affirm their successes.

- Traditional forms of assessment yield a tangible score.

Make the assessment process a positive experience for students.

- Use a variety of assessment techniques.

- Provide opportunities for students to demonstrate their mathematical capabilities in an atmosphere that encourages maximum performance.

- Emphasize what students *do* know and *can* do, not what they do not know and cannot do.

- Motivate students to achieve by using tasks that reflect the value of their efforts.

Authentic assessment focuses on higher-order thinking skills.

- Provides a picture of the student as a critical thinker and problem solver

- Identifies *how* the student does mathematics, not just what answer he or she gets

Provide assessment activities that resemble day-to-day tasks.

- Use activities similar to instructional activities to assess.

- Use assessment activities to further instruction.

- Give students the immediate and detailed feedback they need to further the learning process.

- Encourage students to explore how the mathematics they are learning applies to real situations.

Include each student as a partner in the assessment process.

- Encourage students to reflect on what they have done.

- Encourage students to share their goals.

Portfolios and Notebooks

A portfolio is a collection of a student's work—projects, reports, drawings, reflections, representative assignments, assessment instruments—that displays the student's mathematical accomplishments over an extended period. The following suggestions for use should be adapted to the needs and organizational style of each situation.

A student notebook should reflect the student's day-to-day activities related to the mathematics class. It may include a section for journal entries as well as sections for homework, tests, and notes.

Getting Started

- Provide file folders labeled *Portfolio*.
- Provide guidelines for notebook format.

The Portfolio

- The Portfolio can be used as the basis for assessing a student's achievements. The focus of the Portfolio should be on student thinking, growth in understanding over time, making mathematical connections, positive attitudes about mathematics, and the problem-solving process.

The Notebook

- The notebook is for "work in progress." The student should keep in it all class and reading notes, group work, homework, reports and projects, and various student assessment forms, such as *Student Self-Assessment*.

- Every two to six weeks students review their notebooks to determine the materials they would like to transfer to their Portfolios.

- The teacher also selects student materials for the Portfolio and includes any appropriate assessment instruments.

- The student completes the *About My Portfolio* form.

> **The opportunity to share mathematical ideas through portfolios can mark a real turning point in student attitudes.**
>
> *Mathematics Assessment (NCTM Publication)*

- Portfolios may include:

  student selected items from the notebook; a letter from the student about the work; a math autobiography; other work selected by the teacher including math surveys; various assessment documents.

Evaluating a Portfolio

- Keep in mind that portfolio evaluation is a matter of ongoing discussion.

- Set aside time to discuss the Portfolio with the student.

- Use the Portfolio when discussing the student's progress with his or her family.

- Use it as a basis for identifying strengths and weaknesses and for setting goals for the next block of work.

- Consider developing your own criteria for evaluating portfolios, for example, numeric scales.

Evaluating a Notebook

- Notebooks should be evaluated based on agreed-upon guidelines.

- Notebooks should be evaluated for organization and neatness, completeness, and timeliness.

- Notebooks may be evaluated every week, every chapter, or any time you feel is appropriate.

- You may choose to evaluate notebooks by checking items or by assigning numeric values to specific items.

Precalculus and Discrete Mathematics © Scott Foresman Addison Wesley

Using Free-Response and Multiple-Choice Tests

Teachers use written tests for many purposes. Particularly when it is objective-referenced, a test can be a relatively quick and efficient method of diagnosing the scope of a student's mathematical knowledge. Tests can also provide valuable instructional feedback. And, of course, grades are a traditional instrument for reporting student achievement to parents, administrators, and the community. This *Sourcebook* provides a large number of both free-response and multiple-choice items.

Free-Response Tests

A free-response test, sometimes called a completion test, is a collection of items for which a student must supply requested information. While free-response tests are generally designed for written responses, they may also be used orally with individual students, especially those with limited English proficiency.

Multiple-choice Tests

A multiple-choice test consists of many well-defined problems or questions. The student is given a set of four or five possible answers for each item and is asked to select the correct or best answer. The other choices, often called distractors, usually reflect common misconceptions or errors.

This *Sourcebook* contains:

- Quizzes covering three or four lessons in each chapter. The quizzes are primarily free response in nature.

- Chapter Tests, Forms A and B, which are alternate forms of each other and which test every chapter objective. The tests contain primarily free-response items, but they may also include several multiple-choice items. These tests can be used as chapter pretests and posttests to help implement needed individualized instruction

- Chapter Tests, Cumulative Form, for Chapters 2-13, which are basically free-response assessment

- Comprehensive Tests for Chapters 1-3, 1-6, 1-9, and 1-13, which consist of mostly multiple-choice items and are cumulative in nature

Using Performance Assessment

In order to provide more authentic forms of assessment, this *Sourcebook* provides two forms of chapter tests that focus on students' ability to demonstrate their understanding of mathematical concepts.

Chapter Tests, Form C

The Form C Chapter Test items help you make a judgment of the students' understanding of mathematical concepts and their ability to interpret information, make generalizations, and communicate their ideas. Each assessment contains four to six open-ended questions, each of which is keyed to several chapter objectives.

Administering Form C Tests

The tests can be administered in a way that is best suited for the students. Provide manipulatives, extra paper, and other tools as needed. The use of calculators is assumed.

- Use all the assessment items.
- Use only one or two, along with a free-response or a multiple-choice test.
- Use the assessment items to interview each student.
- Have students give the explanations orally, and then write the answers.

Evaluating Form C Tests

Each test item is accompanied by a list of two or more evaluation criteria that can be used as a basis for judging student responses.

To rate how well students meet each criterion, a simple scale such as this may be used.

+ excellent
✓ satisfactory
− inadequate

Evaluation Guides for these tests are found starting on page 191 of this *Sourcebook*.

Comparison of Form C Tests and Free-Response Tests

	Form C Tests	Free Response Tests
Number of items	4–6	15–35
Sample Format	○ Draw 3 different rectangles that each have an area of 12 square centimeters.	○ Find the area of a rectangle that is 4 centimeters long and 3 centimeters wide.
Mode of administration	○ Interview ○ Written response ○ Combination of interview and written responses	○ Written response
Answers	○ May have more than one ○ May require an explanation by student	○ Single, short
Scoring	○ 2–4 evaluation criteria given ○ Use of simple rating scale	○ One correct answer for each item
Benefits	○ More accurate determination of instructional needs and strengths of students	○ Easy to score

Precalculus and Discrete Mathematics © Scott Foresman Addison Wesley

The Form D Chapter Tests in this *Sourcebook* are composed of large mathematical tasks which allow students to demonstrate a broad spectrum of their abilities:

o how they reason through difficult problems;

o how they make and test conjectures;

o how their number sense helps them give reasonable answers;

o how they utilize alternative strategies.

These performance tasks also give teachers a means of assessing qualities of imagination, creativity, and perseverance.

Administering Form D Tests

Some Classroom Management Tips

o Whenever possible, use Form D Tests as cooperative group activities, listening as students interact in their groups.	o Have any needed mathematical tools or manipulatives readily available. The use of calculators is assumed.
o Ask students questions that will give you information about their thought processes.	o Be sure all students understand the purpose of the task. Offer assistance as needed.

Evaluating Performance Assessments

For each assessment, a set of task-specific performance standards provides a means for judging the quality of the students' work. These standards identify five levels of performance related to the particular task. The specific standards were created using the following characteristics of student performance as general guidelines.

Level 5: Accomplishes and extends the task; displays in-depth understanding; communicates effectively and completely.

Level 4: Accomplishes the task competently; displays clear understanding of key concepts; communicates effectively.

Level 3: Substantially completes the task; displays minor flaws in understanding or technique; communicates successfully.

Level 2: Only partially completes the task; displays one or more major errors in understanding or technique; communicates unclear or incomplete information.

Level 1: Attempts the task, but fails to complete it in any substantive way; displays only fragmented understanding; attempts communication, but is not successful.

Each test is accompanied by a set of teacher notes that identifies the chapter objectives being assessed, as well as the mathematical concepts and skills involved in the performance task. The notes also list any materials that are needed and provide answers where appropriate. Questions to guide students as they seek solutions are provided, along with ideas for extending the activity. These notes, along with the performance standards as described at the left, are found in the Evaluation Guides starting on page 192 of this *Sourcebook*.

Since performance tasks are open-ended, student responses are as varied and individual as the students themselves. For this reason, it may be helpful to use these general guidelines as well as the task-specific standards when determining the level of each student's performance.

Using Assessment Forms

Using Student-Completed Forms

To do meaningful work in our fast-paced and ever-changing technological world, students must learn to assess their own progress. This *Sourcebook* provides four forms that can be used to help students with self-assessment. Use one or more depending on the needs of your students.

Using Teacher-Completed Forms

This *Sourcebook* also provides ten assessment forms that are designed to help you keep a record of authentic assessments. Some forms are for use with individual students, while others are for use with groups of students. Determine which would be best suited for use in your classroom.

	Form	Purpose	Suggested Uses
Student-Completed	Student Survey	Checklist of student attitudes toward various math activities	○ Periodically monitor the change in student attitudes toward math
	Student Self-Assessment	Checklist of student awareness of how well he or she works independently	○ Monitor student progress in working independently
	Cooperative Groups Self-Assessment	Form for students to describe their attitudes and interaction with other students in a cooperative-learning situation	○ Completed at the conclusion of group learning activities ○ Completed by individual students or groups of students
	About My Portfolio	Form for student to describe the contents of his or her portfolio	○ Completed when student transfers work from the notebook to the *Portfolio*
Teacher-Completed	Portfolio Assessment	Form to assess student's mathematical accomplishments over time	○ Use to discuss student's progress in discussions with family
	Notebooks, Individual Assessment	Form to record student's organizational skills and completeness of assignments	○ Describe student's attention to specified daily tasks
	Notebooks, Class Checklist	Checklist to record students' notebook maintenance	○ Use when setting goals for improving study skills
	Problem Solving, Individual Assessment	Form to assess each student in a problem-solving situation	○ Describe level of student performance ○ Modify the level to meet individual needs
	Problem Solving, Class Checklist	Checklist to assess groups of students in problem-solving situations	○ Assess the entire class ○ Assess small groups over time
	Observation, Individual Assessment	Form to determine the student's thought processes, performances, and attitudes	○ Record observation of student in classroom
	Observation, Class Checklist	Checklist for observing several students at one time	○ Provide a mathematical profile of the entire class ○ Identify common strengths and weaknesses ○ Help in modifying content or pace and in determining appropriate groupings
	Cooperative Groups, Class Checklist	Checklist to assess students' abilities to work constructively in groups	○ Assess one or more cooperative groups
	Project Assessment	Form for evaluating extended projects or oral presentations	○ Evaluate an individual or group project or presentation ○ Prepare students for presentations or projects
	Overall Student Assessment, Class Checklist	Checklist summary of students' overall performance	○ Evaluate student performance over an entire instructional period

Precalculus and Discrete Mathematics © Scott Foresman Addison Wesley

Student Survey

Answer the following questions using the rating scale provided.

5 Always
4 Usually
3 Sometimes
2 Rarely
1 Never

_____ 1. I read material more than once if I don't understand it.

_____ 2. I use the reading heads and bold terms to help me preview the material.

_____ 3. I review for a test more than one day before it is given.

_____ 4. I concentrate when I study.

_____ 5. I try all the examples.

_____ 6. I do all of my assigned homework.

_____ 7. I pay attention in class.

_____ 8. I take notes and keep my notebook up-to-date and neat.

_____ 9. I bring the required materials to class.

_____ 10. I really try to get good grades.

_____ 11. I ask questions and try to get help when I need it.

_____ 12. I use the Progress Self-Test and Chapter Review to prepare for tests.

_____ 13. I make up work when I have been absent.

_____ 14. I look for uses of math in real life.

_____ 15. I can solve most problems.

_____ 16. I like to try new strategies.

_____ 17. I give up too easily.

_____ 18. I work cooperatively.

My favorite kind of math is _____

because _____

List some activities in which you have used math.

_____

_____

_____

Student Self-Assessment

Assignment _____

Complete the following sentences to describe your learning experience.

I was supposed to learn _____

_____

I started the work by _____

_____

_____

As a group member, I contributed _____

_____

_____

I learned _____

_____

_____

I am still confused by _____

_____

_____

I enjoyed the assignment because _____

_____

_____

I think the assignment was worthwhile because _____

_____

_____

Check the sentences that describe your work on this assignment.

☐ I was able to do the work.
☐ I did not understand the directions.
☐ I followed the directions but got wrong answers.
☐ I can explain how to do this assignment to someone else.
☐ The assignment was easier than I thought it would be.
☐ The assignment was harder than I thought it would be.

Precalculus and Discrete Mathematics © Scott Foresman Addison Wesley

Cooperative Groups Self-Assessment

Assignment _____

Reader: _____ Writer: _____

Materials handler: _____ Checker: _____

Others in group: _____

Materials: _____

Check the sentences that describe your work.

☐ We had a new idea or made a suggestion.
☐ We asked for more information.
☐ We shared the information we found.
☐ We tried different ways to solve the problem.
☐ We helped others explain their ideas better.
☐ We pulled our ideas together.
☐ We were reminded to work together.
☐ We demonstrated a knowledge of the mathematical concept.
☐ We encouraged those who did not understand.

Complete each sentence.

We learned

_____

_____

We found an answer by

_____

_____

After we found an answer, we

_____

_____

By working together, we

_____

_____

Precalculus and Discrete Mathematics © Scott Foresman Addison Wesley

About My Portfolio

Complete the following sentences about the work you are putting into your portfolio.

Describe the assignment.

_____

_____

_____

I chose this work as part of my portfolio because

_____

_____

_____

I began my work by

_____

_____

_____

Doing this work helped me

_____

_____

_____

The work was ☐ too easy ☐ easy ☐ just right ☐ hard ☐ too hard

because _____

_____

_____

Precalculus and Discrete Mathematics © Scott Foresman Addison Wesley

Portfolio Assessment

The work in this portfolio:

shows growth in the student's mathematical understanding.

exhibits the student's ability to reason mathematically.

makes connections within mathematics.

makes connections to other disciplines.

shows that the student is able to work on mathematical tasks in cooperative groups.

illustrates the appropriate use of a variety of tools.

Notebooks

Rate items, based upon your requirements, as follows:

\+ if excellent
✓ if satisfactory
- if needs improvement
NA if not applicable

Written Assignments   **Comments**

_____ **1.** Assignment sheet

_____ **2.** Daily homework

_____ **3.** Lesson Warm-ups

_____ **4.** Lesson Masters

_____ **5.** Activities

_____ **6.** Projects

Reading and Class Notes   **Comments**

_____ **7.** Definitions

_____ **8.** Properties

_____ **9.** Examples

_____ **10.** Class notes, handouts

Assessment   **Comments**

_____ **11.** Chapter Quizzes

_____ **12.** Chapter Progress Self-Test

_____ **13.** Chapter Review

_____ **14.** Chapter Tests

_____ **15.** Cumulative Chapter Test

_____ **16.** Comprehensive Test

Other   **Comments**

_____ **17.**

_____ **18.**

_____ **19.**

_____ **20.**

Overall Rating/Comments

_____

Precalculus and Discrete Mathematics © Scott Foresman Addison Wesley

Class _____

Rate each item as follows:
+   if excellent
✓   if satisfactory
-     if needs improvement
NA   if not applicable

Students	Date	Written Assignments		Reading/Class Notes		Assessment		
1.								
2.								
3.								
4.								
5.								
6.								
7.								
8.								
9.								
10.								
11.								
12.								
13.								
14.								
15.								
16.								
17.								
18.								
19.								
20.								
21.								
22.								
23.								
24.								
25.								
26.								
27.								
28.								
29.								
30.								

Problem Solving

Check each statement below that accurately describes
the student's work. This list includes suggested student
behaviors to consider. Feel free to modify it to suit your needs.

Reads carefully   **Comments**

☐ Looks up unfamiliar words
☐ Understands lesson concepts and can apply
　them
☐ Rereads
☐ Finds/uses information appropriately
☐
☐

Creates a plan   **Comments**

☐ Chooses an appropriate strategy
☐ Estimates the answer
☐
☐
☐

Carries out the plan   **Comments**

☐ Works systematically and with care
☐ Shows work in an organized fashion
☐ Computes correctly
☐ Rereads the problem if the first attempt is
　unsuccessful
☐ Rereads the problem and interprets the solution
☐ States the answer in required format
☐
☐
☐

Checks the work   **Comments**

☐ Checks by estimating
☐ Tries alternate approaches
☐
☐
☐

Precalculus and Discrete Mathematics © Scott Foresman Addison Wesley

Problem Solving

Class _____

Rate each item as follows:
+   if excellent
✓   if satisfactory
-     if needs improvement
NA   if not applicable

Students	Date	Looks up unfamiliar words	Understands the question/task	Uses information appropriately	Chooses an appropriate strategy	Estimates the answer	Is systematic and careful	Computes correctly	Rereads the problem if necessary	States answer in required format	Tries alternate approaches
1.											
2.											
3.											
4.											
5.											
6.											
7.											
8.											
9.											
10.											
11.											
12.											
13.											
14.											
15.											
16.											
17.											
18.											
19.											
20.											
21.											
22.											
23.											
24.											
25.											
26.											
27.											
28.											
29.											
30.											

Observation

	Usually	Sometimes	Rarely
Understanding			
Demonstrates knowledge of skills	☐	☐	☐
Understands concepts	☐	☐	☐
Selects appropriate solution strategies	☐	☐	☐
Solves problems accurately	☐	☐	☐
Work Habits			
Works in an organized manner	☐	☐	☐
Works neatly	☐	☐	☐
Submits work on time	☐	☐	☐
Works well with others	☐	☐	☐
Uses time productively	☐	☐	☐
Asks for help when needed	☐	☐	☐
Confidence			
Initiates questions	☐	☐	☐
Displays positive attitude	☐	☐	☐
Helps others	☐	☐	☐
Flexibility			
Tries alternative approaches	☐	☐	☐
Considers and uses ideas of others	☐	☐	☐
Likes to try alternative methods	☐	☐	☐
Perseverance			
Shows patience and perseverance	☐	☐	☐
Works systematically	☐	☐	☐
Is willing to try	☐	☐	☐
Checks work regularly	☐	☐	☐
Other			
_____	☐	☐	☐
_____	☐	☐	☐
_____	☐	☐	☐

Observation

Class _____

Rate each item as follows:

+   if excellent
✓   if satisfactory
-    if needs improvement
NA   if not applicable

Students	Date	Demonstrates knowledge of skills	Understands concepts	Works neatly and systematically	Works well with others	Asks for help when needed	Uses time productively	Displays positive attitude	Tries alternative approaches	Considers and uses ideas of others	Shows patience and perseverance
1.											
2.											
3.											
4.											
5.											
6.											
7.											
8.											
9.											
10.											
11.											
12.											
13.											
14.											
15.											
16.											
17.											
18.											
19.											
20.											
21.											
22.											
23.											
24.											
25.											
26.											
27.											
28.											
29.											
30.											

Cooperative Groups

Class

Rate each item as follows:

+ if excellent
✓ if satisfactory
- if needs improvement
NA if not applicable

Students	Date	Works with others in the group	Considers and uses ideas of others	Tutors and helps others	Has a positive attitude	Disagrees but is not disagreeable	Shows patience and perseverance	Works systematically	Initiates questions		
1.											
2.											
3.											
4.											
5.											
6.											
7.											
8.											
9.											
10.											
11.											
12.											
13.											
14.											
15.											
16.											
17.											
18.											
19.											
20.											
21.											
22.											
23.											
24.											
25.											
26.											
27.											
28.											
29.											
30.											

Precalculus and Discrete Mathematics © Scott Foresman Addison Wesley

Project Assessment

Project _____

Rate each item as follows:
+   if excellent
✓   if satisfactory
-     if needs improvement
NA   if not applicable

The Project

_____ Demonstrates mathematical concepts properly

_____ Communicates ideas clearly

_____ Shows connection to another subject

_____ Shows evidence of time spent in planning and preparation

_____ Is original and creative

_____ Includes charts, tables, and/or graphs where appropriate

_____ Uses available technology effectively

_____ Stimulates further investigation of the topic

_____ Includes a short written report if the project is a model or demonstration

_____ Lists resources used

The Oral Presentation

_____ Is organized (includes an introduction, main section, and conclusion)

_____ Uses audio-visual materials where appropriate

_____ Speaks clearly and paces presentation properly

_____ Answers questions and stimulates further interest among classmates

_____ Holds audience's attention

Overall Project Rating/Comments

_____

_____

_____

_____

Precalculus and Discrete Mathematics © Scott Foresman Addison Wesley

Overall Student Assessment

Class

Rate each item as follows:
+   if excellent
✓   if satisfactory
-     if needs improvement
NA   if not applicable

Students	Date	Class Work	Discussion	Cooperative Groups	Problem Solving	Homework	Notebooks	Projects	Tests		
1.											
2.											
3.											
4.											
5.											
6.											
7.											
8.											
9.											
10.											
11.											
12.											
13.											
14.											
15.											
16.											
17.											
18.											
19.											
20.											
21.											
22.											
23.											
24.											
25.											
26.											
27.											
28.											
29.											
30.											

Precalculus and Discrete Mathematics © Scott Foresman Addison Wesley

QUIZ

1. **a.** Rewrite the following statement as an ordinary English sentence:
   $\exists$ *a real number x such that* $x^2 < -x$.

   _____

   b. Is the statement in part **a** true or false?   **b.** _____

2. Multiple choice. Let $p(x)$ be the sentence $2x = 9$.   **2.** _____
   Which one of the following statements is false?

   (a) $p(4.5)$ (b) $\exists$ a real number x such that $p(x)$.

   (c) $\forall$ real numbers $x, p(x)$.   (d) $\exists$ a real number x such that $\sim p(x)$.

3. According to De Morgan's Laws, the   **3.** _____
   negation of $\sim p$ *or* $\sim q$ is equivalent to ___?___.

4. **a.** Write a logical expression that   **4. a.** _____
   corresponds to the network below.

   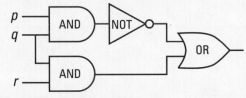

   b. If $p = 1$, $q = 0$, and $r = 1$, what is the   **b.** _____
   output of the network?

5. **a.** Write the negation of the statement $\forall$ *real numbers x,* $\frac{1}{x} \neq x$.

   _____

   b. Which is true, the statement of part **a** or   **b.** _____
   its negation?

6. The following statement is true:
   $\forall$ *real numbers x and y,* $x^2 + y^2 \geq 2xy$.
   Use the Law of Substitution to deduce that
   $\forall$ *positive real numbers k,* $k + \frac{1}{k} \geq 2$.

   _____

   _____

   _____

QUIZ

1. Write the truth table for the logical
   expression $p \Rightarrow q$.

   1.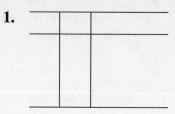

2. Consider the statement $\forall x, x < 5 \Rightarrow |x| < 5$.

   a. Write the converse of the statement.

   2. **a.** _____

   b. Which is true, the statement, its converse,
   or both?

   b. _____

3. *Multiple choice.* Which one of the following
   is logically equivalent to $p \Rightarrow q$?

   3. _____

   (a) $\sim p \Rightarrow q$ (b) $\sim p \Rightarrow \sim q$

   (c) p and $\sim q$ (d) $\sim q \Rightarrow \sim p$

4. Write the negation of the following statement.
   $\forall$ *real numbers a and b, if* $a^2 = b$ *then* $b - a > 0$.

   _____

5. Consider the argument:
   > *If a triangle contains one right angle, then it has exactly two acute angles.*
   > $\triangle ABC$ *does not contain a right angle.*
   > $\therefore \triangle ABC$ *does not have exactly two acute angles.*

   Is the argument valid? Why or why not?

   _____

6. Consider the premises:

   $\forall$ *positive intergers x, x is prime* $\Rightarrow \sqrt{x}$ *is irrational.*
   $\sqrt{961}$ *is rational.*

   a. Draw a valid conclusion.

   6. **a.** _____

   b. Name the form of the argument.

   b. _____

Precalculus and Discrete Mathematics © Scott Foresman Addison Wesley

CHAPTER 1 TEST, Form A

In 1 and 2, select the best description of the sentence.
    (a) statement   (b) universal statement
    (c) existential statement   (d) not a statement

1. *Some birds cannot fly.*   1. _____

2. $0 \leq x < 2\pi$ 2. _____

3. The following statement is true:
    $\forall$ *real numbers* $x \neq 0$, $x^2 > 0$.
    Use the Law of Substitution to show that
    $\forall$ *real numbers n*, $n^{200} > 0$.

_____

_____

In 4 and 5, match the argument with the appropriate argument form and indicate whether the argument is valid or invalid.
    (a) **Law of Detachment (modus ponens)**
    (b) **Law of Indirect Reasoning (modus tollens)**
    (c) **Law of Transitivity**
    (d) **Converse Error**
    (e) **Inverse Error**
    (f) **Improper Induction**

4. $\forall$ *real numbers x*, $|x| > 13 \Rightarrow x > 13$ *or* $x < -13$ 4. _____
    $\forall$ *real numbers x*, $x > 13$ *or* $x < -13 \Rightarrow x^2 > 169$
    $\therefore \forall$ *real numbers x*, $|x| > 13 \Rightarrow x^2 > 169$

5. *If a quadrilateral is a square, then its diagonals*   5. _____
    have equal length.
    Quadrilateral ABCD has diagonals of equal length.
    $\therefore$ *Quadrilateral ABCD is a square.*

6. *True or false.*   6. _____
    $\forall$ *real numbers x*, $|x| - x \geq 0$.

7. Write the negation of the statement in Question **6.**

_____

_____

8. Write the following theorem in an equivalent way using two *if-then* statements:
   The inverse of a function f is itself a function if and only if no horizontal line intersects the graph of f in more than one point.

   _____

   _____

   _____

9. *Multiple choice.* Identify the statement which is   9. _____
   the inverse of
   If the battery is dead, then the car will not start.

   (a) *If the battery is dead, then the car will start.*
   (b) *If the battery is not dead, then the car will start.*
   (c) *If the car will not start, then the battery is dead.*
   (d) *If the car will start, then the battery is not dead.*

10. Rewrite $0 \leq k < 100$, using the words *and* or *or*.   10. _____

11. *Multiple choice.* The statement $p \Rightarrow \sim q$ is   11. _____
    logically equivalent to which of the following?

    (a) *q or p*   (b) $q \Rightarrow \sim p$

    (c) *p and q*   (d) $\sim p \Rightarrow q$

In 12 and 13, consider the network below.

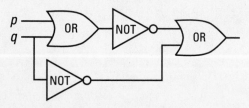

12. Write the logical expression that corresponds   12. _____
    to the network.

13. What is the output if $p = 1$ and $q = 1$?   13. _____

14. Write a truth table to show that $\sim(p \Rightarrow q) \equiv p$ and q

Precalculus and Discrete Mathematics © Scott Foresman Addison Wesley

▶ **CHAPTER 1 TEST, Form A** *page 3*

15. Consider the statement

∀ *real numbers x and y, xy > 0 ⇒ x > 0 and y > 0.*
Is the statement true or false? If true, explain why. If false, give a counterexample.

_____

16. Determine whether the argument is valid or invalid. Justify your reasoning.
If there is a severe frost, then the orange harvest will suffer. The price of orange juice will go up, if the orange harvest suffers. In 1998 there wasn't a severe frost. Therefore, in 1998, the price of orange juice did not go up.

_____

In 17–19, refer to the table below, which lists the states visited by Joan, George, Ibrahim, and Darla. Determine whether each statement is true or false.

	Joan	George	Ibrahim	Darla
Arizona		✓		
California	✓	✓	✓	✓
Florida	✓		✓	
Georgia	✓	✓	✓	✓
Illinois				
Vermont	✓			✓
Wyoming	✓	✓	✓	

17. ∃ *a person p such that p has visited Arizona or p has visited Illinois.*

17. _____

18. ∀ *states s in the list, if s was visited by Darla then s was visited by Ibrahim.*

18. _____

19. ∀ *states s in the list, ∃ person p such that p visited s.*

19. _____

20. Consider the following proof of the statement
If x² − 12x + 36 = x, then x = 4 or x = 9.
The conditional *r ⇒ s* is an instance of what universal conditional?

20. _____

Conclusions	Justifications
p: $x^2 - 12x + 36 = x$	Given
q: $x^2 - 13x + 36 = 0$	Addition Property of Equality
r: $(x - 4)(x - 9) = 0$	Distributive Property
s: $x - 4 = 0$ or $x - 9 = 0$	Zero-Product Property
t: $x = 4$ or $x = 9$	Addition Property of Equality

CHAPTER 1 TEST, Form B

In 1 and 2, select the best description of the sentence.
- (a) statement
- (b) universal statement
- (c) existential statement
- (c) not a statement

1. *No pigs can fly.*

    1. _____

2. *1 + 1 = 3*

    2. _____

3. The following statement is true:
   $\forall$ *real numbers a and b*, $a^3 + b^3 = (a + b)(a^2 - ab + b^2)$.
   Use the Law of Substitution to factor $(x^3 - y^3)$.

   _____

In 4 and 5, match the argument with the appropriate argument form and indicate whether the argument is valid or invalid.
- (a) Law of Detachment (modus ponens)
- (b) Law of Indirect Reasoning (modus tollens)
- (c) Law of Transitivity
- (d) Converse Error
- (e) Inverse Error
- (f) Improper Induction

4. $\forall$ *real numbers x, if x is not a solution to*
   $x^2 - 9x + 18 = 0$ *then x is not a*
   solution to $4 - x = \sqrt{x - 2}$
   3 is a solution to $x^2 - 9x + 18 = 0$
   $\therefore$ *3 is a solution to* $4 - x = \sqrt{x - 2}$

   4. _____

5. *All tea will heat up if placed in a freezer.*
   Jasmine places a cup of tea in the freezer.
   $\therefore$ *Jasmine's cup of tea will heat up.*

   5. _____

6. *True or false.*
   $\forall$ *real numbers x*, $x^2 - |x| \geq 0$.

   6. _____

7. Write the negation of the statement in Question **6**.

   _____

8. Rewrite the following theorem in *if-then* form.
   Having slopes whose product is -1 is a necessary condition for two lines to be perpendicular.

   _____

   _____

Precalculus and Discrete Mathematics © Scott Foresman Addison Wesley

9. *Multiple choice.* Identify the statement which is
the converse of
*If the temperature is not below 0°C, then it will
not snow.*
(a) *If the temperature is below 0°C, then it will snow.*
(b) *If the temperature is not below 0°C, then it will snow.*
(c) *If it will not snow, then the temperature is not below 0°C.*
(d) *If it will snow, then the temperature is below 0°C.*

9. _____

10. Rewrite $-10 < k < 5$, using the words *and* or *or*.

10. _____

11. *Multiple choice.* The statement $\sim p \Rightarrow \sim q$ is
logically equivalent to which of the following?

11. _____

(a) $\sim p \ or \ q$ (b) $q \Rightarrow p$

(c) $p \ and \ q$ (d) $\sim p \Rightarrow q$

In 12 and 3, consider the network below.

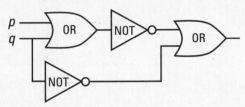

12. Write the logical expression that corresponds
to the network.

12. _____

13. What is the output if $p = 1$ and $q = 0$?

13. _____

14. Write a truth table to show that $\sim p \Rightarrow q \equiv p \ or \ q$.

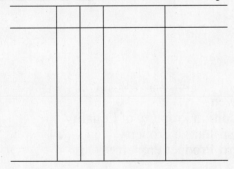

15. Consider the statement.
$\forall$ *real numbers x and y, xy = x $\Rightarrow$ y = 1.*
Is the statement true or false? If true, explain why. If false, give a counterexample.

_____

_____

16. Determine whether the argument is valid or invalid. Justify your reasoning.
There will be an increase in the number of allergy sufferers, if spring pollen levels are higher than average. If spring pollen levels are not significantly higher than average, then the preceding winter was not wetter and warmer than normal. The winter of 1998 was wetter and warmer than normal. Therefore, in the spring of 1998 there was an increase in the number of allergy sufferers.

_____

_____

In 17–19, refer to the table below, which lists the countries visited by Wilbur, Don, Carol, and Jamal. Determine whether each statement is true or false.

	Wilbur	Don	Carol	Jamal
Brazil		✓		✓
Canada	✓	✓	✓	✓
France	✓		✓	✓
Germany	✓	✓	✓	✓
Mexico	✓			✓
Spain	✓	✓	✓	✓

17. ∃ *a person p such that p has visited Brazil and p has not visited Spain.*

17. _____

18. ∀ *countries c in the list, if c was visited by Wilbur then c was visited by Carol.*

18. _____

19. ∀ *countries c in the list, if c was not visited by Don then c was visited by Wilbur.*

19. _____

20. Consider the following proof of the statement
If $8x + 60 = x^2 + 10x + 25$, then $x = -7$ or $x = 5$.
The conditional $p \Rightarrow q$ is an instance of what universal conditional?

20. _____

<u>Conclusions</u>	<u>Justifications</u>
$p:$ $8x + 60 = x^2 + 10x + 25$	Given
$q:$ $0 \quad\;\; = x^2 + 2x - 35$	Addition Property of Equality
$r:$ $0 \quad\;\; = (x + 7)(x - 5)$	Distributive Property
$s:$ $x = -7 \quad$ or $\quad x = 5$	Zero-Product Property

Precalculus and Discrete Mathematics © Scott Foresman Addison Wesley

CHAPTER 1 TEST, Form C

1. a. Write a statement that relates to algebra for each of the following.

  i. a true universal statement.
  ii. a false existential statement.
  iii. neither true nor false.

  b. For each statement in part **a**, write a negation if possible. If it is not possible to write a negation, explain.

  c. Identify each negation you wrote in part **b** as either true or false.

2. Clare's parents made two firm statements:

If you finish your homework, then you may go to the movies.

If you do not finish your homework, then you may not go to the movies.

Clare knows the statements are both true, so she reasons that the second statement is logically equivalent to the first. Use truth tables to explain why her reasoning is incorrect. Then write a statement that *is* logically equivalent to the first.

3. Below you are given the beginning of a logical argument.

If $z = 5$, then $z + 6 > 10$.

$\underline{\quad ? \quad}$

$\therefore \underline{\quad ? \quad}$

  a. Show two different ways to fill in the blanks to create a valid argument. Identify the form of each argument.

  b. Show two different ways to fill in the blanks to illustrate an invalid argument. Identify the type of each argument error.

4. Below are the "mixed-up" steps of a direct proof of a theorem from algebra.

  (i) $-(-x) + (-x + x) = [-(-x) + -x] + x$
  (ii) $-(-x) = -(-x) + 0$
  (iii) $0 + x = x$
  (iv) $[-(-x) + -x] + x = 0 + x$
  (v) $-(-x) + 0 = -(-x) + (-x + x)$

Rearrange the steps in the correct order to create the direct proof. Give a justification for each step. Then write a universal statement of the theorem.

CHAPTER 1 TEST, Form D

A student created a game called *Logical Shapes* that is played with a set of cards, each displaying one statement like those at the right. To score one point, a player must be holding two cards that are the premises of a valid argument and must state the conclusion of the argument and name the valid argument form that justifies it. The first player to score five points wins.

a. Identify two statements in the list that are logically equivalent to each other. Explain your answer.

b. Consider the statement *Some parallellograms are rectangles.*

   i. Is it an existential statement, a universal statement, or neither?

   ii. If possible, rewrite the statement using either *for all* or *there exists,* whichever is appropriate.

   iii. Does a negation of this statement appear anywhere in the list? Explain.

c. Suppose you are holding the cards with these two statements.

   If a figure is a quadrilateral, then it is not a triangle.
   Figure I is a triangle.

   What valid conclusion can you draw from these two cards?
   What is the argument form that justifies this conclusion?

d. Suppose you are holding the cards with these two statements.

   If a figure is a parallelogram, then it is not a rectangle.
   Figure A is a parallelogram.

   A student concluded *Figure A is a rectangle.* Do you agree? Explain.

e. Find two statements that allow you to arrive at a conclusion justified by the Law of Transitivity. What is that conclusion?

f. Find two statements in the list that support the conclusion *Figure B is not a rectangle.* What valid argument form justifies this conclusion?

g. Work with one or two other students. Using the given statements, make a set of *Logical Shapes* playing cards. Decide on a set of rules for playing the game. Then play the game until one student wins, keeping a record of all the valid arguments that have been made.

h. Write six *if-then* statements that can be used to create six additional cards for the game. The statements should be consistent with the statements on the existing cards. For example, a card that states *If a figure has three sides, then it is a rectangle,* is inconsistent with two cards that already exist. However, you may introduce a statement such as *If a figure has three sides, then it is not a quadrilateral,* since that does not contradict any given statement. If you wish, use another figure, and include statements about it.

If a figure is a parallelogram, then it is a quadrilateral.

If a figure is a rectangle, then it is a parallelogram.

If a figure is a quadrilateral, then it is not a triangle.

If a figure is not a parallelogram, then it is not a rectangle.

All triangles have three sides.

Some parallelograms are rectangles.

No figure with three sides is a parallelogram.

Figure A is a parallelogram

Figure B is not a parallelogram.

Figure C is a quadrilateral.

Figure D is not a quadrilateral.

Figure E is a rectangle.

Figure F is not a rectangle.

Figure G has three sides.

Figure H does not have three sides.

Figure I is a triangle.

Figure J is not a triangle.

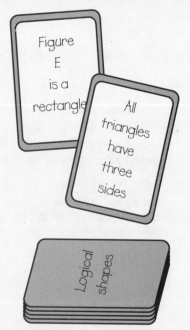

Precalculus and Discrete Mathematics © Scott Foresman Addison Wesley

QUIZ

You will need an automatic grapher for this quiz.

1. Consider the real function g with rule
   $g(x) = \sqrt{9 - x} - 2$. Use interval notation to
   describe the domain and range of g.

   1. _____

   _____

In 2 and 3, refer to the table at the right, which gives a circuit's output voltage V (in volts) and current I (in milliamps) as a function of time t (in milliseconds).

Time (t)	Voltage (V)	Current (I)
0	5.0	50.0
1	10.3	40.5
2	13.6	15.5
3	13.6	-15.5
4	10.3	-40.5
5	5.0	-50.0
6	-0.3	-40.5
7	-3.6	-15.5
8	-3.6	15.5
9	-0.3	40.5

2. Consider the function $C: t \to I$.

   a. Find the largest interval on which
      C is increasing.

      2. a. _____

   b. What is the minimum value of C?
      At what time does it occur?

      b. _____

3. If you map the set of voltage values to the set of current values, will it describe a
   function? Why or why not?

   _____

4. Consider the function h, where $h(x) = 5^x - 7$.

   a. What is $\lim\limits_{x \to -\infty} h(x)$?

      4. a. _____

   b. Give an equation of the horizontal asymptote.

      b. _____

5. A container manufacturer must make a rectangular box with a volume of
   500 cubic centimeters. The end of the box must be twice as wide as it is high.
   Let x be the height of the box.

   a. Express the length ℓ of the box as a function of x.

      5. a. _____

   b. Write a function that gives the surface area S of
      the closed box as a function of x.

      b. _____

   c. Use a graph to estimate the height that produces the
      minimum surface area.

      c. _____

QUIZ

You will need an automatic grapher for this quiz.

1. Consider an object whose position as a
   function of time is described by the
   parametric equations
   $$\begin{cases} x(t) = 4t - 6 \\ y(t) = 3t + 5. \end{cases}$$
   Find the coordinates of the object at times $t = 0$ and $t = 2$.

   1. _____

2. Suppose a volleyball is served at a height of 6 feet with a horizontal speed of 20ft/sec and
   a vertical speed of 15 ft/sec. The position of the ball's center as a function of time is
   described by the parametric equations
   $$\begin{cases} x(t) = 20t \\ y(t) = -16t^2 + 15t + 6. \end{cases}$$
   Will the ball clear the net, if the net is 9 ft high and 15 ft from the point of service?

   _____

   _____

3. Convert $160°$ to radian measure.

   3. _____

4. Consider the real function f defined by
   $f(x) = 7\cos(3x) + 2$.

   a. Give the maximum and minimum
   values of f.

   4. a. _____

   b. What is the fundamental period of f?

   b. _____

5. Consider the function $h: x \rightarrow 7(0.2)^x$.

   a. Use interval notation to describe the
   domain and range of h.

   5. a. _____

   b. Use limit notation to descirbe the end
   behavior of h.

   b. _____

6. On his first birthday, Stafford's parents invest $8,000
   for him in an education fund with an annual yield of 4%.
   At the same time, tuition at a local college is $8,000.

   a. How much will Stafford have in his fund
   when he enrolls at the college at the age of 18?

   6. a. _____

   b. If tuition at the college increases 6% annually,
   what will be the difference between the tuition
   and the amount in the fund at the time Stafford
   enrolls at the college?

   b. _____

Precalculus and Discrete Mathematics © Scott Foresman Addison Wesley

CHAPTER 2 TEST, Form A

You will need an automatic grapher for this test.

1. Let g be the real function defined by $g(x) = \dfrac{-4}{\sqrt{x-3}}$.

   a. Use interval notation to describe the domain of g.

   b. Use interval notation to describe the range of g.

2. Solve for x: $\log_2 4x - \log_2 3 = 5$.

3. Consider the function h: $t \rightarrow 5t^2 - 3t - 2$.

   a. Describe the intervals on which h is increasing and on which h is decreasing.

   b. Find any maximum or minimum values.

4. Consider the function g graphed at the right.

   a. Identify the interval(s) on which g is decreasing.

   b. Find any relative maximum or relative minimum values.

   c. Might the function be even, odd, or neither?

5. A supplier of computer memory chips finds that the number of chips N sold in a month depends on the price p dollars per chip, with $N = 23{,}000 - 1125p$.

   a. Express the monthly revenues $r(p)$ in terms of the price per chip.

   b. Find the price the manufacturer should charge in order to maximize revenues.

   c. About what is the supplier's maximum possible monthly revenue?

1. a. _____

   b. _____

2. _____

3. a. _____

   _____

   b. _____

   _____

4. a. _____

   b. _____

   c. _____

5. a. _____

   b. _____

   c. _____

6. If g is an odd function and $\lim\limits_{x \to -\infty} g(x) = 13$.
   what is $\lim\limits_{x \to \infty} g(x)$?

   6. _____

7. Consider the function $k: t \to 2 - e^{-2t}$.

   a. Use limit notation to describe the end
   behavior of the function k.

   7. a. _____

   b. Give equations for any horizontal
   asymptotes to the graph of $y = k(t)$.

   b. _____

8. Suppose that for a patient who takes 750 mg of a medication
   at a certain time each day, 30% of the drug still remains in
   the bloodstream 24 hours later.

   a. Write a difference equation for the
   amount A of the medication in the
   patient's bloodstream immediately after
   taking the nth dose.

   8. a. _____

   b. Estimate $\lim\limits_{n \to \infty} A_n$.

   b. _____

9. An athlete throws a hammer from a height of 4.5 feet with a
   horizontal velocity of 90 ft/sec and a vertical velocity 20 ft/sec.
   (Assume the acceleration due to gravity is 32 ft/sec².)

   a. Write parametric equations that describe
   the position of the hammer at time t.

   9. a. _____

   _____

   b. Use an automatic grapher to estimate
   the horizontal distance the hammer travels
   before hitting the ground.

   b. _____

10. Use an automatic grapher to plot the graph of $f(x) = \frac{1}{2} \sin (3x) + 5$.

    a. Give the range of the function f.

    10. a. _____

    b. What is the fundamental period of f?

    b. _____

11. A vial contains a 200 mg sample of cobalt-60, a radioactive
    substance with a half-life of 5.26 years.

    a. Write a formula for a function that
    expresses the number of grams of
    cobalt-60 left in the vial after t years.

    11. a. _____

    b. Approximately how many years will
    it take for the sample to decay to 60 mg?

    b. _____

Precalculus and Discrete Mathematics © Scott Foresman Addison Wesley

CHAPTER 2 TEST, Form B

You will need an automatic grapher for this test.

1. Let g be the real function defined by $g(x) = \dfrac{-1}{\sqrt{4-x}}$.

   a. Use interval notation to describe the domain of g.

   1. a. _____

   b. Use interval notation to describe the range of g.

   b. _____

2. Solve for x: $\log_3 9x - \log_3 5 = 4$.

   2. _____

3. Consider the function $g: t \to -7t^2 + 14t - 2$.

   a. Describe the intervals on which g is increasing and on which g is decreasing.

   3. a. _____

   b. Find any maximum and minimum values.

   b. _____

4. Consider the function k graphed at the right.

   a. Identify the interval(s) on which k is increasing and on which k is decreasing.

   4. a. _____

   _____

   b. Find any maximum or minimum values.

   b. _____

   c. Might the function be even, odd or neither?

   c. _____

5. Suppose a clothes manufacturer sells shirts to a retailer at a wholesale price p dollars per shirt that depends on the number N of shirts sold such that $p = 8.50 - .0025N$.

   a. Express the manufacturer's revenues $r(N)$ in terms of N, the number of shirts sold.

   5. a. _____

   b. How many shirts must the manufacturer sell in order to maximize revenues?

   b. _____

   c. What is the manufacturer's maximum possible revenue from the sale?

   c. _____

6. Let s be the sequence defined by the initial condition $s_1 = 8$ and the recurrence relation $s_n = .5s_{n-1} + 2$, for all $n > 1$. What is $\lim\limits_{n \to \infty} s_n$?

6. _____

7. Consider the function $h: x \to 5^{-x^2}$.

   a. Use limit notation to describe the end behavior of the function h.

   7. a. _____

   b. Give equations for any horizontal asymptotes to the graph of $y = h(x)$.

   b. _____

8. Suppose an ant farm is started with a population of 100 ants and each week the population increases by 10%

   a. Write a difference equation for the population P of ants in the farm at the beginning of the nth week.

   8. a. _____

   b. Suppose the ant farm can support only 2,000 ants. Assuming a Logistic Model, write a difference equation for the population P of ants in the farm at the beginning of the nth week.

   b. _____

9. An athlete throws the javelin from a height of 1.5 m. The horizontal velocity of the javelin is 29.6 m/sec and the vertical velocity is 9.8 m/sec. (Assume the acceleration due to gravity if 9.8 m/sec.²)

   a. Write parametric equations that describe the position of the javelin at time t.

   9. a. _____

   b. Use an automatic grapher to estimate the horizontal distance the javelin travels before hitting the ground.

   b. _____

10. Use an automatic grapher to plot the graph of $q(x) = 3 \sin\left(\frac{x}{2}\right) - 5$.

    a. Give the range of the function.

    10. a. _____

    b. What is the fundamental period of q?

    b. _____

11. In 1997, the population of Saudi Arabia was estimated to be about 20 million with an annual growth rate of 3.26%.

    a. Assuming a constant growth rate and a Continuous Change Model, express the population of Saudi Arabia as a function of the number of years after 1997.

    11. a. _____

    b. In what year will the population of Saudi Arabia first exceed 25 million?

    b. _____

Precalculus and Discrete Mathematics © Scott Foresman Addison Wesley

CHAPTER 2 TEST, Form C

1. Peter says that, no matter what the value of n, you need a calculator to evaluate $\log_3 n$. But Pam says that you *cannot* use a calculator to evaluate $\log_3 n$, because calculators only have keys for common logarithms and natural logarithms. Do you agree with Peter, with Pam, or with neither? Justify your answer.

2. The equations below represent the location at time t of a projectile fired from a cannon like the one shown at the right. Graph the equations. Then write a detailed description of the motion of the projectile.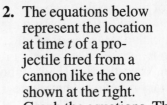

$$\begin{cases} x = 33.9t + 1.9 \\ y = -4.9t^2 + 19.6t + 1.1 \end{cases} \qquad 0 \le t \le T$$

3. Your parents have k feet of fencing, and they want to use it to enclose a rectangular garden. Explain how a function can help determine the dimensions of the garden that will give it the greatest possible area.

4. Write a real-life problem that can be solved by evaluating the nth term of a sequence. Then show how to solve your problem using either an explicit or recursive formula for the sequence.

5. Compare the characteristics of functions f and g graphed at the right. How are the functions alike? How are they different? State as many likenesses and differences as you can.

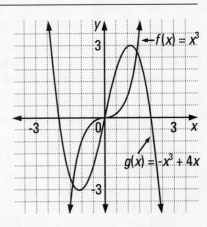

$\leftarrow f(x) = x^3$

$g(x) = -x^3 + 4x$

CHAPTER 2 TEST, Form D

You are a member of the school newspaper staff. This year, the *Math Spotlight* feature of the newspaper will include a series of articles called *Investigating functions*. Each article in the series will be an "investigative report" about one type of elementary function. The article is supposed to identify key characteristics of the function and some important applications of it.

At the right is a proposed article about quadratic functions. The editor knows there are errors and inaccuracies in this article and wants you to rewrite it.

a. The description of an equation of a quadratic function is not complete. How should it be revised? Explain why this revision is necessary.

b. The section called *Examine its graph . . .* implies that all the parabolas shown are graphs of quadratic functions. Is this correct? Explain.

c. Is it accurate to say that the domain of a quadratic function is the set of all real numbers? What about the range? Explain your reasoning.

d. The description of *Maximum (or Minimum) Value . . .* is correct. However, it is possible to give a more specific description of the maximum or minimum, and identify when each occurs. How can this be done?

e. Give a more specific description of:
  i. *Increasing or Decreasing . . .*
  ii. *End Behavior . . .*

f. The editor thinks there is not enough information about the application to physics. What information might be added to it?

g. The editor also thinks it would be helpful to show a second real-life application of quadratic functions. What additional application might you suggest?

h. Using your answers to parts **a** through **g,** rewrite the article so that it describes quadratic functions more accurately.

i. Write an original *Investigating Functions* article about either logarithmic or trigonometric functions. You may use the same format as the article at the right, or you may create a different format. Be sure to discuss all important characteristics of the type of function, and show at least two important applications of it.

Precalculus and Discrete Mathematics © Scott Foresman Addison Wesley

Math Spotlight

Investigating Functions

Quadratic Functions

How to Detect a Quadratic Function

Examine its equation . . .

Can you write it in this form? → $f(x) = ax^2 + bx + c$

Examine its graph . . .

Is it a parabola?

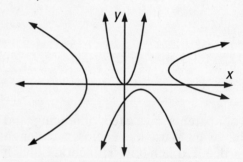

A Quadratic Function's *Modus Operandi**

Domain . . . the set of all real numbers

Range . . . the set of all real numbers

Maximum (or Minimum) Value . . . y-coordinate of the vertex of the parabola

Increasing or Decreasing . . . varies

End Behavior . . . varies

*That's Latin for "method of operating."

Where Quadratic Functions Lurk

In Physics . . . the height of a ball thrown upward →

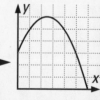

CHAPTER 2 TEST, Cumulative Form

You will need an automatic grapher for this test.

1. Solve for x: $3\log_9 2 + \log_9(x + 1) = 2$.

   1. _____

2. Use limit notation to describe the end behavior of the function f with

   $f(x) = 7 - \dfrac{1}{x^3}$.

   2. _____

3. Consider the following argument.

   *If an employee does not turn in a time card,
   then the employee will not get paid.
   Steve did not get paid.
   ∴ Steve did not turn in a time card.*

   a. Write the form of this argument.

   3. a. _____

   b. Is the argument valid or invalid? Justify your answer.

   _____

   _____

4. Consider the function h graphed at the right.

   a. Give the interval(s) on which h is increasing.

   b. Give the interval(s) on which h is decreasing.

   c. Estimate the values of any relative maxima or relative minima.

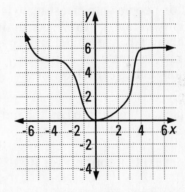

   4. a. _____

   _____

   b. _____

   _____

   c. _____

   _____

5. Compute the output signal for the logic network below for each of the following input signals.

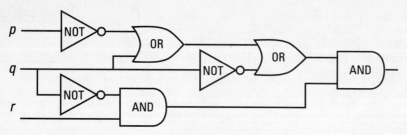

a. $p = 1$ $q = 1$ $r = 0$

b. $p = 1$ $q = 1$ $r = 1$

5. a. _____

   b. _____

6. Consider the universal statement
∀ real numbers x and y, $|x + y| \geq |x| + |y|$.
Is the statement true or false? If true, explain why. If false, give a counterexample.

_____

7. Convert $55°$ to an exact radian measure.

7. _____

8. Jamaica's population in 1996 was about
2.6 million people with an estimated
annual growth rate of 1.67%. Assuming
a Continuous Change Model and a constant
growth rate, estimate the Jamaican
population in the year 2016.

8. _____

9. The sequence V is defined by the initial condition $V_0 = 2$ and
the difference equation $V_{n+1} = V_n - .4V_n$, for $n \geq 0$.

a. Find an explicit formula for V_n.

b. Find the first four terms of V.

c. Find $\lim_{n \to \infty} V_n$.

9. a. _____

   b. _____

   c. _____

In 10 and 11, rewrite the given sentence as the appropriate universal or existential statement using *for all* or *there exists*.

10. *No government is efficient.*

_____

11. *Every state has at least one lake.*

_____

Precalculus and Discrete Mathematics © Scott Foresman Addison Wesley

12. Write the negation of the following statement.
No president was born in Wisconsin.

13. An athlete competing in the long jump takes off
from the fault line and travels according to the
parametric equations:

$$\begin{cases} x(t) = 25t \\ y(t) = 15t - 16t^2. \end{cases}$$

where t is the time measured in seconds and x
and y are the horizontal and vertical distances
traveled, respectively, measured in feet. If the
origin is the point from which the athlete jumped,
at $t = 0$, find the horizontal distance of the
jump to the nearest inch.

13. _____

14. Use interval notation to describe the domain
and range of the real function h with
$h(x) = \sqrt{81 - x}.$

14. _____

_____

Precalculus and Discrete Mathematics © Scott Foresman Addison Wesley

QUIZ

In 1 and 2, let f be the function $f: x \rightarrow \log x$ and g be the function $g: x \rightarrow x^2 - 1$. Find a formula for the given function and state its domain.

1. $\dfrac{f}{g}$

1. _____

    _____

2. $f \circ g$

2. _____

    _____

3. Is the inverse of the function $h: x \rightarrow \dfrac{e^x + e^{-x}}{2}$ a function? Justify your answer.

    _____

    _____

4. Solve $\ln (2t) = \frac{1}{2} \ln(4t + 15)$.

4. _____

5. Suppose that f is a 1-1 function which is continuous over the interval $(-\infty, \infty)$. Suppose further that $f(2) = -7$ and $f(3) = 5$. Prove that $f(4) \neq 0$.

    _____

    _____

    _____

    _____

Precalculus and Discrete Mathematics © Scott Foresman Addison Wesley

QUIZ

In 1 and 2, solve the inequality for all real number solutions.

1. $e^{-x} - 2e^x > 0$

1. _____

2. $m^2 - 8 < -2m$

2. _____

3. Find all zeros of the function f given by
   the rule $f(x) = 2\cos^2 x - \cos x - 1$

3. _____

   _____

   _____

4. **a.** Find an equation in x and y for the
   ellipse with parametric equations

   $\begin{cases} x = 3\sin t - 7 \\ y = 4\cos t + 2 \end{cases}, \quad 0 \le t \le 2\pi$.

4. **a.** _____

   b. What are the coordinates of the center
   of the ellipse?

   b. _____

5. The equation $x^3 + x^2 - 3x - 3 = 0$ has
   real solutions $x = \sqrt{3}$, $x = -\sqrt{3}$, and
   $x = -1$. What are the exact solutions to
   $(2x + 5)^3 + (2x + 5)^2 - 3(2x + 5) - 3 = 0$?

5. _____

   _____

   _____

6. Write an equation for the image of
   $y = \sin x$ under the scale change

   $S: (x, y) \to \left(\frac{2}{3}x, 5y\right)$ followed by

   the translation $T: (x, y) \to (x + 1, y - 4)$.

6. _____

CHAPTER 3 TEST, Form A

You will need an automatic grapher for this test.

In 1 and 2, let r and v be the functions defined by $r(x) = \sqrt{x}$ and $v(x) = e^x$, respectively. Find a rule and state the domain of the given function.

1. $r \circ v$

1. _____

     _____

2. $\dfrac{r}{v}$

2. _____

     _____

3. On the grid at the right are graphed the functions f and g. On the same grid, sketch the graph of the function $f - g$.

3.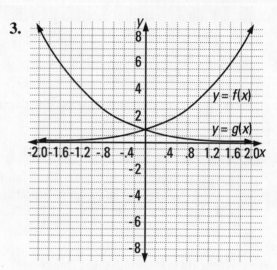

4. Solve for all real values of x:
$(x - 2)\log x = 7x - 14$.

4. _____

5. Is the inverse of the function $f: x \to 4^x$ a function? If so, find a rule for f^{-1}. If not, explain why not.

_____

6. Find an equation for the image of the parabola $y = 3x^2 - 2x + 5$ under the rubberband transformation
$R: (x, y) \to \left(\frac{1}{5}x, 2y + 4\right)$.

6. _____

7. Solve for all real values of z:
$\left|\frac{1}{4}z - 6\right| < 2$.

7. _____

In 8 and 9, the real function f is continuous on the set of real numbers and has exactly three real zeros. The table at the right shows values of $f(x)$ for selected values of x. Indicate whether the given statement's truth value is true, false, or impossible to determine.

x	$f(x)$
-10.0	24.7
-9.5	16.3
-9.0	2.1
-8.5	-3.8
-8.0	-4.8
-7.5	5.6
-7.0	27.0
-6.5	-48.2
-6.0	-0.6
-5.5	-1.2

8. $\exists\, x$ *such that* $-9.5 < x < -8.5$ *and* $f(x) = 0$.

8. _____

9. $f(0) > 0$

9. _____

10. *Multiple choice.* Which of the following is the largest interval over which the function $h: x \to \lceil 4x \rceil$ is continuous?

10. _____

(a) $(.75, 1]$ (b) $(.25, 1]$

(c) $[0, 1]$ (d) $(.5, 1]$

11. Solve for all real values of r:
$$\frac{1}{2r^2 - 7r + 6} = \frac{1}{r^2 + r - 6}.$$

11. _____

12. *Multiple choice.* Applying which one of the following functions to both sides of $f(x) > g(x)$ would preserve the sense of the inequality?

12. _____

(a) $h(x) = -2x^3$ (b) $k(x) = -3x + 2$

(c) $m(x) = .5^x$ (d) $r(x) = \sqrt[5]{x}$

13. Find intervals of length .02 that contain the zeros of the function $f(x) = x^{2.35} - 9 \ln x$.

13. _____

14. A clinical study is being conducted to assess the relative effectiveness of two new drugs in the treatment of cancer. Drug X is administered in a single 500 mg dose and has a half-life in the bloodstream of 32 hrs. Drug Y is administered in a single 700 mg dose and has a half-life in the bloodstream of 25 hrs. How many hours will it take for the concentration of drug X to drop below the concentration of drug Y?

14. _____

15. If an object emitting light at a frequency f is moving toward an observer at a velocity v, then the light's frequency f' as seen by the observer is related to the frequency emitted by the object by the relativistic Doppler shift formula

$$f' = f \cdot \frac{1 + \frac{v}{c}}{\sqrt{1 - \left(\frac{v}{c}\right)^2}}$$

where c is the speed of light. Find the velocity, in terms of the speed of light, at which the observed frequency is twice the emitted frequency.

15. _____

16. The cost C for a manufacturer to produce u units of a new light bulb is given by the function $C(u) = 75{,}000 + .45u$. The manufacturer conducts market research which shows that the number of units sold S is related to the price p by the function $S(p) = 250{,}000 - 86000p$.

16. a.

a. Find a formula for $C \circ S$.

b. What does the function $C \circ S$ represent?

_____

c. Find a formula for the revenue R as a function of the price p.

c. _____

d. Find a formula for the function $F = R - C \circ S$.

d. _____

e. What does the function F represent?

_____

Precalculus and Discrete Mathematics © Scott Foresman Addison Wesley

CHAPTER 3 TEST, Form B

You will need an automatic grapher for this test.

In 1 and 2, let r and v be the functions defined by $r(x) = \sqrt{x}$ and $v(x) = \ln x$, respectively. Find a rule and state the domain of the given function.

1. $v \circ r$

1. _____

   _____

2. $r \circ v$

2. _____

   _____

3. On the grid at the right are graphed the functions f and g. On the same grid, sketch the graph of the function $f + g$.

3.

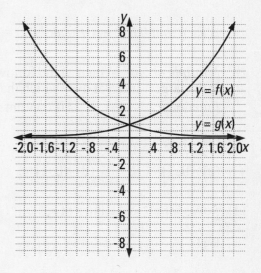

4. Solve for all real values of k:
   $k^6 + 6k^3 = 7$.

4. _____

5. Is the inverse of the function $f: x \rightarrow e^{|x|}$ a function? If so, find a rule for f^{-1}. If not, explain why not.

   _____

6. Find an equation for the image of the graph of $y = |x|$ under the rubberband transformation $R: (x, y) \rightarrow \left(\frac{2}{3}x - 2, y + 6\right)$.

6. _____

7. Solve for all real values of x:
$2x^3 + 3x^2 > 2x$.

7. _____

In 8 and 9, the real function f is continuous on the set of real numbers and has exactly two real zeros. The table at the right shows values of $f(x)$ for selected values of x. Indicate whether the given statement's truth value is true, false, or impossible to determine.

x	$f(x)$
0.0	6.7
0.2	9.4
0.4	12.7
0.6	5.3
0.8	4.2
1.0	-2.8
1.2	-2.0
1.4	-0.6
1.6	-1.0
1.8	2.8
2.0	7.4

8. $\forall\, x,\ 1.2 < x < 1.6 \Rightarrow f(x) < 0$

8. _____

9. $\exists$ *such that* $0.8 < x < 1.0$ *and* $f(x) = 0$

9. _____

10. *Multiple choice.* Which of the following is the largest interval over which the function $h: x \to \lfloor x + 1 \rfloor$ is continuous?

10. _____

(a) $(0, 1)$ 　　　(b) $[0, 1)$

(c) $[0, 1]$ 　　　(d) $(0, 1]$

11. Solve for all real values of r:
$$\frac{1}{\log(r^2 - 3)} = \frac{1}{\log(5r - 9)}.$$

11. _____

12. *Multiple choice.* Applying which one of the following functions to both sides of $f(x) < g(x)$ would reverse the sense of the inequality?

12. _____

(a) $h(x) = x^3$ 　　　(b) $m(x) = 4x$

(c) $v(x) = e^{-x}$ 　　　(d) $k(x) = \sqrt[3]{x}$

13. Find intervals of length .02 that contain the solutions to the equation $x + x^2 + x^3 + x^4 = 1$.

13. _____

Precalculus and Discrete Mathematics © Scott Foresman Addison Wesley

14. In 1998, the population of Ecuador was approximately 11.7 million and increasing at an annual rate of about 1.9%. In 1998, Chile's population was approximately 14.5 million and increasing at an annual rate of 1.2%. Assuming the growth rates for both countries remain constant, approximately how many years will it take for Ecuador's population to exceed Chile's?

14. _____

15. If an object emitting light at a frequency f is moving away from an observer at a velocity v, then the light's observed frequency f' is related to the frequency emitted by the object by the relativistic Doppler shift formula

$$f' = f \cdot \frac{1 - \frac{v}{c}}{\sqrt{1 - \left(\frac{v}{c}\right)^2}}$$

where c is the speed of light. Find the velocity, in terms of the speed of light, at which the observed frequency is two-thirds the emitted frequency.

15. _____

16. The cost C for a manufacturer to produce u units of a new thermometer is given by the function $C(u) = 30{,}000 + 1.25u$. The manufacturer conducts market research which shows that the number of units sold S is related to the price p by the function $S(p) = 8{,}000 - 2500p$.

16. a. _____

a. Find a formula for $C \circ S$.

b. What does the function $C \circ S$ represent?

_____

c. Find a formula for the revenue R as a function of the price p.

c. _____

d. Find a formula for the function $F = R - C \circ S$.

d. _____

e. What does the function F represent?

_____

CHAPTER 3 TEST, Form C

1. **a.** $\forall x$, let $f(x) = x^2$ and let $g(x) = \frac{1}{x}$.
  Show that $f \circ g = g \circ f$.
  b. Identify a third function h for which
  $f \circ h \neq h \circ f$. Give simplified formulas
  for $f \circ h$ and $h \circ f$.

2. Your friend was absent when the class
  studied equation-solving and has asked
  you this question: Why is it that taking the
  logarithm of each side of an exponential
  equation is reversible, while taking the
  square root of each side of a quadratic
  equation is nonreversible? Write an
  explanation for your friend. Be sure to
  give examples.

3. Write a real-life problem that can be solved
  using an inequality of the form $|x - a| \leq b$.
  Write a step-by-step algebraic solution of
  the inequality. Use the solution of the
  inequality to solve your problem.

4. Write two equations *of different types* that
  can be solved by placing each ■ in the
  following equation with the same
  expression.
  $$■^2 + 3■ = 4$$
  Then find all real solutions of each
  equation.

5. Suppose a function f is continuous on the
  interval $[-4, 4]$, with values as given below.

x	-4	-2	0	2	4
$f(x)$	-39	11	5	-9	17

  Write a brief paragraph in which you
  describe what you know about f as a result
  of the Intermediate Value Theorem.

6. Identify transformations T and S for
  which $T \circ S$ maps the unit circle onto an
  ellipse that is not centered at the origin.
  Graph the ellipse on a sheet of grid paper.
  Then show how to represent the ellipse by
  the following:
  a. a pair of parametric equations
  b. a single equation in x and y

Precalculus and Discrete Mathematics © Scott Foresman Addison Wesley

A group of students is starting a wallpaper design business. Their first project is to design a collection of wallpaper borders to be called *Math Paths*. Each border in the collection will be defined by equations in the *xy*-plane. Below is one student's sketch of a suggested pattern of ellipses.

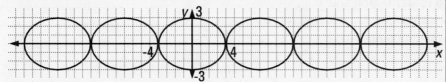

a. Consider the ellipse centered at the origin. Show how to represent it by:
  i. a pair of parametric equations   **ii.** a single equation in *x* and *y*

b. Repeat part **a** for the ellipses centered at (8, 0) and at (-16, 0).

c. Each ellipse is centered at a point (8*n*, 0), where *n* is an integer. Repeat part **a** to write general equations representing any ellipse in the border.

A second student designed the border below. In the interval $-4 \leq x \leq 4$, the equation of the curve is $y = .125x^3 - 2x$. The same cubic curve is then translated right and left.

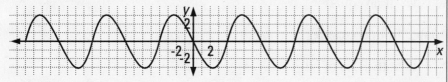

d. Write an equation for the curve in the interval $4 \leq x \leq 12$. What are the zeros of the function in this interval?

e. Write a general equation that can represent any curve in the border. What are the zeros of the function this equation represents.

f. Twelve suggested designs are shown at the right. Choose two of these designs and write equations to generate them. Write each equation so that the design is centered vertically on the *x*-axis. For any equation that represents a function, identify the zeros of the function.

g. Create two original repeating designs for the *Math Paths* collection. Write the general equations that will generate your design. If an equation represents a function, identify all zeros of the function.

(1)

(2)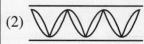

(3)

(4)

(5)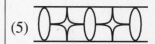

(6)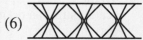

(7)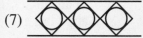

(8)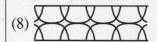

(9)

(10)

(11)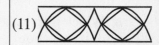

(12)

CHAPTER 3 TEST, Cumulative Form

You will need an automatic grapher for this test.

1. *True or false.* $\forall$ *real numbers* x, $x \le 2 \Rightarrow x < 2$.

    1. _____

2. *True or false.* If f is a real function and
    $\forall$ x_1 and x_2 in the domain of f,
    $x_1 < x_2 \Rightarrow f(x_1) > f(x_2)$, then f is a 1-1
    function.

    2. _____

3. Use limit notation to describe the end
    behavior of the function $g: x \to 8(.6^x)$.

    3. _____

4. Suppose f is an even real function and $f(2) = $ -1.
    Is the inverse of f a function? Justify your answer.

    _____

    _____

5. Which, if any, of the following procedures
    can result in a nonreversible step?
    (a) multiplying both sides of an equation
        by a variable.
    (b) subtracting a variable from both sides
        of an equation
    (c) applying $g(x) = e^x$ to both sides of an
        equation
    (d) dividing both sides of an equation by -1
    (e) All of the above are reversible steps.

    5. _____

6. Let $k(x) = (x + 3)(x - 2)x^2$.
    Solve for x: $k(x) < 0$.

    6. _____

7. Solve for all real values of r:
    $3 = 2\sqrt{r + 11} - r$.

    7. _____

8. **a.** Write the negation of the statement
    $\forall$ *real numbers* x, $ln\,(e^x) = x$.

    8. **a.** _____

    _____

    b. Which is true, the statement of part **a**
    or its negation?

    b. _____

    _____

Precalculus and Discrete Mathematics © Scott Foresman Addison Wesley

9. *Multiple choice.* The statement $\sim p \Rightarrow \sim q$ is logically equivalent to which of the following?

   (a) $\sim q \Rightarrow \sim p$ (b) $q \Rightarrow p$

   (c) $p \Rightarrow \sim q$ (d) $\sim p \Rightarrow q$

9. _____

10. Consider the function defined by the rule $h(r) = 8r - \dfrac{2}{r}$.

   a. Describe the intervals on which h is increasing and on which h is decreasing.

10. a. _____

_____

   b. Find any relative minimum and maximum values of h.

b. _____

_____

11. One set of parametric equations for the circle.

   $x^2 + y^2 = 1$ is $\begin{cases} x = \cos\theta \\ y = \sin\theta \end{cases}$, for $0 \le \theta < 2\pi$.

   a. Describe the rubberband transformation that maps this circle onto the ellipse

   $\begin{cases} x = 5\cos\theta - 6 \\ y = \frac{1}{3}\sin\theta + 2 \end{cases}$, for $0 \le \theta < 2\pi$.

11. a. _____

   b. Find an equation in x and y for the image ellipse.

b. _____

   c. Give the coordinates for the center of the ellipse.

c. _____

12. Suppose for the real function k, $k(10) = -9$ and $k(20) = 1$, yet there exists no real number c in the interval $[10, 20]$ such that $k(c) = -5$. According to the Intermediate Value Theorem, what must be true of k in the interval $[10, 20]$.

_____

13. If $\log_7 20 \approx 1.540$ and $\log_9 7 \approx .886$, what is the approximate value of $\log_9 20$?

13. _____

14. Let the sequences a and b be defined on the interval of integers $[1, \infty)$ by the explicit formulas $a_n = \dfrac{1}{5n}$ and $b_n = \dfrac{1}{2n^2}$.

   a. Find and simplify an explicit formula for the sequence $\dfrac{a}{b}$.

14. a. _____

   b. Is the sequence $\dfrac{a}{b}$ arithmetic, geometric, or neither?

b. _____

15. What, if any, valid conclusion can be drawn from the
following premises?
*If the Chicago Bulls beat the New Jersey Nets and the
Atlanta Hawks beat the Charlotte Hornets in the first
round of the 1998 NBA playoffs, then the Bulls will
play the Hawks in the 1998 NBA Eastern Conference
semifinals. The Bulls did not play the Hawks in the
1998 NBA Eastern Conference semifinals.*

_____

_____

16. A machine makes magnetic disks that are supposed to
have a circumference of 28.3 cm. The absolute error
in the circumference of the disks can be no more than .5 cm.

a. Write an absolute value inequality   **16. a.** _____
that the circumference of the disks
must satisfy.

b. Solve the inequality from part **a.**   **b.** _____

17. In 1998, the population of Boston, Massachusetts, was   **17.** _____
about 548,000 and was declining at an annual rate of 4.6%.
In 1998, the population of Kansas City, Missouri, was
about 444,000 and was growing at an annual rate of
2.1%. If these growth rates remain constant, estimate
the number of years it will take for Kansas City's
population to surpass Boston's.

18. When a company test markets their new product, they   **18.** _____
find that the demand is related to the price by the function
$u = 1400 - 2.5p^2$, where u is the number of units sold
per month and p is the price per unit in dollars. To the
nearest nickel, what should the company charge for their
product to maximize their revenues?

Precalculus and Discrete Mathematics © Scott Foresman Addison Wesley

COMPREHENSIVE TEST, CHAPTERS 1-3

**Write the letter of the correct answer on the line.
You will need an automatic grapher for this test.**

1. Which is the best description of the form of this argument?
   If an animal is a panda, he eats bamboo leaves.
   An animal eats bamboo leaves.
   ∴ This animal is a panda.

   (a) valid argument by the Law of Transitivity

   (b) valid argument by the Law of Detachment

   (c) invalid argument by Inverse Error

   (d) invalid argument by Converse Error

   1. _____

2. Under which of the following conditions will the
   network shown below generate an output
   value of "1"?

   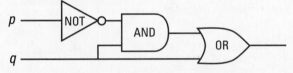

   (a) $p = 0, q = 1$ (b) $p = 1, q = 0$

   (c) $p = 0, q = 0$ (d) none of the above

   2. _____

3. The table at the right shows
   values of a continuous function
   f for selected values of x. In
   which interval must there be a
   value of x with $f(x) = 0$?

x	f(x)
-1.2	-2.6
-1.0	-1.0
-0.8	0.2
-0.6	0.9
-0.4	1.3
-0.2	1.3
0.0	1.0
0.2	0.5
0.4	-0.2

   (a) [-1, -0.9]

   (b) (-0.2, 0.2)

   (c) [0.4, ∞)

   (d) (0, 1)

   3. _____

4. Which of the following describes the domain
   of the real function f with rule $f(x) = \dfrac{\sqrt{x}}{x - 2}$.

   (a) $[2, \infty)$ (b) $[0, 2), (2, \infty)$

   (c) $(0, \infty)$ (d) $(-\infty, \infty)$

   4. _____

5. Which is the range of the function defined by
   $y = 4x^2 + 4x - 13$.

   (a) $\{y: y \geq -14\}$ (b) $\{y: y \geq 14\}$

   (c) $\{y: y \leq 14\}$ (d) the set of all real numbers

   5. _____

6. Which intervals describe all real numbers
   x such that $\frac{x^2 - x - 12}{x - 5} > 0$.

   (a) $(-\infty, 3], [5, \infty)$ (b) $(-3, 4), (5, \infty)$

   (c) $[-3, \infty)$ (d) none of the above

   6. _____

7. The sin function is what kind of function?

   (a) odd   (b) 1-1

   (c) increasing   (d) discrete

   7. _____

8. What is the negation of the statement
   Jack fell down the hill and Jill came tumbling after?

   (a) *Jack fell down the hill or Jill came tumbling after.*
   (b) *Jack didn't fall down the hill and Jill didn't come tumbling after.*
   (c) *Jack didn't fall down the hill or Jill didn't come tumbling after.*
   (d) *Jack fell down the hill and Jill didn't come tumbling after.*

   8. _____

9. The function f and g are
   graphed over the interval
   $[a, b]$ at the right. Consider the
   function $f - g$ over the same
   interval. Which one of the
   following is true?

   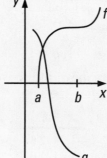

   (a) For all x in $[a, b]$,
        $(f - g)(x) > 0$.

   (b) For all x in $[a, b]$,
        $(f - g)(x) < 0$.

   (c) $(f - g)(b) < 0$.

   (d) There exists x in $[a, b]$
        such that $(f - g)(x) = 0$.

   9. _____

10. Let $h(x) = -3x + 4$ and $k(x) = \frac{1}{2}x^2 + 1$ for
    all real numbers x. Compute $k \circ h(3)$.

    (a) 13.5   (b) 12.5

    (c) -5   (d) 5.5

    10. _____

11. The solution to $2 \log_2 x + \log_2 4 = \log_2 36$ is ___?___.

    (a) 16   (b) 9

    (c) 4.5   (d) 3

    11. _____

12. Which is the largest interval over which
    the function $f(x) = \lfloor 5x + 2 \rfloor$ is continuous?

    (a) $[0, .2]$ (b) $[0, 1)$

    (c) $(-.2, .2)$ (d) $[3, 3.2)$

    12. _____

Precalculus and Discrete Mathematics © Scott Foresman Addison Wesley

13. Which function when applied to both sides of
$f(x) < g(x)$ would reverse the sense of the inequality?

    (a) $h(x) = x^7$ (b) $j(x) = 4^x$

    (c) $k(x) = 6 - 3x$ (d) $m(x) = \log x$

13. _____

14. Suppose $1000 is deposited in an interest
bearing account with an annual rate of 3.65%,
compounded continuously. How much will
there be in the account after 10 years?

    (a) $1,440.51   (b) $2,362.09

    (c) $1,431.18   (d) $1,365.00

14. _____

15. A person takes 200 mg of a medication
once every 24 hrs. The medication has
a half-life in the person's bloodstream of
12 hrs. Which recurrence relation describes
the amount of medication in the person's
bloodstream after the nth dose?

    (a) $a_n = 200 + .25a_{n-1}$ (b) $a_n = 200 + .5a_{n-1}$

    (c) $a_n = 200 + a_{n-1}$ (d) $a_n = 200 + 2a_{n-1}$

15. _____

16. The statement $p \Rightarrow q$ is logically equivalent
to which of the following?

    (a) $\sim p \Rightarrow \sim q$ (b) p and q

    (c) $\sim p$ or q (d) $\sim p$ or $\sim q$

16. _____

17. Let $p(x)$: $x \geq 5$ and $q(x)$: $x > 5$. Which one
of the following is a true statement?

    (a) $\forall x, p(x)$ and $q(x)$ (b) $\forall x, q(x) \Rightarrow p(x)$

    (c) $\forall x, p(x)$ or $q(x)$ (d) $\exists x$ such that, $p(x)$ and $\sim q(x)$

17. _____

18. Over which of the following intervals is
the function h: $x \rightarrow 3 - (x - 3)^2$ decreasing?

    (a) $(-\infty, 0)$ (b) $[3, \infty)$

    (c) $[-1, 1]$ (d) $(2, 3)$

18. _____

19. Approximately how many degrees is 1.5 radians?

    (a) $43°$ (b) $85.9°$

    (c) $270°$ (d) $540°$

19. _____

20. The sentence $|x| > 2$ is equivalent to which of the following?

    (a) $x > 2$ and $x < -2$ (b) $x < 2$ and $x > -2$

    (c) $x > 2$ or $x < -2$ (d) $x < 2$ or $x > -2$

20. _____

21. Let f be the cosine function. Which of the following describes the end behavior of f?

    (a) $\lim_{x \to -\infty} f(x) = 0$, $\lim_{x \to \infty} f(x) = 0$

    (b) $\lim_{x \to -\infty} f(x) = -\infty$, $\lim_{x \to \infty} f(x) = \infty$

    (c) $\lim_{x \to -\infty} f(x) = 1$, $\lim_{x \to \infty} f(x) = 1$

    (d) $\lim_{x \to -\infty} f(x)$ and $\lim_{x \to \infty} f(x)$ do not exist

    21. _____

22. Consider the following solution to the equation $x^2 + 10x = 3x + 18$.

    p: $x^2 + 10x = 3x + 18$
    q: $x^2 + 7x - 18 = 0$
    r: $(x + 9)(x - 2) = 0$
    s: $x = -9$ or $x = 2$

    The conditional $q \Rightarrow r$ is an instance of what universal conditional?

    (a) Multiplication Property of Equality

    (b) Addition Property of Equality

    (c) Distributive Property

    (d) Zero-Product Property

    22. _____

23. If the function g is given by $g(x) = -5x^3 + 2$, which of the following is a rule for g^{-1}?

    (a) $g^{-1}(x) = -\frac{1}{5}\sqrt[3]{x} - 2$ (b) $g^{-1}(x) = -\frac{1}{5}\sqrt[3]{x - 2}$

    (c) $g^{-1}(x) = -\sqrt[3]{\frac{1}{5}x} - 2$ (d) $g^{-1}(x) = \sqrt[3]{-\frac{1}{5}(x - 2)}$.

    23. _____

24. Suppose f is a continuous, real function such that $\forall\, a$ and b in the domain of f, $a < b \Rightarrow f(a) > f(b)$. Which of the following is true?

    (a) f is increasing.   (b) f is 1-1.

    (c) f^{-1} does not exist.   (d) f is discrete.

    24. _____

25. If $\cos \theta = \frac{12}{13}$ and $\frac{3\pi}{2} \leq \theta \leq 2\pi$, then $\sin \theta = \underline{\quad?\quad}$.

    (a) $\frac{5}{13}$ (b) $-\frac{5}{13}$

    (c) $\frac{2}{3}$ (d) $-\frac{4}{5}$

    25. _____

Name _____

1. If $f(x) = -x^4 + 2x^2 - 3x + 8$ and $g(x) = x^4 + 3x^3 - 2x^2 - x + 1$, what is the maximum number of real zeros that the following polynomials can have?

   a. $f(x) \cdot g(x)$

   b. $f(x) + g(x)$

   1. a. _____

   b. _____

2. Find the remainder when $m^3 + 2m^2 + 3m - 5$ is divided by $m + 4$.

   2. _____

3. When n is divided by d, the quotient is 18 and the remainder is 7. Give a possible pair of values for n and d.

   3. _____

4. Juliet wants to copy an article of 23 pages at a copy center that charges 7¢ per copy. If she has $1.65 in her pocket, and each page needs one copy, does she have enough money to copy the whole article? Use the Quotient-Remainder Theorem for Integers to write an equation to describe this situation.

   4. _____

5. Use long division to find the quotient and remainder when $2x^4 + 5x^3 + 7x^2 + 17x + 4$ is divided by $x^2 + 3$.

   5. _____

6. Without dividing, show that $x + a$ is a factor of $x^n + a^n$ where n is an odd positive integer.

   _____

7. Prove the given statement or disprove it by giving a counterexample.
   For integers m, n, and p, if both m and n are factors of p, then $m \cdot n$ is also a factor of p.

   _____

8. Find all zeroes of the function g, where $g(t) = t^3 - 16t^2 + 43t + 60$, given that $g(-1) = 0$.

   8. _____

QUIZ

In 1 and 2, give the smallest positive integer that makes the congruence true.

1. $x \equiv 33 \pmod{21}$

1. _____

2. $y \equiv -5 \pmod{8}$

2. _____

3. Give the standard prime factorization of 660.

3. _____

In 4 and 5, find the base 10 representation of the number.

4. 11011011_2

4. _____

5. $D91_{16}$

5. _____

6. Perform the base 2 addition below.

$$\begin{array}{r} 1010101_2 \\ + \quad 110011_2 \\ \hline \end{array}$$

6. _____

7. **a.** To determine if 243 is prime, what is the largest number that must be tested to see if it is a factor of 243?

7. a. _____

b. Is 243 prime? explain why or why not.

b. _____

8. Give the standard prime factorization of $x^3 - x^2 - 3x + 3$ over the reals.

8. _____

9. Find the last three digits of 7^{49}.

9. _____

10. Prove $x - 2$ is not a factor of $f(x) = x^5 - 2x^4 + 3x^3 - 4x^2 - 5x + 3$.

_____

_____

CHAPTER 4 TEST, Form A

You will need an automatic grapher for this test.

1. A tea manufacturer packages a dozen tea bags in every box. Suppose 20,000 tea bags are manufactured.

    a. How many boxes can be filled, each with a dozen tea bags?

    1. a. _____

    b. How many tea bags will be left unboxed?

    b. _____

    c. Write an equation in the form of the Quotient-Remainder Theorem to describe the situation.

    c. _____

2. Write the base 2 representation of 43.

   2. _____

3. Use long division to find the quotient $q(x)$ and the remainder $r(x)$ when $p(x) = 3x^4 + 2x^3 - 5x^2 + 16x - 9$ is divided by $d(x) = x^2 + 2x - 1$.

   3. _____

4. Prove: *For all integers a, b, and c, if both a and a − b are divisible by c, then b is also divisible by c.*

   _____

   _____

5. Calculate: $1101_2 + 1011_2$. Give your answer in base 2.

   5. _____

6. Find all zeros of $f(x) = 3x^3 - 6x^2 - 24x + 48$, given that $f(2) = 0$.

   6. _____

7. Use the Factor Theorem to show that $x + 3$ is not a factor of $2x^4 - 3x^3 + x^2 - 4x + 9$.

   _____

   _____

8. Give the smallest positive integer solution to $m \equiv \text{-}15 \pmod{12}$.

   8. _____

Precalculus and Discrete Mathematics © Scott Foresman Addison Wesley

9. If a, b, and c are integers, and $a \equiv b \pmod{c}$, how are a, b, and c related?

9. _____

10. *True or false.* The graph at the right could be the graph of a fourth-degree polynomial function with real coefficients. Justify your answer.

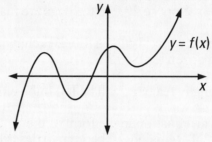

_____

_____

11. Give the standard prime factorization of 9,306.

11. _____

12. Write the base 10 representation of 53241_6.

12. _____

13. Give the prime factorization of $x^4 - 3x^3 - 10x^2$ over the set of polynomials with real coefficients.

13. _____

14. There are 2^{40} ways to answer a true-false test which has 40 questions. Find the last four digits of 2^{40}.

14. _____

15. *True or false.* If a positive integer n has no prime factors between 1 and $\sqrt{n}$ inclusive, then n is prime.

15. _____

16. Consider the statement: *There is no largest degree for a polynomial.*

   a. What assumption would you make to construct a proof by contradiction?

   _____

   b. Complete the proof.

   _____

   _____

   _____

Precalculus and Discrete Mathematics © Scott Foresman Addison Wesley

CHAPTER 4 TEST, Form B

You will need an automatic grapher for this test.

1. A pencil manufacturer packages 12 pencils to each box. Suppose 10,000 pencils have been produced.

   a. How many boxes will be filled?

   1. a. _____

   b. How many pencils will remain unpackaged?

   b. _____

   c. Write an equation in the form of the Quotient-Remainder Theorem to describe the situation.

   c. _____

2. Write the base 2 representation of 59.

   2. _____

3. Use long division to find the quotient $q(x)$ and the remainder $r(x)$ when $p(x) = -2x^4 - 3x^3 + 5x^2 - 11x + 6$ is divided by $d(x) = x^2 - 3x + 1$.

   3. _____

4. Prove: *For all odd integers n and m, $n^2 - m^2$ is divisible by 4.*

   _____

   _____

5. Calculate: $10101_2 + 10111_2$. Give your answer in base 2.

   5. _____

6. Find all zeros of $g(x) = 2x^3 - 3x^2 - 2x + 3$, given that $g(1) = 0$.

   6. _____

7. Use the Factor Theorem to show that $x - 2$ is not a factor of $x^4 - 3x^3 + 2x^2 - 5x + 8$.

   _____

8. Give the smallest positive integer solution to $x \equiv -17 \pmod{11}$.

   8. _____

9. If p and q are integers, and $p \equiv -q \pmod 5$, what can you conclude about $p + q$?

   9. _____

10. At right is the shape of the graph of a polynomial of degree 3 with real coefficients drawn by Zoe. Is Zoe right or wrong? Explain your answer.

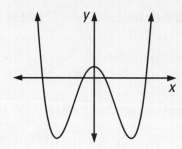

_____

_____

11. Give the standard prime factorization of 3,366.

11. _____

12. Write the base 10 representation of 23771_8.

12. _____

13. Give the prime factorization of $2x^4 + 12x^3 - 14x^2$ over the set of polynomials with real coefficients.

13. _____

14. There are 4^{30} ways to answer a 30-question multiple-choice test with 4 choices for each question. Write the last four digits of 4^{30}.

14. _____

15. *True or false.* If a positive integer n has no prime factors between 1 and $\sqrt{\frac{n}{2}}$ inclusive, then n is prime.

15. _____

16. Consider the statement: *There is no largest odd integer.*

   a. To write a proof by contradiction, with what assumption would you start?

   _____

   b. Complete the proof.

   _____

   _____

   _____

Precalculus and Discrete Mathematics © Scott Foresman Addison Wesley

CHAPTER 4 TEST, Form C

1. **a.** Explain how you know that the following statement is incorrect.
   $$179 \equiv 4 \pmod{16}$$

   Show how to make the statement true by:

   b. replacing 179 with a number other than 4.

   c. replacing 4 with a number other than 179.

   d. replacing 16 with a different number.

2. Let $p(x) = 2x^3 + 5x^2 - x - 6$. Choose a first-degree polynomial $d(x)$ and find $q(x)$ and $r(x)$ such that $p(x) = q(x) \cdot d(x) + r(x)$. Is $d(x)$ a factor of $p(x)$? Explain why or why not.

3. For $f(x) = 2x^4 + 9x^3 - 4x^2 - 36x - 16$, Tran says that the real zeros of f are -4, -2, 1, and 2. Do you agree or disagree? Explain your reasoning. If you disagree, make a corrected list of all the real zeros.

4. Suppose a number k is written in a base other than base 10. Relate the polynomial $5x^3 + x^2 + 7$ to the process of finding the base 10 representation of k. Give a specific example to illustrate your answer.

5. Write an original real-life problem that can be solved by applying the Quotient-Remainder Theorem for Integers. Show how to use the theorem to solve your problem. Be sure to provide a meaning for both the quotient and the remainder in the context of your problem.

6. Consider the interval $2000 \leq n \leq 3000$.

   a. Find an integer n in this interval that is not prime. Give its standard prime factorization.

   b. Find an integer n in this interval that *is* prime. Justify your answer.

CHAPTER 4 TEST, Form D

This statement appeared at the beginning of Chapter 4 in your textbook.

Although integers and polynomials do not look alike, you will see throughout this chapter that they have many structural similarities.

a. The statement asserts that integers and polynomials do not look alike.
   i. Explain why, in general, this assertion is true.
   ii. Give specific cases in which integers and polynomials *do* look like? Explain how they are related.

b. Give a specific example to illustrate each theorem.
   i. Factor of an Integer Sum
   ii. Factor of a Polynomial Sum

c. Choose two "companion" theorems about integers and polynomials other than those mentioned in part **b**. State each theorem and give a specific example to illustrate it.

d. Describe one fundamental way *other than their appearance* in which integers and polynomials are different from each other.

e. Name a theorem related to integers that you studied in this chapter, but that has no counterpart of polynomials. Give a specific example to illustrate the theorem.

f. Name a theorem related to polynomials that you studied in this chapter, but that has no counterpart for integers. Give a specific example to illustrate the theorem.

g. Suppose you are a member of the school debate club. A debate has been scheduled in which teams will argue for and against the statement *Polynomials are very much like integers*. Decide whether you want to be on the team that defends the statement or on the team that challenges it. Write a convincing argument that you might present to support the position you chose. You should create one or more visual displays to illustrate your argument.

The Great Integer/Polynomial Debate

Precalculus and Discrete Mathematics © Scott Foresman Addison Wesley

CHAPTER 4 TEST, Cumulative Form

You will need an automatic grapher for this test.

1. Suppose that the following two statements are true:
   If John went to the movie, so did Bill.
   If Bill went to the movie, Jim stayed home.
   Decide whether the indicated argument is valid or invalid.

   a. John went to the movie,
   ∴ Jim stayed home.

   1. a. _____

   b. Jim stayed home,
   ∴ Bill went to the movie.

   b. _____

2. If $\log_b a = 2$ and $\log_b c = 5$, what is $\log_b c$?

   2. _____

3. A government agency estimates that the number of unemployed in a certain city is 19,982, with error in the estimate of at most 3%. Write an absolute value inequality for the true number N of unemployed persons in the city.

   3. _____

4. Find the base 2 representation of 153_8.

   4. _____

5. Given that $x - 1$ is a factor of the polynomial $p(x) = x^5 - x^4 - 13x^3 + 13x^2 + 36x - 36$, find all zeros of $p(x)$.

   5. _____

6. *Multiple choice.* Which of the following pairs of sentences are not logically equivalent?

   6. _____

   (a) $p \Rightarrow q, \sim q \Rightarrow \sim p$ (b) $\sim(p \ or \ q), \sim p \ or \sim q$

   (c) $\sim(\sim p), p$ (d) $\sim(p \ and \sim q), \sim p \ or \ q$

7. Describe the combined figure obtained by graphing the following parametric equations.
   $$\begin{cases} x = \cos t \\ y = \sin t \end{cases} 0 \le t \le \pi$$

   _____

   _____

8. Given that f and g are both increasing functions and that $g(x) > 0$ for all real values of x, decide whether the function described is increasing or decreasing.

   a. $h(x) = f(-x)$ 　　　　　　　　　　 **b.** $k = g \circ f$

   a. _____ 　 **b.** _____

9. What is the largest prime integer you need to check as a possible factor of 851 to determine whether 851 is prime?

   9. _____

10. Suppose that the quotient $q(x)$ has degree 6 and the remainder $r(x)$ has degree 9, when the polynomial $p(x)$ is divided by the polynomial $d(x)$. What is the minimal possible degree of each?

    a. $d(x)$ 　　　　　　　　　　　　 **b.** $p(x)$

    a. _____ 　 **b.** _____

11. Suppose that g is an odd function and that $\lim_{x \to \infty} g(x) = 2$. What is $\lim_{x \to \infty} \dfrac{1}{g(x)}$?

    11. _____

12. **a.** Find an equation of the image of the ellipse
    $\dfrac{x^2}{4} + \dfrac{y^2}{9} = 1$ under the transformation
    $T: (x, y) \to (3x - 1, 2y + 1)$.

    12. **a.**

    b. Describe the image. 　　　　　　　　 **b.** _____

13. The students in a class are assigned numbers from 1 to 28 and asked to line up in a formation with four rows and seven columns so that students 1–7 stand from left to right in the first row, students 8–14 stand from left to right in the second row, and so on. Let n be the number of a particular student. Write a congruence statement that indicates that this student is in the last column on the right.

    13. _____

Precalculus and Discrete Mathematics © Scott Foresman Addison Wesley

14. Prove that $3c + 3d$ is divisible by 6 if c and d are both odd integers.

_____

_____

_____

15. Find all real solutions to the inequality $x^2 - 3x > 4$.

15. _____

16. A bottling company produced 10,000 bottles of cola and packed as many as possible into cartons holding 24 bottles each.

   a. How many full cartons were packed?

16. a. _____

   b. How many extra bottles were there?

     b. _____

   c. Write an equation in the form $10,000 = pq + r$ to describe the situation.

     c. _____

17. What is the last digit of 7^{53}?

17. _____

18. Factor $x^5 - 81x$ completely into prime polynomials over the reals.

18. _____

1. Is $\dfrac{m+1}{m} - \dfrac{m}{m-1} = \dfrac{-1}{m(m-1)}$ an identity? Justify your answer.
   If it is an identity, state its domain.

   _____

   _____

2. Rewrite as a rational expression in lowest terms and   2. _____
   state any restrictions on the variable:
   $\dfrac{5x^2 + 37x - 24}{5x^2 + 32x - 21}$.

3. Consider the function f defined by $f(x) = \dfrac{1}{(x-8)^4}$.

   a. Give its domain and range.   3. a. _____

                                                            _____

   b. Give equations for any horizontal or vertical   b. _____
      asymptotes.

   c. Use limit notation to describe the behavior of   c. _____
      f near its vertical asymptote(s).

4. Consider the rational function g defined by
   $g(x) = \dfrac{x^2 - 7x + 12}{x^3 - 2x^2 - 8x}$.

   a. State the values of x at which g is discontinuous. 4. a. _____

   b. Which, if any, of the discontinuities are   b. _____
      essential?

5. A factory produces one million plastic containers a year. The manager of the
   plant is considering upgrading from its current machine, which produces
   u containers per kilowatt-hour of electricity, to a more energy-efficient model
   that produces $u + k$ containers per kilowatt-hour. Electricity costs the
   factory 12¢ a kilowatt-hour.

   a. Find a rule for a rational function S which   5. a. _____
      gives the amount that would be saved per
      year, as a function of u, if the factory were
      to upgrade to the new machine.

   b. How much does the factory save per year   b. _____
      if the current machine produces 20 containers
      per kilowatt-hour and the more efficient
      machine produces 52 containers per kilowatt-hour?

Precalculus and Discrete Mathematics © Scott Foresman Addison Wesley

Name _____

QUIZ

1. Use limit notation to describe the end behavior of the rational function *f* given by the rule
$$f(x) = \frac{3x^3}{4x^3 + 5{,}000x + 10{,}000}.$$

    1. _____

2. Let *g* be the rational function defined by $g(x) = \frac{x^2 - 8x - 23}{2x + 4}$. Give equations for any horizontal, vertical, or oblique asymptotes of the graph of $y = g(x)$.

    2. _____

3. Show that $5.8\overline{56}$ is rational by writing it as a ratio of two integers.

    3. _____

4. Rationalize the denominator of $\dfrac{7}{3 - \sqrt{3}}$.

    4. _____

5. Is $\dfrac{2}{2 + \sqrt{2}}$ rational or irrational? Justify your answer.

_____

_____

_____

6. Prove that the secant function is an even function on its domain.

_____

_____

7. Given the triangle at the right, describe the function values in terms of the triangle's two legs.

    7. a. _____

        b. _____

  a. $\cot \alpha$

  b. $\sec \theta$

8. Give the domains on which the following functions are defined.

  a. cotangent

    8. a. _____

  b. secant

        b. _____

  c. cosecant

        c. _____

CHAPTER 5 TEST, Form A

You will need an automatic grapher for this test.

In 1 and 2, an expression is given.   a. Write it as a simple rational expression in lowest terms.   b. State any restrictions on the variable.

1. $\dfrac{z + 6}{5z^2 + 27z - 18} + \dfrac{z - 6}{5z - 3}$

1. _____

2. $\dfrac{2y + 3}{y - 4} \div \dfrac{2y^2 - 9y - 18}{4 - y}$

2. _____

3. Rationalize the denominator to simplify the following expression.

$\dfrac{3\sqrt{3}}{4 - \sqrt{3}}$

3. _____

In 4-6, identify the function as rational or not. If it is rational, state its domain.

4. g with $g(x) = \dfrac{3x^2 + 2x + 1}{4x + 1}$

4. _____

5. f with $f(m) = \dfrac{1 - m}{3 + \sqrt{m}}$

5. _____

6. n with $n(y) = \dfrac{\cos y}{y + 1}$

6. _____

In 7-10, identify the number as rational or irrational. If it is rational, express it as the ratio of two integers.

7. 1.59323

7. _____

8. $\sqrt{28}$

8. _____

9. $5.1\overline{91}$

9. _____

10. $\pi - \dfrac{22}{7}$

10. _____

11. Solve the equation below for x.

$\dfrac{3}{x - 2} + \dfrac{6}{x + 3} = 5$

11. _____

Precalculus and Discrete Mathematics © Scott Foresman Addison Wesley

▶ **CHAPTER 5 TEST, Form A** *page 2*

12. *True or false.* If q is an irrational number and p is a nonzero rational number, then q^p is irrational. Justify your answer.

_____

13. Consider the function k defined by
$$k(x) = \frac{3x^2 - 4x - 15}{x^2 - 9}$$

 a. Use limit notation to describe the behavior of k as $x \rightarrow \text{-}3^+$.

 13. a. _____

 b. Use limit notation to describe the behavior of k as $x \rightarrow \text{-}3^-$.

 b. _____

 c. Use limit notation to describe the end behavior of k.

 c. _____

14. Construct a rule for a rational function c which has a removable discontinuity at $x = 3$ and an essential discontinuity at $x = 5$.

 14. _____

15. Consider the function j graphed below with an asymptote $x = 0$.

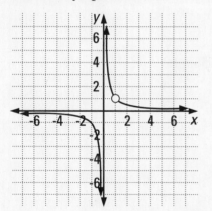

 a. For what values is the function undefined?

 15. a. _____

 b. Use limit notation to describe the behavior of the function near $x = 1$.

 b. _____

 c. Use limit notation to describe the function's end behavior.

 c. _____

Precalculus and Discrete Mathematics © Scott Foresman Addison Wesley

In 16 and 17 consider the graph of the function $p: x \to \dfrac{x^2 + 5x + 2}{x - 20}$.

16. Find the *x*- and *y*-intercepts.

16. _____

17. Give equations for any asymptotes and describe them as horizontal, vertical, or oblique.

17. _____

18. Find the exact value of cot θ.

18. _____

19. Give equations for all asymptotes of the function $h: x \to \csc x$ and describe them as horizontal, vertical, or oblique.

19. _____

20. A trucker was able to average 45 mph on a trip from St. Louis to Detroit.

   a. If the trucker is able to average *A* mph on the return trip from Detroit to St. Louis, give the average speed for the entire trip as a function of *A*.

   20. a. _____

   b. What speed must the trucker average on the return trip so that the average speed for the entire trip is 15 mph?

   b. _____

Precalculus and Discrete Mathematics © Scott Foresman Addison Wesley

CHAPTER 5 TEST, Form B

You will need an automatic grapher for this test.

In 1 and 2, an expression is given.   a. Write it as a simple rational expression in lowest terms.   b. State any restrictions on the variable.

1. $\dfrac{x - 2}{x^2 - 3x - 10} - \dfrac{1}{x - 5}$

1. _____

2. $\dfrac{y}{y + 1} \cdot \dfrac{2y^2 + 3y + 1}{2y^2 - y}$

2. _____

3. Rationalize the denominator to simplify the following expression.

$\dfrac{4}{2 - \sqrt{5}}$

3. _____

In 4–6, identify the function as rational or not. If it is rational, state its domain.

4. $c(x) = \dfrac{3x + 4x + 1}{5}$

4. _____

5. $d(n) = \dfrac{n^2 - 2n + 2}{3n + 5}$

5. _____

6. $g(y) = \dfrac{\cos y}{2 \sin y}$

6. _____

In 7–10, identify the number as rational or irrational. If it is rational, express it as the ratio of two integers.

7. $e - 2$

7. _____

8. $\sqrt{81}$

8. _____

9. $\sqrt{32}$

9. _____

10. $1.\overline{3}$

10. _____

11. Solve the equation below for x.

$\dfrac{7}{x - 5} + \dfrac{1}{x + 5} = 1$

11. _____

12. *True or false.* If p is an irrational number, then $p + p$ is always irrational. Justify your answer.

   _____

13. Consider the function f defined by
   $$f(x) = \frac{3x^2 - x - 70}{3x^2 - 75}.$$

   a. Use limit notation to describe the behavior of k as $x \to -5^+$.

   13. a. _____

   b. Use limit notation to describe the behavior of k as $x \to -5^-$.

   b. _____

   c. Use limit notation to describe the end behavior of f.

   c. _____

14. Construct a rule for a rational function d which has a removable discontinuity at $x = 5$ and essential discontinuities at $x = -8$ and $x = 0$.

   14. _____

15. Consider the function m graphed below with asymptote $x = -1$.

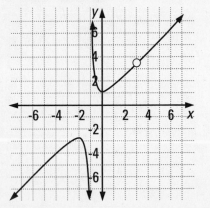

   a. For what values is the function undefined?

   15. a. _____

   b. Use limit notation to describe the behavior of the function near $x = -1$.

   b. _____

   c. Use limit notation to describe the function's end behavior.

   c. _____

Precalculus and Discrete Mathematics © Scott Foresman Addison Wesley

In 16 and 17, consider the graph of the function
$q: x \rightarrow \dfrac{x^3 + 3}{x^2 - 1}$.

16. Find the *x*- and *y*-intercepts.

16. _____

17. Give equations for any asymptotes and
describe them as horizontal, vertical, or
oblique.

17. _____

**In 17 and 18, use the triangle shown below to find the exact
value of the given expression.**

18. csc θ

18. _____

_____

19. Give equations for all asymptotes of
the cotangent function and describe
them as horizontal, vertical, or oblique.

19. _____

20. Two bicyclists were able to average 10 mph on a trip
from their home to a campgrounds.

a. If the bicyclists can average *B* mph for
the trip back, give the average speed
for the entire trip as a function of *B*.

20. a. _____

b. What speed must the bicyclists average
on the return trip so that the average speed
for the entire trip is 15 mph?

b. _____

CHAPTER 5 TEST, Form C

1. **a.** Give an example of an infinite decimal that represents a rational number. Explain how you know it is rational.
   b. Give an example of an infinite decimal that represents an irrational number. Explain how you know it is irrational.

2. Compare the process of simplifying expression (i) to simplifying expression (ii).

   (i) $\dfrac{r^2 - 2r - 3}{r^2 - r - 2} \cdot \dfrac{r - 2}{r + 1}$

   (ii) $\dfrac{r^2 - 2r - 3}{r^2 - r - 2} + \dfrac{r - 2}{r + 1}$

   State as many similarities and differences as you can. Be sure to give the simplified form of each expression.

3. In each part, fill in the blank at the right, so that f is a rational function with the given characteristic.
   $f(x) = \dfrac{x^2 - 2x - 3}{\rule{2cm}{0.4cm}}$
   a. no discontinuities
   b. one removable discontinuity
   c. two essential discontinuities

4. Give an example to show how conjugates can be used to rationalize the denominator of a fraction.

5. Write a step-by-step description of the method you would use to solve a rational equation of the following form.

   $\dfrac{\blacksquare}{x^2 + 3x} + \dfrac{\blacktriangle}{x + 3} = \dfrac{\bullet}{x}$

6. State as many facts as you can about the rational function g graphed below.

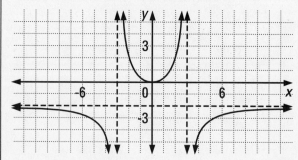

Precalculus and Discrete Mathematics © Scott Foresman Addison Wesley

CHAPTER 5 TEST, Form D

A copy center has six photocopy machines. The manager of the center timed their performance by making 100 copies of the same page on each machine. The results are recorded in the table at the right.

Test Run of 100 Copies	
Copier	Time
A	8 min 20 s
B	5 min 30 s
C	3 min 50 s
D	3 min 35 s
E	2 min 30 s
F	1 min 30 s

a. What fraction of the 100-page run is done in one second by:

  i. copier A?   **ii.** copier B?   **iii.** copier C?

  iv. copier D?   **v.** copier E?   **vi.** copier F?

b. Let x represent the number of seconds required for a given copier to do the 100-page run. Write a rational expression to represent:

  i. the fraction of the job the copier can do in one second.

  ii. the fraction of the job the copier can do in one minute.

c. Assume that a "master" copy is available for both copier A and copier F. What fraction of the 100-page run can be done by the two copiers *working simultaneously* for:

  i. one second?   **ii.** one minute?   **iii.** m minutes?

d. Let x represent the number of seconds required for any one of the copiers to do the 100-page run. Let y represent the number of seconds for a different one of the copiers. Write a rational expression to represent the fraction of the run that can be done by the two copiers working simultaneously for:

  i. one second.   **ii.** one minute.   **iii.** m minutes.

e. Refer to your answers to part **c.**

  i. Write an equation you can use to find the time required for copiers A and F working simultaneously to complete the 100-page run.

  ii. Solve your equation. What amount of time is required?

f. Refer to your answers to part **d.**

  i. Write an equation you can use to find the time required for any two copiers to do the 100-page run working simultaneously.

  ii. Use your equation to find the time required to do the 100-page run if copiers B and E work simultaneously.

g. The copy center is near a large convention center. The manager wants to attract business by advertising how quickly the center can produce copies. Specifically, the manager would like to place a sign in the window that claims the following: *1000 copies in ▓ minutes*

Your job is to recommend to the manager a number of minutes to place in the blank. In making your recommendation, you may assume that some, but not all, of the copiers are available at the time a customer comes to the center. Write a report to the manager explaining the reasoning that justifies your recommendation.

Precalculus and Discrete Mathematics © Scott Foresman Addison Wesley

CHAPTER 5 TEST, Cumulative Form

You will need an automatic grapher for this test.

1. Is the following argument valid? Explain your answer.
   At the intersection of Woodlawn Avenue and 51st Street, you are not allowed to turn right on a red light between 7:00 A.M. and 7:00 P.M. It is 6:00 A.M. Therefore, you are allowed to turn right on red at this intersection.

   _____

2. Rationalize the denominator.   2. _____

   $$\frac{5}{\sqrt{7} + \sqrt{3}}$$

3. Solve $(5n + 2)(n - 2) < 0$.   3. _____

4. Solve the equation below for x.   4. _____

   $$\frac{1}{x - 2} - \frac{6}{x - 3} = 1.$$

5. Find the minimum of the function f given by   5. _____
   the rule $f(x) = x^2 + 10x + 5$.

6. Express $.5\overline{282}$ as a ratio of two integers.   6. _____

7. Let m and d be defined by $m(x) = 3x + 5$ and
   $d(x) = \frac{3}{4}x^3$ for all real numbers x.

   a. Compute $m(d(4))$.   7. a. _____

   b. Give a formula for the function $d \circ m$.   b. _____

8. Consider the function g given by the rule
   $g(x) = x^5 - 3x^4 + x^3 - x^2 + 5x + 2$.

   a. Identify the interval(s) on which g is   8. a. _____
   increasing.

   b. Identify the interval(s) on which g is   b. _____
   decreasing.

9. Write the base 10 representation of 21021_3.   9. _____

Precalculus and Discrete Mathematics © Scott Foresman Addison Wesley

10. Find the quotient and remainder when
$x^3 + 3x^2 + 2x + 1$ is divided by $x - 1$.

10. _____

11. Consider the function $k: x \rightarrow \dfrac{x^2 + 7x - 8}{x^2 + 6x - 16}$.

    a. At what value(s) is k discontinuous?

11. **a.** _____

    b. Which, if any, of the discontinuities are removable?

    b. _____

12. Kelly gets points each time she rents a movie.
For every 30 points she can rents movie free.
Kelly has 428 points.

    a. How many free movies can she rent?

12. **a.** _____

    b. How many points will she have left over
after renting all the movies in part **a**?

    b. _____

13. Only primes less than what integer must be
tested to determine whether 167 is prime?

13. _____

14. Rewrite the expression below as a
rational expression in lowest terms.
$$\frac{z^2 + 7z - 18}{z^2 + 4z - 21} \cdot \frac{z^2 + 3z - 18}{z^2 + 4z - 45}$$

14. _____

15. Find an equation for the oblique asymptote
of $j(x) = \dfrac{5x^2 + 3x + 2}{x + 1}$.

15. _____

16. Use limit notation to describe the end
behavior of $g: x \rightarrow \dfrac{4x^2 + 3x + 2}{2x^2 - 1}$.

16. _____

17. If $p(x) = 5 \csc\left(\dfrac{x}{2}\right)$, find the values at
which p has an essential discontinuity.

17. _____

18. Iris washed 30% of her deck with a cleaning solution
left over from the previous summer. She then washed
the remaining 70% with a new solution which cleans
25 ft^2 per gallon. If, on average, Iris was able to wash
22 ft^2 per gallon of cleaning solution, how many
more square feet per gallon did the new solution
clean? (Round to the nearest ft^2.)

18. _____

QUIZ

You will need an automatic grapher for this quiz.

1. **a.** Give an equation for the graph of the image of
   $y = \sin x$ under the transformation
   $T: (x, y) \to \left(\frac{1}{3}x - .4, -4.2y + 6\right)$.

   1. a. _____

   b. State the amplitude and period for your
   answer to part **a.**

   b. _____

   _____

2. Suppose the output voltage of an AC electrical circuit is
   given by the equation $V = 8 \cos\left(4\pi t + \frac{\pi}{3}\right) + 40$, where
   V is the voltage (in volts) and t is the time (in seconds).

   a. What is the output voltage at time $t = 0$?

   2. a. _____

   b. What is the minimum output voltage
   of the circuit?

   b. _____

   c. How much time elapses between
   successive relative minima?

   c. _____

**In 3 and 4, use an automatic grapher to help decide whether the
equation is an identity. If it appears to be an identity, give its domain
and prove it. If not, illustrate with a counterexample.**

3. $\csc^2 x = \frac{1}{2} \csc (2x)$

4. $\sec^2 x - \tan^2 x = \cos^2 x + \sin^2 x$

Precalculus and Discrete Mathematics © Scott Foresman Addison Wesley

Name _____

In 1 and 2, give an exact value for the expression.

1. $\sin 75°$

    1. _____

2. $\tan \frac{7\pi}{12}$

    2. _____

3. Suppose $\cos \alpha = \frac{3}{5}$ and $\cos \beta = \frac{\sqrt{13}}{7}$ and α and β are both in Quadrant I. Give an exact value for $\cos(\alpha + \beta)$.

    3. _____

4. If $\cos \theta = -\frac{2}{3}$ and $\frac{\pi}{2} < \theta < \pi$, find $\cos(2\theta)$.

    4. _____

5. In the right triangle below, solve for θ in terms of x.

    5. _____

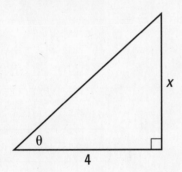

6. Prove the identity $\cos 2x = 2 \sin\left(x + \frac{\pi}{4}\right) \cos\left(x + \frac{\pi}{4}\right)$.

CHAPTER 6 TEST, Form A ▶

You will need an automatic grapher for this test.

In 1 and 2, use an appropriate trigonometric identity to find an exact value for the expression.

1. tan 195°

    1. _____

2. cos $\frac{11\pi}{12}$

    2. _____

3. Evaluate tan $\left(\cos^{-1}\left(-\frac{\sqrt{2}}{2}\right)\right)$.

    3. _____

4. If cos θ = -.4 and $\pi \leq \theta \leq \frac{3\pi}{2}$, find the exact value of sin θ.

    4. _____

5. Solve tan θ + $\sqrt{3}$ = 0 over the interval -π ≤ θ ≤ π.

    5. _____

6. Solve $\left(\cos x + \frac{1}{2}\right)(\sin x - 1) = 0$ over the given domain.

    a. 0 ≤ x < 2π

        6. a. _____

    b. the set of real numbers

        b. _____

7. Use an automatic grapher to find all solutions to sin x + cos x = $\frac{1}{2}$ (to the nearest tenth) in the interval 0 ≤ x < 2π.

    7. _____

    _____

8. The sinusoidal graph at the right is the image of the graph of y = sin x under a rubberband transformation.

    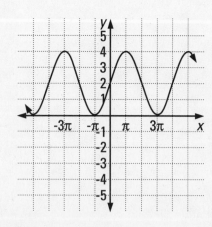

    a. Find an equation for the transformation.

        8. a. _____

    b. Find an equation for the graph.

        b. _____

Precalculus and Discrete Mathematics © Scott Foresman Addison Wesley

9. The seat of a swing is suspended by a rope 5 m long from a horizontal pole which is 6 m above the ground, as shown at the right. Find a formula for the angle θ that the seat makes with the vertical in terms of *h*, the height of the seat above the ground.

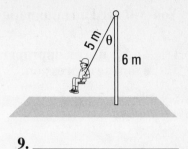

9. _____

10. For a certain AC circuit, the output voltage is given by the formula $V = 25 \sin(\pi t) + 10$, where *V* is the voltage in volts and *t* is the time in seconds. Approximate the values of *t* in the interval $0 \le t \le 2$ for which the voltage is greater than 30 volts.

10. _____

11. Use an automatic grapher to determine whether $\tan \frac{\theta}{2} = -\cot \theta + \csc \theta$ appears to be an identity. If it does, state its domain. If not, find a counterexample.

11. _____

In 12 and 13, prove the identity and give its domain.

12. $2 \cos^2 \alpha = (1 + \sec 2\alpha) \cos 2\alpha$

13. $\sin 2x = 2 \sin^2 \left(x + \frac{\pi}{4}\right) - 1$

CHAPTER 6 TEST, Form B

You will need an automatic grapher for this test.

In 1 and 2, use an appropriate trigonometric identity to find an exact value for the expression.

1. $\sin 195°$

    1. _____

2. $\tan \frac{11\pi}{12}$

    2. _____

3. Evaluate $\cos\left(\sin^{-1}\left(-\frac{\sqrt{2}}{2}\right)\right)$.

    3. _____

4. If $\cos \theta = -.2$ and $\pi \le \theta \le \frac{3\pi}{2}$, find the exact value of $\sin 2\theta$.

    4. _____

5. Solve $\cos x + \frac{\sqrt{3}}{2} = 0$ over the interval $-\pi \le x < \pi$.

    5. _____

6. Solve $\cos^2 x = \frac{\sqrt{2}}{2} \cos x$ over the given domain.

    a. $0 \le x < 2\pi$

    6. a. _____

    b. the set of real numbers

    b. _____

7. Use an automatic grapher to find all solutions to $\sin (2x) = \sin (.5x)$ (to the nearest tenth) in the interval $0 \le x < 2\pi$.

    7. _____

8. The sinusoidal graph at the right is the image of the graph of $y = \cos x$ under a rubberband transformation.

    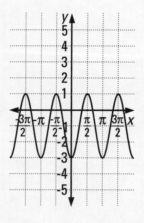

    a. Find an equation for the transformation.

    8. a. _____

    b. Find an equation for the graph.

    b. _____

Precalculus and Discrete Mathematics © Scott Foresman Addison Wesley

9. A ground-based observer has sighted an airplane which is flying at an altitude of 20,000 ft. Find a formula for θ, the angle the observer's line-of-sight makes with the horizontal, in terms of d, the airplane's horizontal distance from the observer.

9. _____

10. At 40° N latitude, the amount of daily sunlight can be approximated by the formula
$m = 170.5 \cos\left(\frac{2\pi(d + 193)}{365}\right) + 730.5$, where m is the number of minutes between sunrise and sunset and d is the day of the year (January 1 = day 0). For approximately how many days of the year are there at least 840 minutes (14 hr) of sunlight at 40° N latitude?

10. _____

11. Use an automatic grapher to determine whether $\tan\frac{\theta}{2} = \sqrt{\frac{1 - \cos\theta}{1 + \cos\theta}}$ appears to be an identity. If it does, state its domain. If not, find a counterexample.

11. _____

In 12 and 13, prove the identity and give its domain.

12. $\sin\alpha + \cot\alpha \cos\alpha = \csc\alpha$

13. $\frac{2}{\sin 2x} = \tan x + \cot x$

CHAPTER 6 TEST, Form C

1. Show algebraically that

$$\frac{\sec x}{\cos x} - 1 = \frac{\cot x}{\tan x}$$

is *not* an identity. Show two different ways to create an identity by changing the right side. Identify the domain of each identity.

2. Explain how to find $\sin 2x$ if you know $\cos x$ and the quadrant in which x lies. Give an example to illustrate your method.

3. At the right, a ladder is shown resting against a building. Write a problem about the situation that can be solved by evaluating an inverse trigonometric function. Show how to solve the problem.

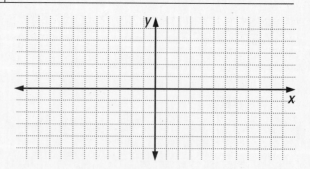
12 ft
θ

4. Jerry wrote the following.

$$\sin x = \frac{1}{2} \text{ or } \sin x = \text{-}1$$

What trigonometric equation might he have been solving? Give two possible equations, one involving just the sine function, the other involving both the sine and cosine functions. Then solve each equation over the set of real numbers.

5. Create a rubberband transformation *T* that can be applied to a circular function:

$$T(x, y) = (\rule{1cm}{0.4pt}, \rule{1cm}{0.4pt})$$

On the axes at the right, graph the image of the graph of $y = \sin x$ under your transformation *T*. Find an equation for the image. Then state its amplitude, period, phase shift, and vertical shift.

Precalculus and Discrete Mathematics © Scott Foresman Addison Wesley

CHAPTER 6 TEST, Form D

The *bearing* of a ship at sea is the measure of the angle formed by the course of the ship and a *reference meridian* that points due north. A bearing is measured in a clockwise direction from the reference meridian, as shown in the diagrams at the right. The bearing of due north is 0°.

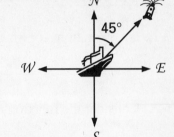

a. The captain of a ship determines that a buoy is 7 miles north and 5 miles east of the ship's present position.

   i. How far is the buoy from the ship, to the nearest tenth of a mile?

   ii. On what bearing, to the nearest degree, should the captain set the ship's course to sail directly toward the buoy?

b. Suppose the captain wants to set a course for a buoy that lies relatively close to the ship at a location *N* miles north and *E* miles east. Write a formula the captain can use to calculate:

   i. the distance *d* in miles.   **ii.** the bearing *b* in degrees.

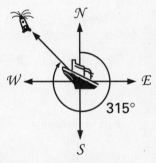

c. Repeat part **b** for a buoy that lies *N* miles north and *W* miles west of the ship.

Nautical positions often are identified by degrees of *latitude* and *longitude*, which are assigned to Earth's surface as follows.

Degrees of Latitude

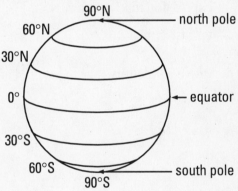

- There are 90 degrees of latitude north of the equator, and 90 degrees south.
- The *prime meridian* is a great circle of Earth that passes through Greenwich, England. There are 180 degrees of longitude west of the prime meridian, and 180 degrees east.
- Each degree (°) of latitude or longitude is divided into 60 minutes (').
- At any point on Earth, the distance spanned by one degree of latitude is approximately 69 miles.
- At a given latitude *x*°, the distance spanned by the degree of longitude is approximately [69(cos *x*)] miles.

d. Suppose the latitude of a ship is 46°30'N, and its longitude is 124°20'W. The captain wants to sail directly toward a buoy at latitude 46°32'N and longitude 124°15'W.

Degrees of Longitude

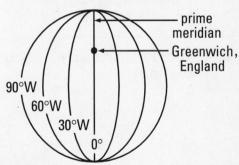

   i. How far is the buoy from the ship, to the nearest tenth of a mile?

   ii. On what bearing should the captain sail? Give the answer to the nearest degree.

e. Create a set of formulas the captain can use to determine the distance and bearing needed to sail the ship to a buoy that is relatively close and *within the same degree of latitude.* Assume that the latitude and longitude of the ship and the buoy are known to the nearest minute. Also assume that the ship and the buoy are on the same side of the prime meridian.

Precalculus and Discrete Mathematics © Scott Foresman Addison Wesley

CHAPTER 6 TEST, Cumulative Form

You will need an automatic grapher for this test.

1. Is $\dfrac{\sqrt{50}}{\sqrt{32}}$ rational or irrational? Justify your answer.

   _____

2. Consider the function $r: x \to \dfrac{5x + 2}{5x^2 + 32x + 12}$.

   a. At what value(s) is r discontinuous?   2. a. _____

   b. Which, if any, of the discontinuities   b. _____
   are removable?

3. Give an exact value for $\sin 22.5°$.   3. _____

4. Suppose $\sin \alpha = \frac{2}{7}$ and $\sin \beta = 1$ and α 4. _____
   is in Quadrant II. Give an exact value for
   $\sin (\alpha + \beta)$.

5. Rewrite the expression below as a rational   5. _____
   expression in lowest terms.

   $\dfrac{14}{5x + 1} - \dfrac{3}{x}$

6. Prove an identity for $\tan \left(x - \dfrac{\pi}{4}\right)$ and state its domain.

7. Solve. $e^{2t} - 8e^t + 15 = 0$ 7. _____

8. Find the remainder when $x^{12} + 3x^9 - 4x^4$ 8. _____
   is divided by $x + 1$.

Precalculus and Discrete Mathematics © Scott Foresman Addison Wesley

9. Consider the image of $y = \cos x$ under
   the transformation $T(x, y) = (-2x + \pi, 3y - 2)$.

   a. Find an equation for the image.

   9. a. _____

   b. State the period and the phase shift
   of the image.

   b. _____

10. Solve $\cos^2 x + \frac{1}{2} \cos x = 0$ over the
    interval $0 \le x < 2\pi$.

    10. _____

11. Prove the identity $\sin (\alpha + \beta) - \sin (\alpha - \beta) = 2 \cos \alpha \sin \beta$
    and give its domain.

12. Use limit notation to describe the behavior

    of $g(x) = \dfrac{4x^2 + 3x + 2}{4x^2 - 1}$ as x approaches
    .5 from the left and from the right.

    12. _____

13. Suppose each time water is passed through a special
    filter, 35% of the dissolved lead is removed. If a
    sample of tap water initially has a lead concentration
    of 55 micrograms/liter, what is the minimum number
    of times it must be passed through the filter to ensure
    its lead concentration is less than 2 micrograms/liter?

    13. _____

14. In human depth perception, stereoscopic judgments
    of distance depend on the parallactic angle, the angle
    from one eye to the object and back to the other eye.
    If the average adult eyes are spaced about 6.5 cm
    apart, find a formula for the parallactic angle θ in
    terms of the distance d of the object from the viewer.

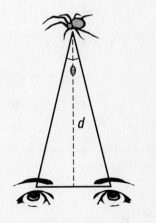

    14. _____

COMPREHENSIVE TEST, CHAPTERS 1-6

1. To prove that the statement $\forall x, p(x)$ is false, which of the following statements do you have to prove is true?

  (a) $\forall x, p(x)$ (b) $\exists x, \sim p(x)$

  (c) $\exists x, p(x)$ (d) $\forall x, \sim p(x)$

1. _____

2. Which of the described functions defined on the set of real numbers has a minimum value?

  (a) $h(x) = e^x$ (b) $g(x) = x^3$

  (c) $k(x) = |x|$ (d) $f(x) = -x^2$

2. _____

3. Given $f(x) = x^2 - 1$ and $g(x) = \frac{1}{2x} + 3$, what is $g(f(x))$?

  (a) $g(f(x)) = \frac{3}{x} + \frac{1}{4x^2} + 12$ (b) $g(f(x)) = \frac{1}{2x^2 - 2} + 3$

  (c) $g(f(x)) = \frac{1}{4x^2} + 8$ (d) $g(f(x)) = \frac{1}{2x^2 - 1} + 3$

3. _____

4. $2x - 2$ is a factor of $12x^3 + 26x^2 - 18x - 20$. Find another factor.

  (a) $3x - 2$ (b) $2x + 3$

  (c) $2x + 2$ (d) $3x + 2$

4. _____

5. Rewrite the expression $\frac{1}{y + 2} - \frac{y}{y - 3}$ as a rational expression in lowest terms.

  (a) $\frac{-y^2 - y - 3}{y^2 - y - 6}$ (b) $\frac{y^2 + y + 3}{y^2 - y - 6}$

  (c) $\frac{-y^2 + y + 3}{y^2 - y - 6}$ (d) $\frac{-y^2 - 2y + 2}{y^2 - y - 6}$

5. _____

6. What is the domain of the identity $1 + \cot^2 x = \csc^2 x$?

  (a) the set of real numbers

  (b) $\{x: x \neq \frac{n\pi}{2}, n \text{ an integer}\}$

  (c) $\{x: x \neq n\pi, n \text{ an integer}\}$

  (d) $\{x: x \neq \frac{(2n + 1)\pi}{2}, n \text{ an integer}\}$

6. _____

7. What is the negation of the statement: *If a car enters Indiana, then the driver must pay a toll?*

  (a) *If a car enters Indiana, then the driver does not have to pay a toll.*

  (b) *If a car does not enter Indiana, then the driver does not have to pay a toll.*

  (c) *A car enters Indiana and the driver does not pay a toll.*

  (d) *A car does not enter Indiana and the driver does not pay a toll.*

7. _____

8. Describe the domain and range of the function h given by $h(x) = \sqrt{x - 6}$.

   8. _____

   (a) domain: $[6, \infty)$
       range: $[0, \infty)$

   (b) domain: $(6, \infty)$
       range: $[0, \infty)$

   (c) domain: $[-6, \infty)$
       range: $(-\infty, \infty)$

   (d) domain: $[0, \infty)$
       range: $[6, \infty)$

9. Find an equation for the inverse of the function k given by $k(x) = x^3 + 2$.

   9. _____

   (a) $k^{-1}(x) = \sqrt[3]{x} - 2$

   (b) $k^{-1}(x) = \sqrt[3]{x - 2}$

   (c) $k^{-1}(x) = \sqrt[3]{x + 2}$

   (d) $k^{-1}(x) = \sqrt[3]{x} - \sqrt[3]{2}$

10. Use long division to determine the remainder when $p(x) = 3x^3 + 4x^2 + 5x + 1$ is divided by $x^2 + 1$?

    10. _____

    (a) 0

    (b) $\dfrac{2x - 3}{x^2 + 1}$

    (c) $3x + 4$

    (d) $2x - 3$

11. Find the equation for the oblique asymptote of $j(x) = \dfrac{5x^3 + 4x^2 + 2x + 1}{x^2 + 4}$.

    11. _____

    (a) $y = 0$

    (b) $y = -18x - 15$

    (c) $y = 5x + 4$

    (d) $y = 5$

12. If $\cos \theta = -\dfrac{1}{4}$ and $\pi \le \theta \le \dfrac{3\pi}{2}$, what is the value of $\cos 2\theta$?

    12. _____

    (a) $\dfrac{1}{16}$

    (b) $\dfrac{\sqrt{15}}{4}$

    (c) $-\dfrac{1}{2}$

    (d) $-\dfrac{7}{8}$

13. What type of reasoning is being used in the following argument?
    If a student is a member of the ski team,
    then the student has been to Utah.
    Tyler is not a member of the ski team.
    ∴ Tyler has not been to Utah.

    13. _____

    (a) Converse Error

    (b) Inverse Error

    (c) Law of Detachment

    (d) Law of Indirect Reasoning

14. Which of the described functions is increasing on
its entire domain?

14. _____

    (a) $c(x) = x^2 + 5$ (b) $d(x) = -5x^4 + 3$

    (c) $b(x) = \log x$ (d) $r(x) = e^{-x}$

15. Solve the inequality $\frac{1}{t} < \frac{5}{t+1}$ for t.

15. _____

    (a) $t < -1, t > \frac{1}{4}$ (b) $-1 < t$

    (c) $-1 < t < \frac{1}{4}$ (d) $-1 < t < 0, t > \frac{1}{4}$

16. Which of the following is not congruent to
7 (mod 11)?

16. _____

    (a) 19   (b) 62

    (c) 128   (d) 150

17. Evaluate $\lim\limits_{x \to \infty} \dfrac{3x^5 + 7x^4 + 5x^3 + 1}{2x^5 + x^2 + 1}$.

17. _____

    (a) ∞ (b) $-\infty$

    (c) $\frac{3}{2}$ (d) 0

18. Which equation represents the image of
$y = \sin x$ under the transformation
$T: (x, y) \to \left(\frac{x}{4} - 2, 3y + 5\right)$?

18. _____

    (a) $y = \frac{1}{3} \sin (4x + 2) - 5$

    (b) $y = 3 \sin (4x + 8) + 5$

    (c) $y = \frac{1}{3} \sin \left(\frac{1}{4}x - 2\right) - 5$

    (d) $y = 3 \sin (4x - 2) - 5$

19. The N-Det credit card company compounds
interest continuously at an annual rate of 18%.
If Redd Inc. charges $2,000 on its N-Det card
and does not make any payments, how much
will it owe in interest after one year?

19. _____

    (a) $360.00   (b) $391.24

    (c) $394.43   (d) $394.33

20. A manufacturer specifies that a bolt must
have a radius of .5 cm, with an error not
to exceed .02 cm. Which inequality
expresses the radius r of acceptable bolts?

20. _____

    (a) $|r - .5| \le .02$ (b) $|r - .5| \ge .02$

    (c) $|r - .02| < .5$ (d) $|r - .02| \ge .5$

Precalculus and Discrete Mathematics © Scott Foresman Addison Wesley

21. A calculator displays 6^{24} in scientific notation as 4.738381E18. Find the last three digits of this number.

    (a) 936   (b) 896

    (c) 296   (d) 656

    21. _____

22. A train going from Philadelphia to New York travels 60% of the distance at x miles/hr and the remaining 40% of the distance at y miles/hr. Which expression gives the average rate of the train for the entire trip?

    (a) $.6x + .4y$ (b) $\dfrac{xy}{.6y + .4x}$

    (c) $\dfrac{.6}{x} + \dfrac{.4}{y}$ (d) $\dfrac{1}{.6x + .4y}$

    22. _____

23. For all α, $\sin\left(\alpha - \dfrac{\pi}{3}\right) = $ ___?___ .

    (a) $\dfrac{1}{2}\sin\alpha - \dfrac{\sqrt{3}}{2}\cos\alpha$

    (b) $\sin\alpha - \dfrac{\sqrt{3}}{2}$

    (c) $\dfrac{1}{2}\cos\alpha - \dfrac{\sqrt{3}}{2}\sin\alpha$

    (d) $\dfrac{1}{2}\cos\alpha$

    23. _____

24. Identify the converse of the statement.
    If it is later than three, then I am leaving.

    (a) *If I am not leaving, then it is not later than three.*

    (b) *If I am leaving, then it is later than three.*

    (c) *If it is not later than three, then I am leaving.*

    (d) *If it is not later than three, then I am not leaving.*

    24. _____

QUIZ

1. Find a recursive formula for the sequence with explicit formula $b_n = 4n^2 + 2$.

   1. _____

2. Consider the sum S_n defined by
   $S_n = 2 \cdot 4 + 3 \cdot 5 + \cdots + n(n + 2)$.

   a. Use summation notation to write an expression for S_n.

   2. a. _____

   b. Write a formula that expresses S_{k+1} in terms of S_k for $k \geq 2$.

   b. _____

   c. Given that $S_{100} = 348{,}447$, find S_{101}.

   c. _____

3. Prove by mathematical induction that the sequence defined by $\begin{cases} c_1 = 6 \\ c_{k+1} = 7c_k + 6 \end{cases}$
   satisfies the explicit formula $c_n = 7^n - 1$ for all integers $n \geq 1$.

4. Prove by mathematical induction that 3 is a factor of $n^3 + 3n^2 + 2n$ for every positive integer n.

Precalculus and Discrete Mathematics © Scott Foresman Addison Wesley

QUIZ

1. Evaluate $\sum_{k=0}^{\infty} 6\left(\frac{1}{4}\right)^k$.

1. _____

2. For what values of r does $\lim\limits_{n \to \infty} \sum\limits_{i=0}^{n} 2r^i$ not exist?

2. _____

3. Consider the computer program at the right.

   ```
   10  B = 3
   20  S = B
   30  FOR J = 1 TO 25
   40  B = 2 * B
   50  S = S + B
   60  NEXT J
   70  PRINT S
   80  END
   ```

   a. Write an expression using summation notation for the sum printed by the computer.

   3. a. _____

   b. Evaluate the sum.

   b. _____

4. Use the Strong Form of Mathematical Induction to prove that if a is the sequence defined by the recursive formula at the right, then a_n is divisible by 3 for every positive integer n.

$$\begin{cases} a_1 = 6 \\ a_2 = 18 \\ a_{k+1} = 3a_k + 9a_{k-1}, \text{ for } k \geq 2. \end{cases}$$

CHAPTER 7 TEST, Form A

You will need a calculator for this test.

1. Find the first five terms of the sequence
   defined by $p_n = \left\lfloor \dfrac{n}{2} \right\rfloor + n$.

   1. _____

2. **a.** Find the first five terms of this
   recursively defined sequence:
   $$\begin{cases} a_1 = 3 \\ a_2 = 6 \\ a_{k+2} = 2a_{k+1} - a_k, \text{ for } k \geq 1. \end{cases}$$

   2. **a.** _____

   b. Conjecture an explicit formula for
   this sequence.

   b. _____

3. Rewrite $\displaystyle\sum_{k=-2}^{10} k(k+1) - \sum_{k=6}^{10} k(k+1) + \sum_{k=6}^{n} k(k+1)$
   using the summation symbol only once.

   3. _____

4. Express $\displaystyle\sum_{j=1}^{2k+1} j^2$ in terms of $\displaystyle\sum_{j=1}^{2k} j^2$.

   4. _____

5. Find the value of $\displaystyle\sum_{i=0}^{15} \frac{1}{5} \cdot 3^i$.

   5. _____

6. Find the value of $\displaystyle\sum_{n=0}^{\infty} \frac{12}{7^n}$.

   6. _____

7. Prove that the sequence defined by $\begin{cases} a_1 = 3 \\ a_{k+1} = a_k + 3(k+1), \forall\, k \geq 1 \end{cases}$

   satisfies the explicit formula $a_n = \dfrac{3}{2}n(n+1)$.

Precalculus and Discrete Mathematics © Scott Foresman Addison Wesley

8. Suppose that John places coins in a row according to the following procedure. First he puts down two coins. Then he inserts another coin between the first two. At each subsequent stage, he inserts an additional coin between each pair of adjacent coins. Let c_n be the number of coins after the nth stage.

   a. Find the first five terms of the sequence.   8. a. _____

   b. Write a recursive formula for the sequence.   b. _____

9. Prove by mathematical induction that 3 is a factor of $n^3 - n$ for all integers $n \geq 1$.

10. Use the Bubblesort algorithm to arrange the list 4, -1, 3, 2, 5 in increasing order. Show the results of each step.

11. Consider the computer program at the right. Give a recursive formula for the sequence of values printed by the computer.

```
10 SUM = 10
20 K = 1
30 PRINT SUM
40 SUM = SUM + 10 • (1/5)^K
50 K = K + 1
60 GOTO 30
```

11. _____

Precalculus and Discrete Mathematics © Scott Foresman Addison Wesley

CHAPTER 7 TEST, Form B

You will need a calculator for this test.

1. Find the first five terms of the sequence
   defined by $t_n = \left\lceil \dfrac{n}{2} \right\rceil - n$.

   1. _____

2. **a.** Find the first five terms of this
   recursively defined sequence.
   $$\begin{cases} b_1 = 3 \\ b_2 = 9 \\ b_{k+2} = 2b_{k+1} + 3b_k \text{ for } k \geq 1. \end{cases}$$

   2. a. _____

   b. Conjecture an explicit formula for
   this sequence.

   b. _____

3. Rewrite $\displaystyle\sum_{j=5}^{13}(j^3 - j) - \sum_{j=8}^{13}(j^3 - j) + \sum_{j=-10}^{4}(j^3 - j)$
   using one summation symbol.

   3. _____

4. Express $\displaystyle\sum_{k=1}^{2n}(-x)^k$ in terms of $\displaystyle\sum_{k=1}^{2n-1}(-x)^k$.

   4. _____

5. Approximate $\displaystyle\sum_{j=0}^{20} 1.5^j$
   to the nearest thousandth.

   5. _____

6. Find the value of $\displaystyle\sum_{n=0}^{\infty} \dfrac{20}{11^n}$.

   6. _____

7. Prove that the sequence defined by $\begin{cases} c_1 = -5 \\ c_{k+1} = c_k - 5(k+1), \forall\, k \geq 1 \end{cases}$

   satisfies the explicit formula $c_n = \dfrac{-5n(n+1)}{2}$.

Precalculus and Discrete Mathematics © Scott Foresman Addison Wesley

8. Suppose that Jane places coins in a row according to the following procedure. First she puts down two coins. Then she inserts one coin between the first two, another at the left end of the row, and another at the right end of the row. At each subsequent stage, she places one coin between each pair of adjacent coins, one at the left end of the row, and one at the right end of the row. Let c_n be the number of coins in the row after the nth stage.

   a. Find the first five terms of the sequence.　　　　　　**8. a.** _____

   b. Write a recursive formula for the sequence.　　　　　**b.** _____

9. Prove by mathematical induction that for all $n \geq 2$,
   $$s_n = \left(1 - \frac{1}{4}\right)\left(1 - \frac{1}{9}\right)\left(1 - \frac{1}{16}\right)\cdots\left(1 - \frac{1}{n^2}\right) = \frac{n+1}{2n}.$$

10. Use the Quicksort algorithm to arrange the list 8, 3, 1, 11, 9 in increasing order. Show the results of each step.

11. Consider the computer program at the right. Give a recursive formula for the sequence of values printed by the computer.

    ```
    10 SUM = 2
    20 K = 1
    30 PRINT SUM
    40 SUM = SUM + 2 • (1/3)^K
    50 K = K + 1
    60 GOTO 30
    ```

    11. _____

    _____

CHAPTER 7 TEST, Form C

1. Compare the computer programs at the right with respect to what you have seen in this chapter. How are the two programs alike? different?

Program A	Program B
10 FOR N = 1 TO 8	10 TERM = 1
20 TERM = 4*N − 3	20 PRINT TERM
30 PRINT TERM	30 FOR N = 2 TO 8
40 NEXT N	40 PRINT TERM
50 END	50 TERM = TERM + 4
	60 NEXT N
	70 END

2. Fill in the blanks to create two different examples of writing a sum recursively:

$$\sum_{i=1}^{6} \blacksquare = \sum_{i=1}^{5} \blacksquare + 41$$

For each example, write the sum in expanded form and find its value.

3. Del's class proved the following statement.

$$\sum_{i=1}^{n} i = \frac{n(n + 1)}{2}$$

So Del made the following conjecture.

$$\sum_{i=1}^{n} (3i) = \frac{3n \cdot 3(n + 1)}{2}$$

Show that Del's conjecture is false. Correct it to make a true statement, and prove your new statement using mathematical induction.

4. To evaluate an infinite geometric series, Ali wrote the expression at the right. What series could Ali have been evaluating? Write the series using summation notation. Find the first four partial sums, then evaluate the series.

$$\frac{6}{1 - \frac{1}{5}}$$

5. Explain the purpose of the Bubblesort and Quicksort Algorithms. Then create a list of five different numbers, choose one of the algorithms, and show how the algorithm can be applied to the list. Be sure to show intermediate results of each step.

CHAPTER 7 TEST, Form D

Spreadsheet software often is used to generate and analyze lists of numbers. In many cases, these lists actually are sequences arising from explicit or recursive formulas.

For example, column B of *Table 1* at the right was generated by entering the formula =4*A1+21 in cell B1. Then, using the "Fill Down" command on cells B1 through B12, the formula for cell B2 became =4*A2+21, the formula for cell B3 became =4*A3+21, and so on.

Table 1		
	A	**B**
1	1	25
2	2	29
3	3	33
4	4	37
5	5	41
6	6	45
7	7	49
8	8	53
9	9	57
10	10	61
11	11	65
12	12	69

Enter =4*A1+21 in cell B1.

Highlight cells B1 through B12 and choose "Fill Down."

a. Has the sequence in column B been generated explicitly or recursively? Explain.

b. Let p represent a term of the sequence in column A. Let b_p represent is value. Write a formula for b_p in terms of p.

Column B of *Table 2* at the right looks exactly the same as column B of *Table 1*. This time, however, column B was generated by entering 25 in cell B1 and using the formula =B1+4 for Cell B2. Then, using the "Fill Down" command on cells B2 through B12, the formula for cell B3 became =B2+4, the formula for cell B4 became =B3+4, and so on.

Table 2		
	A	**B**
1	1	25
2	2	29
3	3	33
4	4	37
5	5	41
6	6	45
7	7	49
8	8	53
9	9	57
10	10	61
11	11	65
12	12	69

Enter 25 in cell B1.

Enter =B1+4 in cell B2.

Highlight cells B2 through B12 and choose "Fill Down."

c. Has the sequence in column B been generated explicitly or recursively? Explain.

d. Let q represent a term of the sequence in column A. Let c_q represent its value. Write a formula for c_q in terms of q.

e. Describe how to adjust the commands in *Table 1* and *Table 2* to generate the first 12 terms of this sequence: 25, 5, 1, .2, .04, . . .

f. Consider the series 25 + 5 + 1 + .2 + .04 + ... Describe how to adjust the formulas for either *Table 1* or *Table 2* to generate the first twelve partial sums.

g. Spreadsheets like those above are used extensively for financial analysis. For example, consider this situation: Your friend wants to buy a new car after college graduation, four years from now, and is interested in several models that are currently available. Design a set of spreadsheets your friend can use to:

 • estimate the cost of each model four years from now, assuming that inflation increases car costs 3% per year.

 • determine how much money can be saved toward a down payment by depositing d dollars per month in an account that pays r% annual interest, compounded monthly.

Write a set of detailed instructions that tells your friend exactly what formulas to enter, and in which cells they should be entered.

CHAPTER 7 TEST, Cumulative Form

You will need a calculator for this test.

1. Write the logical expression that corresponds
    to the following network.

    1. _____

    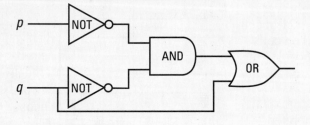

2. Prove that the equation $\sec x - \cos x = \sin x \tan x$ is an identity and state its domain.

3. Give an explicit formula for the sequence defined by
    $\begin{cases} t_1 = \pi \\ t_{k+1} = t_k^2, \text{ for } k \geq 1 \end{cases}$

    3. _____

4. Express this sum of an arithmetic sequence,
    $3 + 6 + 9 + \cdots + 81$, using summation notation.

    4. _____

5. Use limit notation to describe the end
    behavior of the function f defined by
    $f(x) = \dfrac{5 - 4x}{2x + 5}$.

    5. _____

6. Describe a transformation under which the image
    of the graph of the circle $x^2 + y^2 = 1$ is the
    ellipse $\dfrac{(x + 2)^2}{64} + \dfrac{(y - 1)^2}{36} = 1$.

    6. _____

Precalculus and Discrete Mathematics © Scott Foresman Addison Wesley

7. Use chunking to solve the equation
   $e^x + 9e^{-x} = 6$.

7. _____

8. Give the exact value of sin 435°.

8. _____

9. Give the exact value of $\sum_{j=0}^{9} \left(\sqrt{2}\right)^j$.

9. _____

10. Evaluate $\sum_{n=1}^{\infty} \frac{5}{6^n}$.

10. _____

11. How many passes by the Bubblesort algorithm
    are required to arrange the list 9, 4, 11, 6, 2
    in increasing order?

11. _____

12. Prove: for all integers $n \geq 3$, $2^n > 2n + 1$.

Precalculus and Discrete Mathematics © Scott Foresman Addison Wesley

QUIZ

1. Let $z = 5 - 4i$ and $w = -7 + i$. Perform the indicated operations and write the result in $a + bi$ form.

   a. $z - w$

   1. a. _____

   b. $z \cdot \overline{w}$

   b. _____

2. Use Ohm's Law $I = \dfrac{V}{Z}$ to find the current in an AC circuit when a voltage of 8 volts is applied across a circuit with an impedance of $2 + 4i$ ohms. Give your answer in $a + bi$ form.

   2. _____

3. Write the complex number $-6 - 6i$ in each form.

   a. rectangular

   3. a. _____

   b. polar

   b. _____

   c. trigonometric

   c. _____

In 4–6, sketch all the solutions (r, θ) to the equation.

4. $\dfrac{1}{3}r = 2$

   4.

   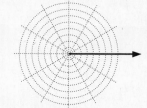

5. $\theta = \dfrac{3}{4}\pi$

   5.

   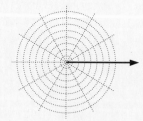

6. $r = 2 + 6\cos\theta$

   6.

   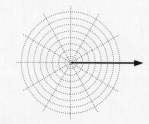

Precalculus and Discrete Mathematics © Scott Foresman Addison Wesley

QUIZ

1. Compute z^3 when $z = 4\left(\cos\frac{3\pi}{8} + i\sin\frac{3\pi}{8}\right)$.

2. **a.** Find all fourth roots of $-8 + 8\sqrt{3}\,i$.
   Write the answers in polar form.

   b. Graph your answers to part **a** on the polar grid at the right.

3. The fifth roots of $6 + 6i$ form the vertices of what type of figure? Be as specific as possible.

4. A cube root of z is $3(\cos 30° + i\sin 30°)$.

   a. Find the other two cube roots of z.

   b. Find z.

5. How many zeros (counting multiplicities) does the polynomial $r(x) = (x^3 - 8)(x^2 + 4)(5x + 1)$ have in the given set of numbers?

   a. integers

   b. rational numbers

   c. real numbers

   d. complex numbers

6. Sketch the polar graph of $r = 6\cos 2\theta$.

1.  _____

2. a.  _____

   _____

b.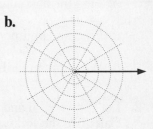

3.  _____

4. a. _____

   b. _____

5. a. _____

   b. _____

   c. _____

   d. _____

6.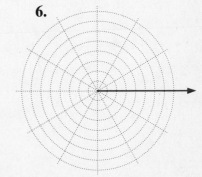

CHAPTER 8 TEST, Form A

You will need a graphing calculator for this test.

1. Let $z = -4i$.

   a. Write z in rectangular coordinate form. 1. a. _____

   b. Find the absolute value of z. b. _____

   c. Find the argument θ of z if $0 < \theta < 2\pi$. c. _____

   d. Write z in polar form. d. _____

2. Let $z = 3 - 5i$ and $w = -2 + 7i$.
   Calculate the following and express
   the results in $a + bi$ form.

   a. $z^2 + w$ 2. a. _____

   b. $\frac{z}{w}$ b. _____

3. Prove: $\forall$ complex numbers $z = a + bi$, $|z - \bar{z}| = 2|b|$.

   _____

4. If $P = \left[r, \frac{2\pi}{3}\right] = (x, 5\sqrt{3})$, solve for r and x. 4. _____

5. Use Ohm's Law $I = \frac{V}{Z}$ to find the voltage in an 5. _____

   AC circuit with current $\frac{2}{5} + \frac{4}{5}i$ amps and

   impedance $4 - 3i$ ohms. Give your answer in $a + bi$ form.

6. Find all fourth roots of $81i$. Write your 6. _____
   answers in trigonometric form.

   _____

   _____

   _____

Precalculus and Discrete Mathematics © Scott Foresman Addison Wesley

7. Let $w = [.8, 45°]$.

   a. Calculate w^2, w^3, and w^4. Write
      your answers in polar form.

7. a. _____

   b. Graph w, w^2, w^3, and w^4 on
      the polar grid at the right.

b.

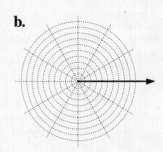

**In 8 and 9, sketch the graph of the given polar equation
and identify the curve obtained.**

8. $r = 4 \sin 3\theta$

8. _____

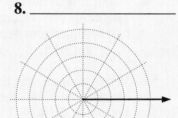

9. $r = -1 - 2 \sin \theta$

9. _____

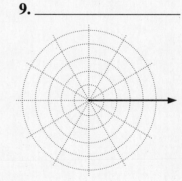

10. Find all zeros and their corresponding
    multiplicities for the polynomial
    $k(x) = x^4 + 2x^3 + 4x^2 + 6x + 3$,
    given that $\sqrt{3}\,i$ is a zero of $k(x)$.

    10. _____

    _____

11. How many zeros (counting multiplicities) does
    the polynomial $r(x) = (x + 7)^2(x^2 + 5)(x^2 - 6)$
    have in the given set of numbers?

    a. integers

    11. **a.** _____

    b. rational numbers

    b. _____

    c. real numbers

    c. _____

    d. complex numbers

    d. _____

12. **a.** According to the Geometric Addition
    Theorem, what figure is formed when
    two complex numbers, their sum, and
    0 are plotted in the complex plane?

    12. **a.** _____

    b. Verify your answer to part **a** by
    plotting the points representing
    $z = -3 + 2i$, $w = 2 + i$, $z + w$, and
    0, and then drawing in the figure.

    b.

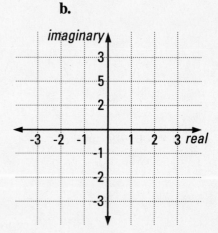

Precalculus and Discrete Mathematics © Scott Foresman Addison Wesley

CHAPTER 8 TEST, Form B

You will need a graphing calculator for this test.

1. Let $z = -2\sqrt{3} + 2i$.

   a. Write z in rectangular coordinate form.

   b. Find the absolute value of z.

   c. Find the argument θ of z if $0 \leq \theta < 2\pi$.

   d. Write z in polar form.

   1. a. _____

   b. _____

   c. _____

   d. _____

2. Let $z = 5 - 4i$ and $w = 3i$.
   Calculate the following and express
   the results in $a + bi$ form.

   a. $2z \cdot \overline{w}$

   b. $\dfrac{w}{w + z}$

   2. a. _____

   b. _____

3. Prove: $\forall$ nonzero complex numbers $z = \dfrac{a + bi}{\sqrt{a^2 + b^2}}$, $|z| = 1$.

4. Express $[-2, 300°]$ in rectangular coordinates.

   4. _____

5. Use Ohm's Law $I = \dfrac{V}{Z}$ to find the current

   in an AC circuit with voltage 12 volts and
   impedance $6 + 2i$ ohms. Give your answer in $a + bi$ form.

   5. _____

6. Find all fourth roots of $-\dfrac{1}{2} + \dfrac{\sqrt{3}}{2}i$. Write your

   answers in binomial form.

   6. _____

   _____

7. Let $w = [1.5, 30°]$.

    a. Calculate w^2, w^3, and w^4. Write
    your answers in polar form.

7. a.

    b. Graph w, w^2, w^3, and w^4 on
    the polar grid at the right.

    b.

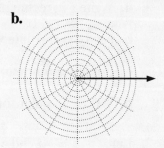

In 8 and 9, sketch the graph of the given polar equation and identify the curve obtained.

8. $r = 3 \cos \theta$

8.

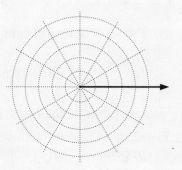

9. $r = -2 - 2 \sin \theta$

9.

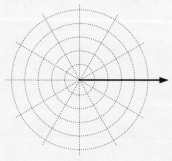

Precalculus and Discrete Mathematics © Scott Foresman Addison Wesley

10. Find all zeros and the corresponding
    multiplicities for the polynomial
    $p(x) = x^3 + 3x^2 - 15x + 91$,
    given that $2 - 3i$ is a zero of $p(x)$.

    10. _____

    _____

11. How many zeros (counting multiplicities) does
    the polynomial $r(x) = x^2(x + 3i)^2(2x - 7)^3$
    have in the given set of numbers?

    a. integers

    11. a. _____

    b. rational numbers

    b. _____

    c. real numbers

    c. _____

    d. complex numbers

    d. _____

12. **a.** Graph $\triangle ABC$ in the complex
    plane when $A = 2i$, $B = -2 + 2i$,
    and $C = -2$.

    b. Multiply each vertex by $-1 + i$ and graph
    the result as $\triangle A'B'C'$.

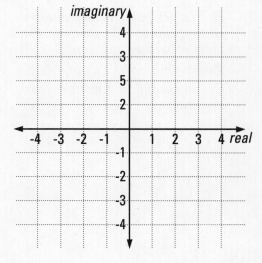

    c. Fill in the blanks. The transformation that
    maps $\triangle ABC$ to $\triangle A'B'C'$ is a composite
    of a size change of magnitude __?__ and a
    rotation of __?__ about the origin.

    c. _____

CHAPTER 8 TEST, Form C

1. Choose any two of the complex numbers below and find their product. Then write the product in each of the four forms shown.

   $(-3\sqrt{3}, -3)$ $-2\sqrt{3} + 2i$

   $[8, 60°]$ $12\left(\cos\frac{\pi}{6} + i\sin\frac{\pi}{6}\right)$

2. Explain how this diagram can be related to complex numbers. Be as specific as possible.

   [2, 90°]
   [2, 210°]   [2, 330°]

3. Explain the meaning of this statement in your own words.

   For a given point in the plane, the rectangular coordinate representation is unique, but the polar coordinate representation is not.

   Give an example to illustrate your response.

4. Celia listed all the zeros of the polynomial $x^4 - 8x^3 + 23x^2 - 26x + 10$ as $1, i - 3$ and $i + 3$. Explain how you know this list is incorrect.

   To help her correct the list, Celia's teacher gave her these clues.

   Two of the entries in the list *are* correct. One of these correct zeros has multiplicity 2.

   Show how to use the clues to correct the list.

5. Shown at the right is a circle graphed in a polar coordinate system. Write a polar equation whose graph will be a circle in this position. Now, by modifying your circle equation, find an equation whose graph has the given shape and position.
   (*Note:* The graphs are not drawn to scale relative to one another.)

   a.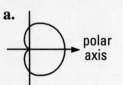

   b.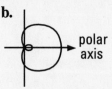

   c.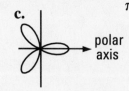

   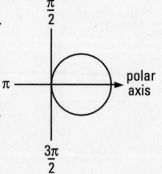

Precalculus and Discrete Mathematics © Scott Foresman Addison Wesley

CHAPTER 8 TEST, Form D

A friend of your family is a craftsperson who creates decorative items made of stained glass. At the right is a design your friend saw in a magazine and would like to adapt as a sun-catcher. Your friend has asked you to help make a full-size template of the design. The outer border of the template is to be a square with sides that are approximately 8 inches in length.

a. On a sheet of polar coordinate paper, or on a plain sheet of paper about $8\frac{1}{2}$ inches wide and 11 inches long, create a polar coordinate system like the one shown below the design.

b. The middle of the design actually is the union of two graphs, which are sketched in reduced form as graphs A and B at the right.

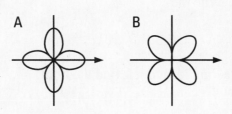

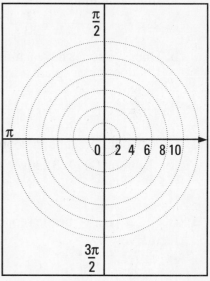

   i. What is the name of each type of graph?

   ii. Give the general form of the polar equation for each graph

   iii. To recreate the design at the desired size, graph A should pass through $\left[10, \frac{\pi}{2}\right]$, and graph B through $\left[10, \frac{\pi}{4}\right]$. Write specific equations that will generate graphs A and B.

   iv. Graph the equations on your coordinate system from part **a**.

c. There are two circles around the central design. (One is partially hidden by the square border.) Each circle should be centered at [0, 0]. One should pass through [10, 0], and the other through [12, 0]. Write equations for the circles. Then add them to your graph from part **b**.

d. In a polar coordinate system, the general equation of a horizontal line passing through $\left[a, \frac{\pi}{2}\right]$ is $r = a \csc \theta$. The general equation of a vertical line passing through [a, 0] is $r = a \sec \theta$. Write specific equations to generate the sides of the squares around the design. Then complete the template by adding these lines to your graph from part **c**.

e. Suppose a complex plane is superimposed on the real plane you created in part **a**. The complex plane is coordinatized with a polar grid drawn to the same scale. Graphed on the complex plane are all the fourth roots of 1296. What would this add to the design?

f. Create an original sun-catcher design that is defined by polar equations. Draw a full-size template of your design on a polar coordinate system. List all the equations that you used and identify which part of the design each equation generates. If you wish, you may also add elements of interest to your design by graphing numbers in a complex plane superimposed on your real plane.

95

CHAPTER 8 TEST, Cumulative Form

You will need a calculator for this test.

1. Let $z = -3 - i$ and $w = -2i$. Compute $\frac{w}{z}$ and write the answer in $a + bi$ form.

   1. _____

2. Let $z = 1.5(\cos 50° + i \sin 50°)$ and $w = 2(\cos 47° + i \sin 47°)$. Calculate $z \cdot w$ and write the answer in trigonometric form.

   2. _____

3. **a.** Use summation notation to write the following infinite series.

   $2 + \frac{2}{3} + \frac{2}{9} + \frac{2}{27} + \frac{2}{81} + \cdots$

   3. a. _____

   b. Does the series have a finite limit? If it does, find the limit. If it does not, explain why not.

   _____

4. Give two different polar coordinates $[r, \theta]$ for the point $(-1, \sqrt{3})$, given that $0 \leq \theta < 2\pi$.

   4. _____

5. Let $a_1, a_2, a_3, \cdots$ be the sequence defined recursively by

   $\begin{cases} a_1 = 0 \\ a_{k+1} = a_k + 2k + 1. \end{cases}$

   a. Write the first six terms of the sequence.

   5. a. _____

   b. Prove that $a_n = n^2 - 1$ is an explicit formula for the sequence.

6. a. Convert the polar equation
$r(\sin \theta + \cos \theta) = 4$ to an equation
in rectangular coordinates.

6. a. _____

b. Sketch the polar graph of the equation.

b.

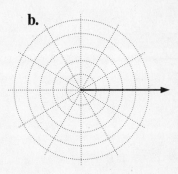

7. a. The fourth roots of $-8 - 8\sqrt{3}\, i$,
when plotted in the complex plane,
lie at the vertices of what type of figure?
Be as specific as possible.

7. a. _____

b. Find those fourth roots and graph
them in the complex plane.

b. _____

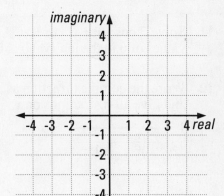

8. Find all zeroes and their multiplicities for the
polynomial $f(x) = x^6 - 5x^5 + 8x^4$.

8. _____

9. Apply the Quicksort algorithm to the list 4, 3, 9, 7, 1, 2. Draw a diagram to show your work.

10. *Multiple choice.* Which of the following defines a 1-1 function?

    10. _____

    (a) $f(x) = \sin x$ (b) $g(x) = 3x^4$

    (c) $h(x) = \dfrac{1}{x}$ (d) $d(x) = |x|$

11. Solve $2\cos^2\theta + 3\cos\theta + 1 = 0$ for all values of θ in the interval $0 \le \theta < 2\pi$.

    11. _____

12. Write the complex fraction as a simple fraction and give all restrictions on x.

    12. _____

    $$1 + \dfrac{1}{\dfrac{1}{1+x} + \dfrac{1}{1-x}}$$

Precalculus and Discrete Mathematics © Scott Foresman Addison Wesley

Name _____

QUIZ

1. The graph at the right shows an object's distance d (in cm) from its starting point as a function of time t (in sec).

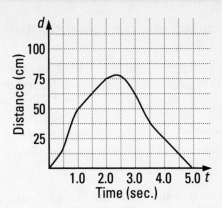

    a. What was the change in the object's directed distance from $t = 1$ to $t = 4$?

1. a. _____

    b. What was the average velocity of the object over the interval $1 \leq t \leq 4$?

b. _____

    c. What does the sign of your answer to part **b** indicate about the average motion of the object in the interval $1 \leq t \leq 4$?

_____

2. Determine the average rate of change of the function h defined by $h(x) = \sqrt{x}$ over the interval $4 \leq x \leq 9$.

2. _____

3. Let g be the function with $g(x) = x^2 - 1$. What is the slope of the tangent line to the graph of g at $x = .25$?

3. _____

4. **a.** Find a simplified rational expression for the difference quotient, $\dfrac{f(x + \Delta x) - f(x)}{\Delta x}$, for the function f defined by $f(x) = \dfrac{1}{x}$.

4. a. _____

    b. Find a simplified rational expression for the derivative function f'.

b. _____

CHAPTER 9 TEST, Form A

You will need a graphing calculator for this test.

Year	Price, including taxes (cents per gallon)
1976	61.4
1980	124.5
1984	121.2
1988	94.6
1992	112.7
1996	123.1

1. The table at the right shows the average urban retail price of unleaded regular gasoline from 1976 to 1996.

   a. Find the average rate of change in the price of gasoline from 1976 to 1980.

   1. a. _____

   b. Find the average rate of change from 1980 to 1996.

   b. _____

   c. What does the sign of your answer to part **b** tell you about the change in gasoline prices from 1980 to 1996?

   _____

2. Let $D(x) = -8x^2 - 5$.

   a. Find an expression for the average rate of change of function D from 2 to $2 + \Delta x$.

   2. a. _____

   b. Use the answer to part **a** to find the average rate of change from 2 to 2.05.

   b. _____

3. *Multiple choice.* At the right is graphed the function f and its tangent line at $x = -1$. Which most closely approximates $f'(-1)$?

   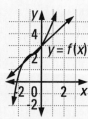

   3. _____

   (a) 1 (b) 2
   (c) 0 (d) -2

Precalculus and Discrete Mathematics © Scott Foresman Addison Wesley

4. *Multiple choice*. The graph at the right is the graph of h', the derivative of h. Which of the graphs below could be the graph of h?

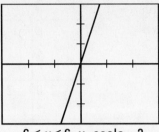

$-6 \leq x \leq 6$, x-scale = 2
$-3 \leq y \leq 3$, y-scale = 1

4. _____

(a)

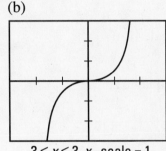

$-6 \leq x \leq 6$, x-scale = 2
$-3 \leq y \leq 3$, y-scale = 1

(b)

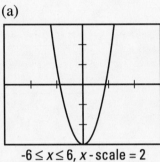

$-3 \leq x \leq 3$, x-scale = 1
$-3 \leq y \leq 3$, y-scale = 1

(c)

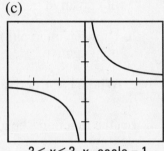

$-3 \leq x \leq 3$, x-scale = 1
$-3 \leq y \leq 3$, y-scale = 1

5. Refer to the graph of the function g at the right.

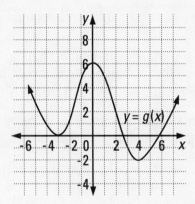

a. Find the average rate of change from $x = -3$ to $x = 2$.

5. a. _____

b. *Multiple choice*. Over which interval is the average rate of change zero?
   (a) $x = -3$ to $x = 0$
   (b) $x = 3$ to $x = 5$
   (c) $x = 0$ to $x = 6$
   (d) $x = -2$ to $x = 2$

b. _____

6. Suppose the derivative of a function g is given by $g'(x) = 3x^2 - 4x$.

a. Find the interval(s) on which g is increasing.

6. a. _____

b. Find the interval(s) on which g is decreasing.

b. _____

7. Refer to the graph of the function f at the right.

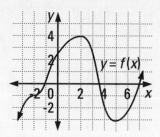

a. On what interval(s) is the derivative of f positive?

7. a. _____

b. On what interval(s) is the derivative of f negative?

b. _____

c. Where is the derivative equal to zero?

c. _____

8. Let the function k be given by $k(x) = \ln x$.

a. The derivative of k at $x = 3$ is $\lim\limits_{\Delta x \to 0} \underline{\ \ ?\ \ }$.

8. a. _____

b. Approximate $k'(3)$ to three decimal places.

b. _____

9. Consider a situation in which a ball is thrown so that its height (in meters) after t seconds is approximated by $h(t) = -5t^2 + 20t + 15$.

a. Estimate the instantaneous velocity of the ball 3 seconds after it is thrown.

9. a. _____

b. Estimate the acceleration of the ball 3 seconds after it is thrown.

b. _____

c. Estimate the maximum height reached by the ball.

c. _____

d. Estimate the instantaneous velocity when the ball reaches its maximum height.

d. _____

Precalculus and Discrete Mathematics © Scott Foresman Addison Wesley

CHAPTER 9 TEST, Form B

You will need a graphing calculator for this test.

Year	Number of complaints
1987	40,985
1988	21,493
1989	10,553
1990	7,703
1991	6,106
1992	5,639
1993	4,438
1994	5,179
1995	4,629

1. The Table at the right gives the total number of consumer complaints against the U.S. airlines for the years 1987–1995.

    a. Find the average rate of change from 1987 to 1991.

    b. Find the average rate of change from 1991 to 1995.

    c. Does the acceleration in the number of complaints per year from 1987 to 1995 appear to be positive, negative, or zero.

1. a. _____

    b. _____

    c. _____

2. Let $R: x \rightarrow 4x^2 - 9$.

    a. Find an expression for the average rate of change of R from 3 to $3 + \Delta x$.

    b. Use the answer to part **a** to find the average rate of change from $x = 3$ to 3.5.

2. a. _____

    b. _____

3. *Multiple choice.* At the right is graphed the function h and its tangent line at $x = 1$. Which most closely approximates $h'(1)$?

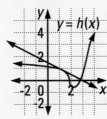

    (a) 1   (b) 2

    (c) 2   (d) $-\frac{1}{2}$

3. _____

    _____

4. *Multiple choice.* The graph at the right is the graph of f', the derivative of f. Which of the graphs below could be the graph of f?

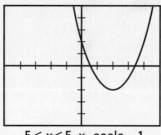

$-5 \le x \le 5, x\text{-scale} = 1$
$-5 \le y \le 5, y\text{-scale} = 1$

4. _____

(a)

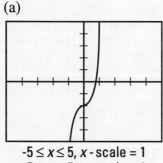

$-5 \le x \le 5, x\text{-scale} = 1$
$-5 \le y \le 5, y\text{-scale} = 1$

(b)

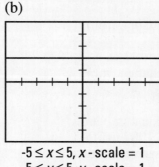

$-5 \le x \le 5, x\text{-scale} = 1$
$-5 \le y \le 5, y\text{-scale} = 1$

(c)

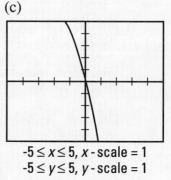

$-5 \le x \le 5, x\text{-scale} = 1$
$-5 \le y \le 5, y\text{-scale} = 1$

5. Refer to the graph of the function g at the right.

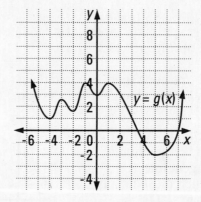

$y = g(x)$

a. Find the average rate of change from $x = -4$ to $x = -1$.

5. a. _____

b. *Multiple choice.* Over which interval is the average rate of change zero?
   (a) $x = -1$ to $x = 1$
   (b) $x = 3$ to $x = 5$
   (c) $x = 0$ to $x = 6$
   (d) $x = -6$ to $x = 0$

b. _____

6. Suppose the derivative of a function f is given by $f'(x) = 3x^2 - 2x - 1$.

a. Find the interval(s) on which f is increasing.

6. a. _____

b. Find the interval(s) on which f is decreasing.

b. _____

Precalculus and Discrete Mathematics © Scott Foresman Addison Wesley

7. Refer to the graph of *f* shown at the right.

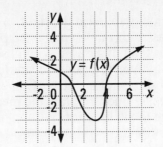

    a. On what interval(s) is the derivative of *f* positive?

    b. On what interval(s) is the derivative of *f* negative?

    c. For what values of *x* is the derivative equal to zero?

7. a. _____

b. _____

c. _____

8. Let the function k be given by $k(x) = \tan x$.

    a. The derivative of *k* at $x = \frac{\pi}{4}$ is
    $\lim\limits_{\Delta x \to 0} \underline{\ ?\ }$.

    b. Approximate $k'\left(\frac{\pi}{4}\right)$ to two decimal places.

8. a. _____

b. _____

9. A ball is thrown so that its height (in meters) after *t* seconds is approximated by $h(t) = 5t^2 + 30t + 20$.

    a. Estimate the instantaneous velocity of the ball 1 second after it is thrown.

    b. Estimate the acceleration of the ball 1 second after it is thrown.

    c. Estimate the maximum height reached by the ball.

    d. Estimate the ball's instantaneous velocity when it reaches its maximum height.

9. a. _____

b. _____

c. _____

d. _____

CHAPTER 9 TEST, Form C

1. Refer to the function graphed at the right. **a.** Draw a secant line that passes through two named points and whose slope is positive. **b.** Draw a second secant line whose slope is negative. **c.** Draw a secant line whose slope is neither positive nor negative. Calculate the slope of each of your secant lines. Explain the meaning of each slope relative to the function.

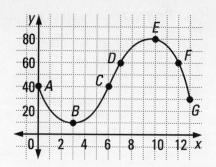

2. A student drew the graph at the right and arrived at this conclusion.

$$f'(3) = \frac{-3 - (-7)}{3 - .5} = \frac{4}{2.5} = 1.6$$

Do you agree or disagree? If you agree, justify your answer. If you disagree, show how to find a correct value for $f'(3)$ and describe what adjustment, if any, you would make to the graph.

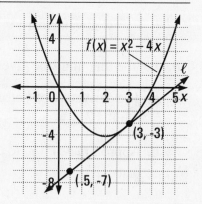

3. A projectile is shot upward so that its height in feet above the ground after t seconds is given by $h(t) = 16t^2 + 92t + 24$. Choose any time t during which the projectile is in motion and state as many facts as you can about its position and movement. Be as specific as possible, and justify each fact.

4. Consider the functions f and g graphed below. Compare the functions f' and g'. How are they alike? How are they different?

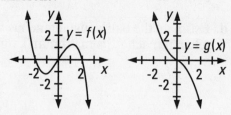

Precalculus and Discrete Mathematics © Scott Foresman Addison Wesley

CHAPTER 9 TEST, Form D

The figure at the right shows a rectangular sheet of cardboard. Congruent squares are to be cut from the four corners of the sheet. Then the sheet will be folded along the dashed lines to form an open-top box.

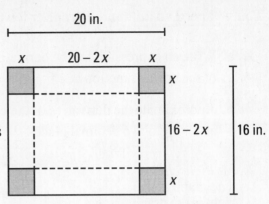

Recall that the formula for the volume V of a rectangular prism of length ℓ, width w, and height h is $V = \ell wh$. So you can calculate the volume of the box formed by the sheet of cardboard as follows.

$$\begin{aligned} V &= \ell wh \\ &= (20 - 2x)(16 - 2x)x \\ V &= 4x^3 - 72x^2 + 320x \end{aligned}$$

a. The graph of the function $V(x) = 4x^3 - 72x^2 + 320x$ is shown below at the right. Estimate where the derivative of V is:

    i. positive   **ii.** negative   **iii.** zero

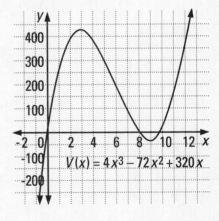

b. On which interval(s) does the function have meaning in the context of the situation described? Explain.

c. Find the average rate of change in V from:

    i. $x = 0$ to $x = 2$ **ii.** $x = 4$ to $x = 8$.

d. Interpret your answers to part **c** in the context of the situation described.

e. Estimate the value(s) of x for which it appears the box will have the maximum volume. Estimate the volume for each value of x you identify.

f. The following theorem shows the derivative of a cubic function.

If $f(x) = ax^3 + bx^2 + cx + d$, where a, b, c, and d are real numbers and $a \neq 0$, then $f'(x) = 3ax^2 + 2bx + c$ for all real numbers x.

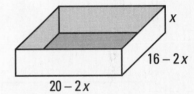

$V(x) = 4x^3 - 72x^2 + 320x$

Show how you can use the theorem to identify the value(s) of x that you were only able to estimate in part **e**. Then give the maximum volume of the box.

g. Suppose you are an industrial designer in a company that manufactures paper products. You have been asked to design a set of three gift boxes that can "nest" inside each other. Each box is to have a cover and one simple flap, as shown at the right. Write a report to your supervisor in which you specify sizes for the three boxes. For each box, give a layout like the one above in which you show how it will be cut from a sheet of cardboard. (Assume that the box will hold its shape by means of tape attached at the vertical edges.) Demonstrate that you have maximized the volume for at least one of the boxes. Can you maximize the sum of the volumes of all three boxes?

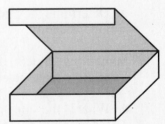

CHAPTER 9 TEST, Cumulative Form

You will need an automatic grapher for this test.

1. **a.** Write an expression for the derivative
   of the cosine function at $x = \frac{\pi}{6}$.

   1. a. _____

   b. Approximate the derivative of the cosine function
   at $x = \frac{\pi}{6}$ to two decimal places.

   b. _____

2. *Multiple choice.*
   The graph at the
   right is the graph
   of f. Which of the
   graphs below
   could be the graph
   of f', its
   derivative?

   2. _____

   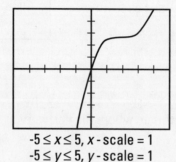

   $-5 \le x \le 5, x\text{-scale} = 1$
   $-5 \le y \le 5, y\text{-scale} = 1$

   (a)

   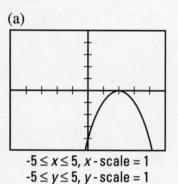

   $-5 \le x \le 5, x\text{-scale} = 1$
   $-5 \le y \le 5, y\text{-scale} = 1$

   (b)

   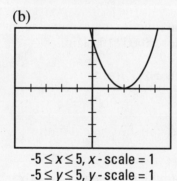

   $-5 \le x \le 5, x\text{-scale} = 1$
   $-5 \le y \le 5, y\text{-scale} = 1$

   (c)

   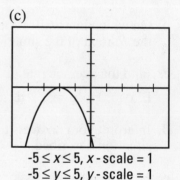

   $-5 \le x \le 5, x\text{-scale} = 1$
   $-5 \le y \le 5, y\text{-scale} = 1$

3. Write $-12 - 12i$ in each form.

   a. rectangular

   3. a. _____

   b. polar

   b. _____

   c. trigonometric

   c. _____

4. Suppose that the derivative of a function f
   is given by $f'(x) = 3x^2 - 2x - 8$.

   a. Determine the interval(s) on which f
   is increasing.

   4. a. _____

   b. At what value(s) of x could f have
   relative maxima or minima?

   b. _____

   c. What is the slope of the tangent line to
   the graph of f at the point $(0, f(0))$?

   c. _____

Precalculus and Discrete Mathematics © Scott Foresman Addison Wesley

5. Find a polynomial of smallest degree with
   real coefficients that has zeros 2 and $1 - i$.

   5. _____

6. An object is propelled upward with an initial velocity
   of 160 ft/sec. Its height (in feet) after t seconds
   is given by $h(t) = 160t - 16t^2$.

   a. Find an expression for the velocity
      function $v(t)$.

      6. a. _____

   b. What is the object's velocity after 4 seconds?

      b. _____

   c. What is the maximum height it reaches?

      c. _____

7. a. $-2 + 2\sqrt{3}\,i$ is a cube root of what
      real number?

      7. a. _____

   b. What are the other cube roots?

      b. _____

   c. Graph these cube roots on the polar grid
      at the right.

      c.

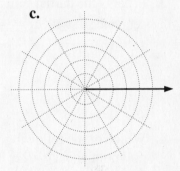

8. Find a recursive formula for the sequence
   with explicit formula $s_n = n^2 - n$ for $n \geq 1$.

   8. _____

9. Let $h : u \rightarrow \dfrac{u^2 + 3u - 10}{u - 2}$.

   a. Use limit notation to describe the
      behavior of h as u approaches 2.

      9. a. _____

   b. Is the discontinuity at $u = 2$ essential
      or removable?

      b. _____

10. Prove the identity $\cos(\alpha + \beta)\cos(\alpha - \beta) = \cos^2\alpha - \sin^2\beta$.

COMPREHENSIVE TEST, CHAPTERS 1-9

You will need an automatic grapher for this test.

1. Which of he following statements represents the logical form of the Law of Detachment?

   1. _____

   (a) $((p \Rightarrow q) \text{ and } \sim q) \Rightarrow \sim p$

   (b) $((p \Rightarrow q) \text{ and } p) \Rightarrow q$

   (c) $((p \Rightarrow q) \text{ and } \sim p) \Rightarrow \sim q$

   (d) $((p \Rightarrow q) \text{ and } q) \Rightarrow p$

2. Which of the following is a factor of $x^6 - 2x^5 + x - 2$?

   2. _____

   (a) $x + 2$ (b) $x + i$

   (c) $x - 1$ (d) $x - 2$

3. What is the partial sum S_5 of the sequence a, with $a_k = \frac{3}{2^k}$ for all integers $k \geq 1$?

   3. _____

   (a) $\frac{31}{32}$ (b) 3

   (c) $\frac{93}{32}$ (d) 2

4. Which of the following is the remainder of polynomial $p(x) = 2x^5 + x^3 - x - 3$ when divided by $x - 1$?

   4. _____

   (a) 1 (b) -3

   (c) 1 (d) 0

5. Which of the following is the exact range of the function g given by $g(x) = -5x^2 + 4x - 4$?

   5. _____

   (a) $\{g: g \leq -\frac{16}{5}\}$ (b) $\{g: g \geq -3\}$

   (c) $\{g: g \leq 7.2\}$ (d) $\{g: g \geq -4\}$

6. If the height h (in meters) of an object as a function of time t (in seconds) is described by the equation $h(t) = 7 - 4.9t^2$, which equation describes the velocity of the object as a function of time?

   6. _____

   (a) $v(t) = 4.9t$ (b) $v(t) = -9.8t$

   (c) $v(t) = -9.8t^2$ (d) $v(t) = 7 - 9.8t$

7. Which of the following equals $\frac{i}{2-i}$?　　　　　　　　7. _____

(a) $\frac{1}{2} - i$　　　　　　　(b) $1 + 2i$

(c) $1 - 2i$　　　　　　　(d) $-\frac{1}{5} + \frac{2}{5}i$

8. If $a_n = \frac{4n}{n-2}$ for all integers $n \geq 1$, find $\lim\limits_{n \to \infty} a_n$.　　8. _____

(a) 4　　　　　　　(b) $\frac{1}{2}$

(c) ∞　　　　　　　(d) 0

9. Suppose that for all real numbers x,　　　　　　　　9. _____
$f(x) = x^2 + 3$, $g(x) = \log_5 x$, and
$h(x) = \log_5(x^2 + 3)$. Which is true?

(a) $f = g \circ h$　　　　　　　(b) $g = f \circ h$

(c) $h = g \circ f$　　　　　　　(d) $f = h \circ g$

10. Which of the following is equal to　　　　　　　　10. _____
$(\sec x + \tan x)(\sec x - \tan x)$ for all x for
which $\cos x \neq 0$?

(a) 1　　　　　　　(b) $\cot^2 x$

(c) $\csc^2 x$　　　　　　　(d) $\sin^2 x$

11. Find the base 10 representation of the number　　　11. _____
110100_2.

(a) 56　　　　　　　(b) 52

(c) 104　　　　　　　(d) 11010

12. Mathematical induction is closely related to　　　　12. _____
which one of the following?

(a) Law of Detachment

(b) Law of Indirect Reasoning

(c) Improper Induction

(d) recursion

13. Consider the statement.　　　　　　　　13. _____
If Jean is on the softball team,
then she practices every day.
Which would tell you the statement is false?

(a) Jean is not on the softball team, and she practices every day.

(b) Jean is on the softball team, and she does not practice every day.

(c) Jean is not on the softball team, and she does not practice every day.

(d) Jean is not on the basketball team, and she does not practice every day.

14. What is the slope of the line tangent to the graph of the function $f(x) = -3x^2 + x$ at the point $(1, -2)$?

    (a) 3   (b) -6

    (c) 13   (d) -5

14. _____

15. $\frac{1}{2} + \frac{1}{2}i$ is an eighth root of what real number?

    (a) $\frac{1}{16}$ (b) $\frac{1}{2}$

    (c) $\frac{1}{4}$ (d) $\frac{1}{8}$

15. _____

16. For which value of k is $\sum_{i=0}^{\infty} 2k^i$ finite?

    (a) 1   (b) -1.5

    (c) -.5   (d) e

16. _____

17. Which one of the following functions, when applied to both sides of $r(x) < s(x)$, would reverse the sense of the inequality?

    (a) $g(x) = x^3$ (b) $h(x) = \sqrt[3]{x}$

    (c) $f(x) = 3^{-x}$ (d) $k(x) = 3x$

17. _____

18. Which of the following defines a function that is continuous on the interval $[-1, 3]$?

    (a) $h(x) = \lfloor x \rfloor$ (b) $f(x) = \frac{x}{x - 2}$

    (c) $g(x) = x^3 - 3x - 2$ (d) $b(x) = -\tan x$

18. _____

19. If $\sin x = \frac{2}{3}$ and $\cos x = \frac{\sqrt{5}}{3}$, then $\cot x = $ ___?___.

    (a) $\frac{3}{2}$ (b) $\frac{3}{\sqrt{5}}$

    (c) $\frac{\sqrt{5}}{5}$ (d) $\frac{\sqrt{5}}{2}$

19. _____

20. On which of the following intervals is f increasing, given $f'(x) = (x - 1)(x + 3)$?

    (a) $x < -3$ (b) $-3 < x < 1$

    (c) $x < 1$ (d) $-1 < x < 3$

20. _____

21. A polynomial $p(x)$ is defined by $p(x) = x^3 + 2x^2 + x + 2$. Which of the following is a zero of $p(x)$?

(a) $x = 2$ (b) $x = -i$

(c) $x = 1$ (d) $x = -1$

21. _____

22. Which of the following equations is graphed at the right?

(a) $y = \sin 4\theta$ (b) $y = 4 \sin \theta$

(c) $y = 4 \sin \frac{\theta}{4}$ (d) $y = 4 \sin 4\theta$

22. _____

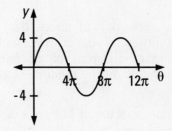

23. Suppose a person drives 25,000 miles a year and a gallon of gasoline costs \$1.25 on average. About how much would this person save in a year by driving a car that gets $30 \frac{mi}{gal}$ over one that gets $25 \frac{mi}{gal}$?

(a) \$1040   (b) \$200

(c) \$800   (d) \$6250

23. _____

24. Which of the following is an equation for the asymptote of the graph of
$$k(x) = \frac{3x^3 - 2x^2 + x - 4}{x^2 + x + 2}?$$

(a) $y = 0$ (b) $y = 3$

(c) $y = 3x - 2$ (d) $y = 3x - 5$

24. _____

25. If $\cos x = -\frac{2}{5}$, find $\cos 2x$.

(a) $-\frac{21}{25}$ (b) $\frac{4}{25}$

(c) $-\frac{17}{25}$ (d) $-\frac{4}{5}$

25. _____

QUIZ

You will need a calculator for this quiz.

In 1–3, a problem in combinatorics is presented.
a. Identify the essential features of the items to be counted.
b. Solve the problem.

1. How many different 10-letter code words
    can be constructed from the English alphabet?

    1. a. _____

    b. _____

2. A TV network is planning to air 3 of
    12 commercials during a 90-second slot.
    How many different sequences of 3 commercials
    are possible during the time slot?

    2. a. _____

    b. _____

3. Emma wants to put 11 books on a shelf. Four of
    the books are by her favorite author. How
    many arrangements are possible, if Emma keeps
    all the books by her favorite author together?

    3. a. _____

    b. _____

4. A model of car comes in 3 styles, GLE, GXE, and LX.
    Each style also has the option of manual or automatic
    transmission. Construct a possibility tree for the
    possible types of this model.

5. Evaluate $P(8,4)$.

    5. _____

6. Among the integers from 300 through 999, how
    many contain at least one digit which is 1, 4, or 7?

    6. _____

7. Find n so that $P(11, n) = \frac{11!}{7!}$.

    7. _____

Precalculus and Discrete Mathematics © Scott Foresman Addison Wesley

QUIZ

You will need a calculator for this quiz.

1. Consider the following problem:
   How many different 4-element subsets can be
   constructed from an 8-element set?

   a. Identify the essential features of the
   problem.

   1. a. _____

   b. Solve the problem.

   b. _____

2. If $C(11, 6) = C(11, r)$ and $r \neq 6$, what is the
   value of r?

   2. _____

3. A council has 11 Democrats and 13 Republicans.
   A committee is to be comprised of 5 Democrats
   and 7 Republicans. How many different
   committees are possible?

   3. _____

4. What is the coefficient of the term a^7b^7 in
   the expansion of $(a + b)^{14}$?

   4. _____

5. How many different subsets does a
   12-element set have?

   5. _____

6. A coin is tossed 7 times. How many of
   the possible sequences of heads and tails
   have no more than 2 heads?

   6. _____

7. A lottery has a probability of $\frac{1}{10}$ that a ticket is
   a winner. If someone buys 15 tickets, what is
   the probability that exactly 4 are winners?

   7. _____

Precalculus and Discrete Mathematics © Scott Foresman Addison Wesley

CHAPTER 10 TEST, Form A

You will need a calculator for this test.

In 1 and 2, evaluate the expression.

1. $P(10, 5)$

1. _____

2. $_{12}C_3$

2. _____

3. Find the sixth term of $(3a - b)^{11}$.

3. _____

4. What binomial coefficient, expressed as a combination, gives the number of 7-element subsets that can be formed from a 17-element set?

4. _____

In 5–8, a counting problem is given. a. Identify the essential features of the problem. b. Solve the problem.

5. A planning committee has to choose four speakers from a group of six. How many different programs are possible, if the program lists the speakers in order of appearance?

5. a. _____

   b. _____

6. Suppose a computer account password must be 6 characters long, and each character may be any uppercase letter, any lowercase letter from the English alphabet, or any digit 0-9. How many possible passwords are there?

6. a. _____

   b. _____

7. A House committee consists of 12 members, seven from the majority party and five from the minority party. If there are 228 in the majority and 206 in the minority, how many different committees are possible?

7. a. _____

   b. _____

8. A deli serves 5 types of sandwiches: tuna salad, egg salad, cheese, turkey, and salami. A customer orders 16 sandwiches for a picnic. How many different ways can the customer's order be filled?

8. a. _____

   b. _____

Precalculus and Discrete Mathematics © Scott Foresman Addison Wesley

9. A carnival game gives a prize when the bottom of a duck has a blue mark. If one-fourth of the ducks have a blue mark, and the game is played 13 times, what is the probability that at least two of the ducks drawn will be prize winners?

9. _____

10. A certain microwave popcorn bag has a probability of .02 that the bag is defective. If a family pack with 12 bags is purchased, what is the probability that exactly 2 of the bags are defective? (Round your answer to the nearest thousandth.)

10. _____

11. An airline has a choice of 3 different main courses: regular, low-salt, and vegetarian; and a choice of beverage: soda, juice, or water. However, the low-salt meal does not come with soda. Make a possibility tree displaying the possible meals.

In 12 and 13, consider the integers from 1000 to 9999.

12. How many of the integers have at least one even digit?

12. _____

13. How many of the integers have the property that the sum of their digits is 9?

13. _____

14. Prove that $\binom{r + (n - 1)}{r} = \binom{n + r - 1}{n - 1}$.

CHAPTER 10 TEST, Form B

You will need a calculator for this test.

In 1 and 2, evaluate the expression.

1. $P(11, 4)$

1. _____

2. $_{13}C_2$

2. _____

3. Find the seventh term of $(3a + b)^{12}$.

3. _____

4. What binomial coefficient, expressed as a combination, gives the number of 5-element subsets that can be formed from a 16-element set?

4. _____

In 5–8, a problem is given. a. Identify the essential features of the problem. b. Solve the problem.

5. A popular game show picks its contestants from its studio audience. If 10 people must be chosen for the panel and there are 75 people in the audience, how many different panels are possible?

5. a. _____

   b. _____

6. A multiple-choice quiz has 12 questions, each with three choices. If you may only choose one answer for each question, how many possible ways are there to answer the 12-question quiz?

6. a. _____

   b. _____

7. A circus has seven acts, but only five perform each night. If acts performing in a different order are considered a different show, how many possible shows are there?

7. a. _____

   b. _____

8. Jim has 4 different colored papers on which to make 50 copies of a flyer. In how many ways can he make these copies?

8. a. _____

   b. _____

Precalculus and Discrete Mathematics © Scott Foresman Addison Wesley

9. A furniture company is having a balloon contest
during which a customer pops a balloon at the time
of purchase. If the balloon contains a "free!" tag, the
purchase is free. One out of every fifty balloons
contains the tag. If there are 14 purchases during
the day of the sale, what is the probability that 2 or
more of the purchases are free?

9. _____

10. Suppose 2% of a shirt manufacturer's shirts have
defective stitching. If you buy 20 shirts, what is the
probability that exactly 3 have defective stitching?

10. _____

11. A housing developer is building custom-made homes.
The buyer has a choice of one, two, or three bathrooms
and a choice of carpet or wood flooring. Make a possibility
tree displaying the possible houses.

**In 12 and 13, consider an election in which there are
12 candidates and you are allowed to vote for 5 of them.**

12. In how many ways can you cast your 5 votes
if each vote must be for a different candidate?

12. _____

13. In how many ways can you cast your 5 votes
if you can vote for any candidate a repeated
number of times?

13. _____

14. Show that $r! \cdot C(n, n - r) = P(n, r)$.

CHAPTER 10 TEST, Form C

1. Write a paragraph that explains what is illustrated in the diagram at the right. Include a statement of a conclusion that can be drawn from the diagram.

	Select first letter	Select second letter	Select third letter	Code Word
	B	A	C	BAC
		C	A	BCA
Start	C	A	B	CAB
		B	A	CBA

2. Compare $_4P_3$ and $_4C_3$. How are they alike? How are they different? State as many likenesses and differences as you can.

3. Identify a "counting situation." Write a problem about it that can be solved using:

   a. permutations.   **b.** combinations.

   Show how to solve each problem.

4. In the past 0.3% of the microwave ovens manufactured at a certain factory have been defective. Assume this is the probability that an oven in a new shipment of 20 microwave ovens is defective. A student calculated the probability that this shipment contains at least one defective oven as shown below. Do you agree or disagree? If you agree, justify your answer. If you disagree, find a correct probability.

   $$\binom{20}{1}(.997)^{19}(.003)^1 \approx .0567$$

5. The expression $(x + y)^n$ is expanded for a certain value of n. One term in the expansion is $2024x^{21}y^3$. What is the next term? Explain your reasoning. (*Note:* Assume the terms are written as customary, with the exponents of x in decreasing order.)

Precalculus and Discrete Mathematics © Scott Foresman Addison Wesley

CHAPTER 10 TEST, Form D

Two older friends of yours are planning to open a new restaurant in the town where you live. There already are several popular restaurants in the area, so a marketing consultant suggested that they create a slogan to set their restaurant apart from the others. Your friends decided they would like to advertise their restaurant as "The Home of a Million Meals." They are considering the menu shown at the right.

Appetizer
   Grandma's Vegetable Soup

Main Courses
   Old-Fashioned Chicken Bake
   Home-Style Pot Roast of Beef

Potatoes
   Crispy Corkscrew French Fries
   Creamy Mashed Potatoes
   Twice-Baked Potato

Vegetables
   Honey-Glazed Carrots
   Garden-Fresh Peas
   Buttered Golden Corn
   Lemon-and-Herb Broccoli

Dessert
   Grandpa's Apple Pie
   (served with or without ice cream)

a. Make a possibility tree to show the number of different meals a restaurant patron can order from this menu if choosing exactly one item from each category. How many possible meals are there?

b. Suppose a patron decides to order exactly two different items from the *Vegetables* category.

   i. In how many ways can the choice of two different vegetables be made? Show your work.

   ii. Suppose the patron orders exactly two different items from the *Vegetables* category and exactly one item from each other category. How would this change your possibility tree from part **a**?

   iii. How many possible meals are there under these conditions?

c. Suppose a patron decides to order exactly three different items from the *Vegetables* category and exactly one item from each other category. Use Pascal's triangle to explain why the number of possible meals under these conditions is exactly the same as the number of meals in part **a**.

d. What is the total number of possible meals if a patron orders either one, two, three, four, or no items from the *Vegetables* category and exactly one item from each other category? Assume that there is no repetition among the items ordered.

e. What is the total number of possible meals that can be ordered from this menu? Assume there is no repetition among the items ordered, and assume that at least one item is ordered.

f. Do you think the slogan "The Home of a Million Meals" is realistic? Is it honest advertising? If you think it is, write an argument to support that conclusion. Then create a menu that will generate all the meals.

If you think the slogan is *not* realistic, or if you think it is not honest advertising, suggest a number that you think your friends can use in place of "a million." Create a menu that will generate your suggested number of meals. Then write an argument to explain why your choice is more realistic or honest.

CHAPTER 10 TEST, Cumulative Form

You will need a calculator for this test.

1. Evaluate $_{11}P_3$.

   1. _____

2. What is the sum of the entries in the twelfth row of Pascal's Triangle?

   2. _____

3. Find all solutions to the equation $x^4 = 81$ over the complex numbers.

   3. _____

4. Consider the function g defined by $g(x) = 3x^2 + 4x + 1$.

   a. Find an equation for the derivative of the function.

   4. a. _____

   b. What is the slope of the graph of g at the point $(5, 96)$?

   b. _____

5. How many subsets containing 3 elements or less can be formed from a 9-element set?

   5. _____

6. Find the remainder when $p(x) = 3x^6 + 5x^5 + 3$ is divided by $q(x) = x - 1$.

   6. _____

7. A standardized test has 20 questions, each of which has four choices. If a student can only select one answer for each question, in how many ways can the test be answered?

   7. _____

8. Write an equation whose graph is a rubberband transformation image of the graph of $y = \sin x$ and has amplitude 4, period $\frac{2\pi}{3}$, vertical shift 0, and phase shift $-\frac{2}{3}$.

   8. _____

9. Find an equation for any oblique asymptote(s) of the function k defined by $k(x) = \frac{3x^3 + 4x^2 + 2x + 1}{x^2 - 2}$.

   9. _____

10. If a car goes from 0 to 60 mph in 4 seconds, what is its average acceleration during this time interval?

    10. _____

11. The derivative m' of a function m is graphed at the right. On which interval(s) is m decreasing?

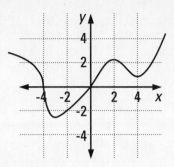

11. _____

12. Consider the following counting problem: A candy display has 20 different kinds of candy. If a customer fills a bag with 40 candies, how many different bags of candies are possible?

   a. Identify the essential features of the problem.

12. a. _____

   b. Solve the problem.

b. _____

13. a. Write a recursive formula for the arithmetic sequence with initial term 5 and common difference of 7.

13. a. _____

   b. Write an explicit formula for the sequence.

b. _____

14. Fifteen percent of a company's packages of crackers contain a coupon for a free package. If you buy 20 packages, what is the probability that you will find more than one coupon?

14. _____

15. Find the exact x-value at which the function p defined by $p(x) = 3x^2 + \sqrt{2}\,x + 1$ reaches its maximum.

15. _____

16. A raffle has 50 different entries. There are 10 prizes. How many groups of winners are possible if an entry can win only one prize and all the prizes are the same.

16. _____

17. Expand $(1 - 2k)^6$.

17. _____

QUIZ

1. Of one thousand Americans surveyed, 65% gave the President
   a favorable approval rating. Of those who gave a favorable rating,
   80% were Democrats, 18% were Republicans, and 2% were Independents.
   Of those who did not give a favorable rating, 25% were Democrats,
   74% were Republicans, and 1% were Independents.

   a. Draw a probability tree representing this situation.

   b. What percentage of those surveyed were   **b.** _____
   Democrats?

   c. What is the probability that a Democrat in   **c.** _____
   this survey did not give the President
   a favorable approval rating?

2. **a.** Draw a picture of a directed
   graph with the adjacency
   matrix shown at the right.

$$\begin{array}{c} \\ v_1 \\ v_2 \\ v_3 \\ v_4 \\ v_5 \end{array} \begin{array}{ccccc} v_1 & v_2 & v_3 & v_4 & v_5 \\ \begin{bmatrix} 0 & 0 & 0 & 1 & 0 \\ 1 & 0 & 1 & 1 & 0 \\ 0 & 1 & 0 & 1 & 0 \\ 0 & 1 & 0 & 1 & 0 \\ 0 & 0 & 0 & 0 & 0 \end{bmatrix} \end{array}$$

   b. Is this a simple graph? Explain your answer.

   _____

   c. List all isolated vertices.   **c.** _____

   d. Give the degree of each vertex.   **d.** _____

   e. Determine the total degree of the graph.   **e.** _____

Precalculus and Discrete Mathematics © Scott Foresman Addison Wesley

3. A small editorial office is trying to network their six computers and one printer so that each computer is connected to the printer and only two of the other five computers. Is this possible? Use graph theory to justify your answer.

_____

_____

_____

4. Consider the graph below.

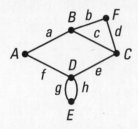

a. Is the graph connected?

b. Find a walk from *A* to *C* which is not a path and which goes through *E*.

c. Find a path from *A* to *C* that goes through *E*.

d. Find a circuit beginning at *A* that goes through *E*.

e. Does the graph have an Euler Circuit? If it does, describe the circuit. If it does not, state which edge could be removed or added to make an Euler Circuit.

_____

_____

4. a. _____

b. _____

c. _____

d. _____

CHAPTER 11 TEST, Form A

1. Draw the graph defined below.
   set of vertices: $\{v_1, v_2, v_3, v_4\}$
   set of edges: $\{e_1, e_2, e_3, e_4, e_5\}$
   edge-endpoint function:

edge	endpoint
e_1	$\{v_1, v_2\}$
e_2	$\{v_1, v_4\}$
e_3	$\{v_2\}$
e_4	$\{v_3, v_4\}$
e_5	$\{v_2, v_4\}$

2. Consider Graph 1 pictured at the right.

   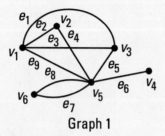

   Graph 1

   a. List all vertices adjacent to v_3.

   b. Identify all parallel edges.

   c. Is this a simple graph? If not, tell how to make the graph simple.

   d. What is the degree of v_5?

   e. What is the total degree of the graph?

   2. a. _____

   b. _____

   c. _____

   d. _____

   e. _____

In 3 and 4, *multiple choice*. Consider Graph 2 pictured at the right. Decide which of the following best describes the given alternating sequence of adjacent vertices and edges.
   (a) a walk but not a path
   (b) a path but not a circuit
   (c) a circuit
   (d) none of the above

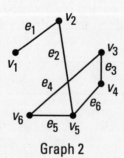

Graph 2

3. $v_1 e_1 v_2 e_2 v_5 e_6 v_4 e_3 v_3 e_4 v_6 e_5 v_5$

   3. _____

4. $v_6 e_5 v_5 e_6 v_4 e_6 v_5 e_2 v_2$

   4. _____

5. Add an edge to Graph 2 to make an Euler Circuit possible and describe the Euler Circuit.

   _____

Precalculus and Discrete Mathematics © Scott Foresman Addison Wesley

6. Does there exist a graph with 5 vertices of degrees 0, 1, 3, 2, and 1? If so, draw one, If not, explain why not.

7. A police survey finds that 98% of those who own bikes lock them. Of the bikes that are locked, 10% will be stolen at some point. Of those left unlocked, 50% will be stolen.

   a. Draw and label a probability tree representing this situation.

   b. If the city has 10,000 bikes, how many should be expected to be stolen?

   7. b. _____

8. The President of a high school chess club wants to rank the club's 11 members. To do this, she suggests that each member play exactly 5 different matches. Is this possible? Justify your answer.

   _____

   _____

9. Marla has a paper route. The map at the right outlines her route; each vertex is a corner and the edges are the streets. Is there a route Marla can take so that she can traverse each street exactly once and return to where she began? Explain your answer.

10. If Tyler Erd works late on any given evening, there is a
10% chance he will work late the following evening. If he
does not work late on any given evening, there is a 60% chance
he will work late the following evening.

    a. Draw a graph for this situation, and label the edges with the correct probabilities.

    b. Find the corresponding stochastic
       matrix.

10. b. _____

    c. What is the probability that Tyler works
       late any given evening?

c. _____

In 11 and 12, use the following adjacency matrix.

$$\begin{bmatrix} 1 & 2 & 1 \\ 0 & 0 & 1 \\ 2 & 3 & 0 \end{bmatrix}$$

11. Draw a graph for the adjacency matrix.

12. How many walks of length 3 go from
v_1 to v_3?

12. _____

CHAPTER 11 TEST, Form B

1. Draw the graph defined below.
   set of vertices: $\{v_1, v_2, v_3, v_4, v_5\}$
   set of edges: $\{e_1, e_2, e_3, e_4\}$
   edge-endpoint function:

edge	endpoint
e_1	$\{v_1, v_3\}$
e_2	$\{v_4, v_5\}$
e_3	$\{v_2\}$
e_4	$\{v_3, v_5\}$

2. Consider Graph 1 pictured at the right.

   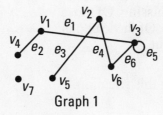

   Graph 1

   a. List all vertices adjacent to v_6.

   2. a. _____

   b. Identify any isolated vertices.

   b. _____

   c. Is this a simple graph? If not, tell how to make the graph simple.

   c. _____

   d. What is the degree of v_3?

   d. _____

   e. What is the total degree of the graph?

   e. _____

In 3 and 4, *multiple choice*. Consider Graph 2 pictured at the right. Decide which of the following best describes the given alternating sequence of vertices and edges.

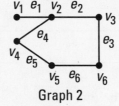

Graph 2

   (a) a walk but not a path
   (b) a path but not a circuit
   (c) a circuit
   (d) none of the above

3. $v_3 e_3 v_6 e_6 v_5 e_5 v_4 e_4 v_2 e_2 v_3$

   3. _____

4. $v_1 e_1 v_2 e_2 v_2 e_4 v_4$

   4. _____

5. Add an edge to Graph 2 to make an Euler Circuit possible and describe the Euler Circuit.

   _____

6. Does there exist a graph with 3 vertices of degrees 1, 3, and 5?
   If so, draw one, If not, explain why not.

7. A library database provides the following information:
   4% of the books requested are reported missing. Of those
   that are reported missing, 80% are found. Of those books
   not reported missing, 10% are checked out.

   a. Draw and label the graph representing this situation.

   b. If 5,000 books are requested, how many   **7. b.** _____
       should be expected to be checked out?

8. A softball tournament has 7 teams. The organizers would
   like each team to play exactly 4 different teams to determine
   who will advance to the next round. Is this possible? Justify your answer.

   _____

   _____

9. A bus tour uses the routes in the graph below.

   Is it possible for a bus to begin and end in the same city,
   covering each route exactly once? Justify your answer.

   _____

Precalculus and Discrete Mathematics © Scott Foresman Addison Wesley

10. A devoted basketball fan noted that when her home team won a game, the probability that they won the next game was .75. However, whenever they lost a game, the probability that they lost the next game was .60.

   a. Draw a graph for this situation, and label the edges with the correct probabilities.

   b. Find the corresponding stochastic matrix.

   10. b. _____

   c. Approximately how many basketball games would the team win over the course of an 80-game season?

   c. _____

11. Give the adjacency matrix for the graph below.

   11. _____

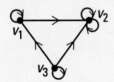

12. The adjacency matrix for a graph is

$$\begin{bmatrix} 1 & 1 & 1 \\ 0 & 0 & 1 \\ 1 & 2 & 1 \end{bmatrix}.$$

   How many walks of length 2 go from v_1 to v_2?

   12. _____

CHAPTER 11 TEST, Form C

1. Consider all that you have learned about graphs in Chapter 11. State five significant facts about the graph at the right.

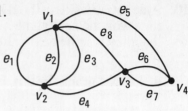

2. Consider this statement: A graph has 5 vertices of degree 3, 2, ▨, ▨, and ▨.

   a. Replace each ▨ with a number so that such a graph exists. Draw the graph.

   b. Replace each ▨ with a number so that no such graph exists. Justify your answer.

3. a. Explain why the graph at the right below *does* have an Euler circuit.

   b. Write a real-life problem that can be solved by finding an Euler circuit in this graph. Show how to solve your problem.

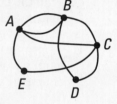

4. Matrix A at the right is the adjacency matrix for a graph. A student says it shows there are three walks of length 2 from v_2 to v_3 of the graph. Do you agree or disagree? Explain.

$$A = \begin{bmatrix} 1 & 0 & 1 \\ 0 & 2 & 3 \\ 1 & 3 & 0 \end{bmatrix}$$

5. The matrix B at the right shows the probabilities that Sarah will go to the movies (M) or will not go (N) on consecutive Saturdays. Explain each entry. Then show how you can use this matrix to make a prediction.

$$B = \begin{matrix} & M \ \ N \\ \begin{matrix} M \\ N \end{matrix} & \begin{bmatrix} .4 & .6 \\ .8 & .2 \end{bmatrix} \end{matrix}$$

Precalculus and Discrete Mathematics © Scott Foresman Addison Wesley

CHAPTER 11 TEST, Form D

Below is a map of a local zoo, showing all its exhibits and walkways.

a. Construct a graph to model the exhibits and walkways.

b. Identify which, if any, of these adjectives describe the graph you made in part **a**: *simple, complete, directed, connected.* Justify your answer.

c. Use the graph you made in part **a** to identify a walk from the main entrance to the *Bears* exhibit:

    i. that is a path.   **ii.** that is not a path.

d. The manager of the zoo would like to identify a "Zoo Trail" that visitors could follow starting at the main entrance, covering each walkway exactly once, and returning to the main entrance. Explain why this is not possible with the existing configuration of walkways.

e. After a fund-raising campaign, the zoo's board of directors has decided to add four new attractions: a rhinoceros/hippopotamus exhibit, a chimpanzee house, a children's zoo, and a gift shop. There also is money available to change the configuration of some of the walkways.

Suppose you work at the zoo as an assistant to the manager. Create a new map of the zoo in which you assign reasonable locations to the four new attractions. (Keep all the existing attractions in their current locations.) The map should include a new configuration for the system of walkways so the manager can advertise the "Zoo Trail" described in part **c**. Be sure to clearly indicate the trail on your map.

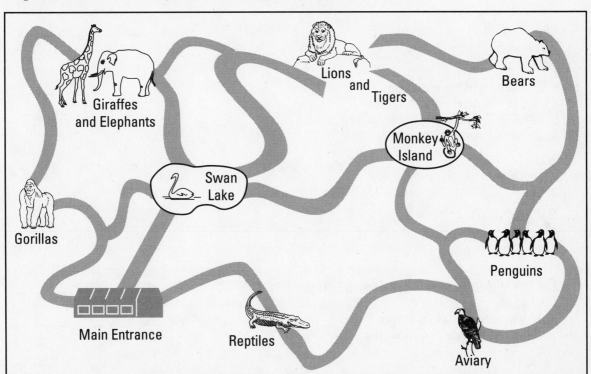

CHAPTER 11 TEST, Cumulative Form

You will need a calculator for this test.

In 1 and 2, use the the graph pictured at the right.

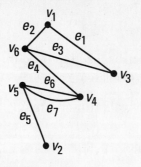

1. **a.** Name the edges adjacent to e_3.

    1. a. _____

    b. Is the graph simple? Justify your answer.

    b. _____

    c. What is the degree of v_3?

    c. _____

    d. What is the total degree of the graph?

    d. _____

2. Does the graph have an Euler circuit? Justify your answer.

    _____

3. Find the coefficient of the term a^3b^4 in the expression of $(a + 2b)^7$.

    3. _____

4. Find $f'(-1)$ if f is defined by $f(x) = 3x^2 - 3x + 2$.

    4. _____

5. One solution to the equation $x^4 - 11x^3 + 46x^2 - 86x + 60 = 0$ is $x = 3 + i$. Find all other solutions in the set of complex numbers.

    5. _____

6. Consider the graph below.

    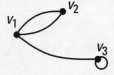

    a. Give the adjacency matrix for the graph.

    6. a. _____

    b. How many walks of length 5 are there from vertex v_1 to vertex v_3?

    b. _____

Precalculus and Discrete Mathematics © Scott Foresman Addison Wesley

In 7 and 8, a counting problem is given. a. Identify the essential features of the problem. b. Solve the problem.

7. How many different 4-letter strings can be constructed from the English alphabet if any letter can be used at most once?

7. a. _____

b. _____

8. How many 4-element subsets can be constructed from the set of letters in the English alphabet?

8. a. _____

b. _____

9. A computer program generates a sequence of "1s" and "0s" in the following manner. If the program generates a "1," the probability is 50% that the next term in the sequence is a "1." If the program generates a "0," the probability is 75% that the next term will be a "1."

a. Find a stochastic matrix to represent this situation.

9. a. _____

b. If the program generates 100 terms in the sequence, how many of the terms should you expect to be "1"?

b. _____

10. Use limit notation to describe the behavior of the function f given by $f(x) = \frac{3x^2 + 4x + 1}{x - 2}$ as x approaches 2.

10. _____

11. Write $-\frac{5\sqrt{3}}{2} - \frac{5}{2} i$ in polar form.

11. _____

12. Bob is buying 10 apples to make an apple pie. He has a choice of any combination of red, green, or yellow apples. How many different combinations of apples are possible?

12. _____

13. In a physics class of 23 students, the teacher would like each student to work with exactly 9 different lab partners over the course of the year. Is this possible? Justify your answer.

_____

_____

14. A tire manufacturer knows that 2% of all the tires they produce contain a minor flaw. To maintain a high level of quality control, the manufacturer tests every tire. Their test rejects 98% of the flawed tires and 5% of the tires which are not flawed.

   a. Draw and label a probability tree to represent the situation.

   b. What percent of rejected tires are not flawed?

14. b. _____

15. How many 3-digit positive integers have at least one digit which is a 6?

15. _____

16. Consider the map of the nature preserve below.

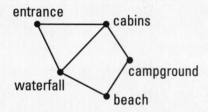

Is it possible to start at the entrance, traverse each trail exactly once, and end at the entrance? Justify your answer.

_____

Precalculus and Discrete Mathematics © Scott Foresman Addison Wesley

QUIZ

1. **a.** Find the component representation of the vector pictured at the right.

   b. Find its polar representation.

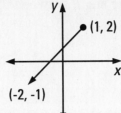

1. a. _____

   b. _____

2. Let $\vec{u} = (2, -3)$ and $\vec{v} = (-4, 2)$. Sketch the vectors $\vec{u}, \vec{v}, \vec{u} + \vec{v}$, and $\vec{u} - \vec{v}$ in their standard positions on the grid at the right.

2.

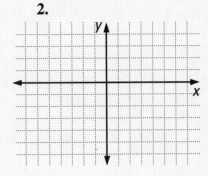

3. Given that $\vec{u} = [\sqrt{2}, 45°]$ and $\vec{v} = [2, -30°]$, write $3\vec{u} + 2\vec{v}$ in component form.

3. _____

4. Write a vector equation for the line through $(4, -7)$ that is parallel to the line with vector equation $(x + 1, y - 1) = t(2, 1)$.

4. _____

5. An aircraft flying across the Atlantic toward Europe is headed 30° north of east at a constant airspeed of $800 \frac{k}{hr}$. In a $\frac{1}{2}$-hour period, the aircraft encounters a $200 \frac{k}{hr}$ wind coming directly from the west.

   a. How far east does the aircraft travel in the $\frac{1}{2}$-hour period?

   b. How far north does it travel in the half hour?

5. a. _____

   b. _____

QUIZ

In 1 and 2, find the exact measure of the angle between the indicated vectors.

1. $\vec{u} = (\sqrt{3}, 3)$ and $\vec{v} = (1, -\sqrt{3})$

1. _____

2. $\vec{w}_1 = (2, -3, \sqrt{3})$ and $\vec{w}_2 = (2, -5, -\sqrt{3})$

2. _____

3. Let $\vec{u} = (5, r)$ and $\vec{w} = (3, 1)$. Find r if the vectors $\vec{u}$ and $\vec{w}$ are orthogonal.

3. _____

4. Let $\vec{u} = (1, 2, 0)$ and $\vec{v} = (0, 2, 3)$.

   a. Find the component representation of $\vec{u} \times \vec{v}$.

   4. a. _____

   b. Sketch $\vec{u}, \vec{v}$, and $\vec{u} \times \vec{v}$ in the figure at the right.

   b.

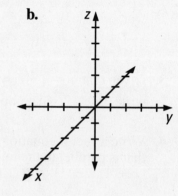

5. Find the center and the radius of the sphere with equation $x^2 + y^2 + z^2 + 6x - 8y + 10z = 50$.

5. _____

Precalculus and Discrete Mathematics © Scott Foresman Addison Wesley

CHAPTER 12 TEST, Form A

You will need a calculator for this test.

1. Find the magnitude and direction of the
   vector from (3, 5) to (9, -3).

   1. _____

**In 2 and 3, let $\vec{a}$ = [7, 65°] and $\vec{b}$ = [4, 125°].
Compute each.**

2. $\vec{a} + 3\vec{b}$

   2. _____

3. $\vec{a} \cdot \vec{b}$

   3. _____

4. Prove: For all real numbers r and 3-dimensional vectors $\vec{u} = (x, y, z)$, $|r\vec{u}| = |r||\vec{u}|$.

   _____

   _____

5. Approximate the degree measure
   of the angle between the vectors
   $\vec{u} = (-2, -3, 0)$ and $\vec{v} = (-6, 0, 4)$.

   5. _____

6. Determine whether the vectors
   $\vec{u} = (3, -5)$ and $\vec{v} = (-12, 20)$
   are orthogonal, parallel, or neither.

   6. _____

7. A quarterback releases a football with an initial velocity of
   12.2 m/sec at an angle of 34° with the horizontal. Find each.

   a. the horizontal component of the
      football's initial velocity

   7. a. _____

   b. the vertical component of the
      football's initial velocity

   b. _____

8. An aircraft flies with an airspeed of 400 $\frac{mi}{hr}$ and a heading 30° north of east.
   The wind comes directly from the north and has a speed of 100 $\frac{mi}{hr}$. Find the
   true speed and direction of the aircraft with respect to the ground.

   _____

   _____

9. Find the component representation of
   the vector $\vec{v} = [4, 240°]$.

9. _____

10. Consider the vectors $\vec{u}$ and $\vec{v}$ shown in
    the figure at the right. Sketch the following
    vectors. Label each vector and its endpoint.

    a. $-2\vec{u}$

    b. $\vec{u} + \vec{v}$

    c. $\vec{u} - \vec{v}$

10.

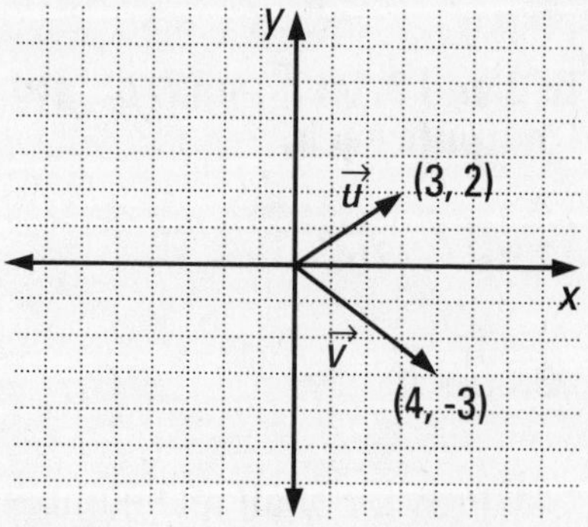

11. Sketch the vector $\vec{w} = (3, -2, 4)$.

11.

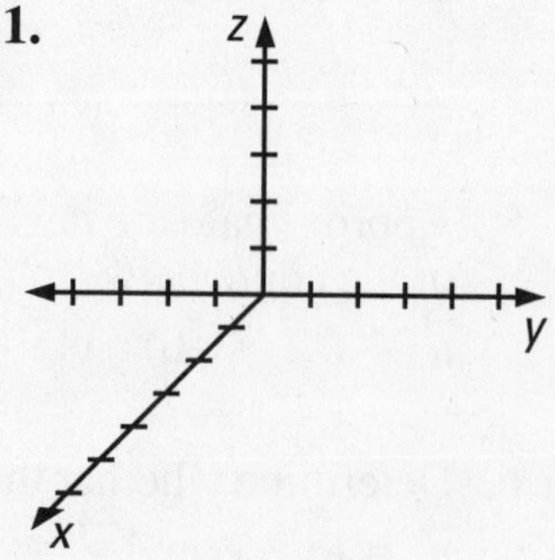

12. Write a vector equation for the line
    through the point $(4, -1)$ that is parallel
    to the vector $\vec{w} = (-2, -3)$.

12. _____

13. Find an equation of the plane through the
    point $(2, -1, 1)$ that is perpendicular to
    $\vec{u} = (-5, 4, -1)$.

13. _____

14. *Multiple choice.* Let $3x - 4y + 5z = 2$ be an equation
    for the plane M_1 and $2x + 3y - 4z = 6$ be an equation
    for the plane M_2. If $\vec{w} = (3, -4, 5) \times (2, 3, -4)$, then $\vec{w}$ is

    (a) perpendicular to both M_1 and M_2

    (b) parallel to both M_1 and M_2

    (c) perpendicular to M_1 and parallel to M_2

    (d) parallel to M_1 and perpendicular to M_2

14. _____

Precalculus and Discrete Mathematics © Scott Foresman Addison Wesley

CHAPTER 12 TEST, Form B

You will need a calculator for this test.

1. Find the magnitude and direction of the
   vector from (6, 1) to (-6, 6).

   1. _____

In 2 and 3, let $\vec{a} = [3, 22°]$ and $\vec{b} = [4, 52°]$. Compute each.

2. $2\vec{a} - \vec{b}$

   2. _____

3. $\vec{a} \cdot \vec{b}$

   3. _____

4. Prove: For all real numbers r and s and 3-dimensional vectors $\vec{u} = (u_1, u_2, u_3)$ and
   $\vec{v} = (v_1, v_2, v_3)$, $(r\vec{u}) \cdot (s\vec{v}) = (rs)(\vec{u} \cdot \vec{v})$.

   _____

   _____

5. Approximate the degree measure of
   the angle between the vectors
   $\vec{w} = (0, -4, 1)$ and $\vec{t} = (2, 0, 8)$.

   5. _____

6. Determine whether the vectors
   $\vec{u} = (-\sqrt{13}, 3, \sqrt{13})$ and $\vec{v} = (2, \sqrt{13}, -1)$
   are orthogonal, parallel, or neither.

   6. _____

7. A child pulls a wagon by exerting a force of 25 pounds
   at an angle of 38° with the horizontal.
   Find the approximate values of each.

   a. the horizontal component of the force

   7. a. _____

   b. the vertical component of the force

   b. _____

8. An aircraft pilot wishes to fly due west with a ground speed of 320 $\frac{k}{hr}$. If the wind is blowing
   directly from the south with a speed of 80 $\frac{k}{hr}$, what air speed and compass heading should
   the pilot maintain?

   _____

   _____

9. Find the polar representation of the vector $\vec{u} = (-3, 4)$

9. _____

10. Consider the vectors $\vec{v}$ and $\vec{w}$ shown in the figure at the right. Sketch the following vectors. Label each vector and give its endpoint.

10.

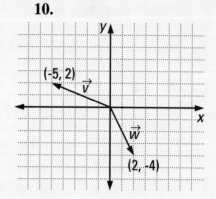

    a. $-1.5\vec{w}$

    b. $\vec{v} + \vec{w}$

    c. $\vec{w} + \vec{v}$

11. Sketch the vector $\vec{u} = (-2, 3, -3)$.

11.

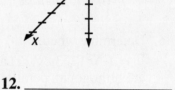

12. Find parametric equations for the line containing $(-3, 5)$ and parallel to the vector $\vec{v} = (7, -2)$.

12. _____

13. Find an equation for the plane that passes through the point $(-1, 2, -3)$ and is perpendicular to $\vec{g} = (1, 1, -1)$.

13. _____

14. Find a vector that is orthogonal to both $\vec{u} = (6, -1, 3)$ and $\vec{v} = (-4, 2, -1)$.

14. _____

Precalculus and Discrete Mathematics © Scott Foresman Addison Wesley

CHAPTER 12 TEST, Form C

1. Let $\vec{w}$ be the vector from $(1, -1)$ to $(-2, 5)$. Give the magnitude and direction of $\vec{w}$. Then find two nonzero vectors $\vec{u}$ and $\vec{v}$, such that $\vec{u} + \vec{v} = \vec{w}$, and $\vec{u}$ and $\vec{v}$ are neither parallel nor perpendicular to each other. Find the measure of the angle between $\vec{u}$ and $\vec{v}$.

2. Describe a situation that can be represented by the vectors in this figure. What do the components and the sum of the vectors represent in the situation? (Be specific.)

N
$\vec{w}$
40 mph
$\vec{v}$
160 mph
60°
W ← → E
S

3. Give parametric equations for a line parallel to the vector $\vec{q} = (-2, 5)$. Use the theorem that describes parallel vectors to verify that the line you specified is parallel to $\vec{q}$.

4. Give components of three 3-dimensional vectors $\vec{r}$, $\vec{s}$, and $\vec{t}$ so that each vector is orthogonal to the other two. Justify your answer.

5. Jameel says that the vector $\vec{j} = (-3, 6, 3)$ is perpendicular to the plane defined by the equation $x - 2y - z = -6$. Do you agree?

If you agree, explain. If you disagree, identify a vector $\vec{k}$ that *is* perpendicular to the plane, and justify your answer. Then sketch the plane and perpendicular vector on the axes at the right. Be sure to label the axes and all important points of your sketches.

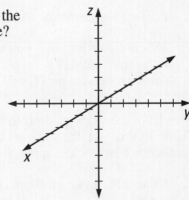

CHAPTER 12 TEST, Form D

A group of students is creating a study guide about vectors. They plan to call it *A Tale of Two Vectors in a Plane.* Part I of the study guide will be *Meet the Vectors,* and it will begin with the "vector profile" shown at the right.

a. Assume that the initial point and end point of $\vec{v}$ are correct as given. Is each part of the profile accurate? If you think a part is accurate, justify your answer. If you think it is not accurate, show how to correct it.

  i. magnitude

  ii. direction

  iii. component representation

  iv. polar representation

  v. opposite

  Modify the profile, incorporating your corrections.

b. Suppose $\vec{w} = [4, 60°]$ and has initial point $(3, 2)$. Create a profile for $\vec{w}$. Call it *Vector Profile #2.*

Part II of the study guide is to be called *When Two Vectors Get Together.* A plan for the first page of Part II is shown at the right, but it has yet to be completed.

c. Use $\vec{v}$ and $\vec{w}$ as given above. Copy and complete the page at the right. Be sure to draw an appropriate diagram, or appropriate diagrams, to illustrate the sum.

d. Use $\vec{v}$ and $\vec{w}$ as given above. Create pages for each of the following titles that the students have chosen. Be sure to draw a diagram or diagrams whenever appropriate.

  i. *Two Vectors in the Plane Have a Difference*

  ii. *Two Vectors in the Plane Have a Dot Product*

  iii. *Two Vectors in the Plane Form an Angle*

e. Is there any other page you would include in Part II of the study guide? If so, plan and write the page(s). If not, proceed to part **f.**

Part III of the study guide is to be called *When Two Vectors Go to Work.* In this part, the students hope to include at least two pages that show how vectors apply to real-life situations.

f. Write at least two problems that can be solved by using $\vec{v}$ and $\vec{w}$. For each problem, plan and write a page for the study guide. When you are finished, assemble all the pages to form the study guide.

Vector Profile #1

name: vector *v*

symbol: vector $\vec{v}$ or *v*

initial point: $(-1, -3)$

end point: $(-7, 5)$

magnitude: 10

direction: $\approx -53.1°$

component representation:
  $(6, -8)$

polar representation:
  $\approx -[10, -53.1°]$

opposite:
  $(-6, 8)$ or $\approx -[10, -53.1°]$

Two Vectors in the Plane Have a Sum

$\vec{v} + \vec{w}$

$= (v_1 + w_1, v_2 + w_2)$

$= \sim\!\sim\!\sim\!\sim\!\sim\!\sim$

$= \sim\!\sim\!\sim\!\sim\!\sim\!\sim$

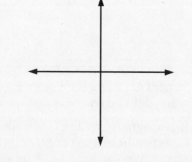

A Tale of Two Vectors in the Plane

Precalculus and Discrete Mathematics © Scott Foresman Addison Wesley

CHAPTER 12 TEST, Cumulative Form

You will need a calculator for this test.

1. Write the logical expression that corresponds
   to the following network.

   1. _____

   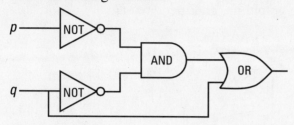

2. In a city with 9 high school basketball teams, is it possible
   to schedule the games for the season so that each team
   plays exactly 7 games and each game is against a different
   team? Justify your answer.

   _____

   _____

3. If $\vec{u} = (-2, -3)$ and $\vec{v} = (-3, -3)$,
   find and graph $\vec{w} = \vec{u} - 2\vec{v}$.

   _____

   3.

   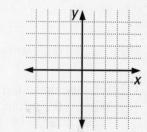

4. Find the polar representation of the vector (-14, 25).

   4. _____

5. Prove: For all 3-dimensional vectors $\vec{u}$, $\vec{v}$, and $\vec{w}$, if $\vec{w}$ is orthogonal to both $\vec{u}$ and
   $\vec{v}$, then $\vec{w}$ is orthogonal $\vec{u} + \vec{v}$.

6. If Mrs. Smith drove to her office at an average speed of 30 mph, at what speed must she drive back to average 36 mph for the round trip?

6. _____

7. *Multiple choice.* Which of the following graphs has an Euler circuit?

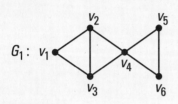

(a) G_1

(b) G_2

(c) both G_1 and G_2

(d) neither G_1 nor G_2

7. _____

8. Find all vectors in the plane that are orthogonal to (-1, 2) and have length 5.

8. _____

9. Find an equation for the plane through the point (2, -1, 0) that is parallel to the plane with equation $3x - y + z = 5$.

9. _____

10. Find all cube roots of -8.

10. _____

11. Imagine that a fair coin is tossed 20 times. What is the probability of the coin landing heads exactly 10 times?

11. _____

12. Find parametric equations for the line through the point (-1, 0, 2) that is orthogonal to both the vectors $\vec{u} = (2, 1, 0)$ and $\vec{v} = (1, 0, 1)$.

12. _____

13. Two tugboats are towing a ship into port, as shown in the figure. The larger tug exerts a force of 5,000 pounds on its cable, and the smaller tug exerts a force of 4,000 pounds on its cable. If the ship is to travel due east, find the angle θ that the smaller tug's cable must make with the eastward direction.

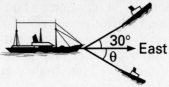

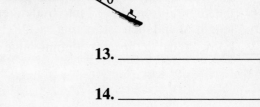

13. _____

14. Find the center and radius of the sphere with equation

$$x^2 - 6x + y^2 + 4y + z^2 - 2z = 86.$$

14. _____

15. **a.** Give the adjacency matrix for the graph below.

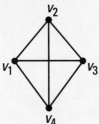

15. a. _____

b. How many walks of length 5 go from v_1 to v_2?

b. _____

QUIZ Lessons 13-1 Through 13-4

1. The graph at the right represents a household's electric power usage (in kilowatts) as a function of time (in hours). Estimate the total energy consumption (in kilowatt-hours) over the 12-hour period by partitioning the interval from 0 to 12 into 6 subintervals of equal length Δt and then estimating each $P(z_i)$ to the nearest kilowatt, using the left endpoint value for each z_i.

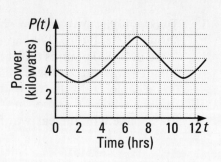

1. _____

2. Find the exact value of the definite integral
$\int_{-2}^{3}(5 - 2x)\,dx.$

2. _____

3. Use the points on the graph of $y = x^3$ shown at the right. Consider Riemann sums on the interval from 0 to 1.

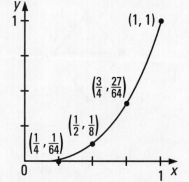

   a. Compute the value of the upper Riemann sum with 4 equal-width subintervals.

   _____

   b. Compute the value of the lower Riemann sum with 4 equal-width subintervals.

   _____

   c. According to parts **a** and **b**, $\int_{0}^{1}x^3\,dx$ is between __?__ and __?__ .

3. c. _____

4. Suppose g is a continuous function such that $\int_{-4}^{-2} g(x)\,dx = 5$, $\int_{-4}^{0} g(x)\,dx = 8$, and $\int_{0}^{3} g(x)\,dx = 6$. Find each.

   a. $\int_{-4}^{3} g(x)\,dx$

4. a. _____

   b. $\int_{-2}^{0} g(x)\,dx$

   b. _____

▶ **QUIZ for Lessons 13-1 Through 13-4** *page 2*

5. Shown below are the graphs of the functions *h* and *g*.
Express the area of the shaded region between
the two graphs using integral notation.
You do not have to evaluate the integral.

5. _____

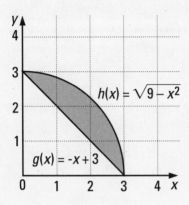

CHAPTER 13 TEST, Form A

1. When $f(x) = 2x^2$, evaluate $\sum\limits_{i=1}^{5} f(z_i)\Delta x$ over the interval from 0 to 10, using the right endpoint of the subinterval for each z_i.

_____

2. Find the exact value of the definite integral $\int_{-10}^{10} \sqrt{100 - x^2}\, dx$.

2. _____

3. Express the area of the shaded region as an integral.

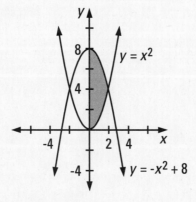

3. _____

4. *True or False*. Justify your answer.

$\int_2^3 \frac{1}{x-1}\, dx = \int_3^4 \frac{1}{x-1}\, dx - \int_2^4 \frac{1}{x-1}\, dx$

_____

5. Find the distance traveled over the 2-hour period by a train with the velocity-time graph below.

5. _____

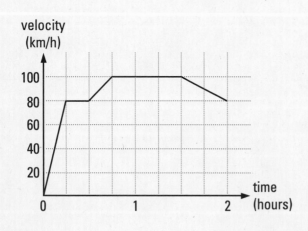

Precalculus and Discrete Mathematics © Scott Foresman Addison Wesley

6. The velocity (in ft/sec) of an object at t seconds is $3t^2 - 5t + 1$. Estimate the distance traveled by the object from $t = 5$ to $t = 10$ seconds to the nearest ten feet.

6. _____

7. Give an integral expressing the volume of the right circular cone generated by revolving the shaded region about the x-axis. Then find the value of the integral.

7. _____

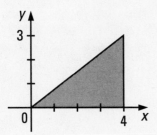

8. Consider the region bounded by the x-axis and the lines $x = -2$, $x = 2$, and $y = -x + 4$.

   a. Sketch the region.

   b. Set up and evaluate an integral that describes the area of this region.

8. a.

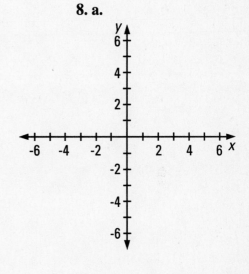

b. _____

9. The table at the right shows the rate (in gallons per minute) at which a jet engine is consuming fuel as a function of time (in minutes). What are the maximum and minimum possible values for the engine's total fuel consumption over the 8-minute period, if the rate of fuel consumption is constantly increasing?

t	$f(t)$
0	5.3
2	7.8
4	8.8
6	9.4
8	9.8

10. a. Rewrite the following expression as a
single integral.

$$\int_2^6 \frac{1}{x}\, dx + \int_2^6 \frac{x^2 - 1}{x}\, dx$$

b. Evaluate your answer to part **a**.

10. a. _____

b. _____

Precalculus and Discrete Mathematics © Scott Foresman Addison Wesley

CHAPTER 13 TEST, Form B

1. When $f(x) = 3x^2$, evaluate $\sum_{i=1}^{4} f(z_i)\Delta x$ over the interval from 0 to 8, using the right endpoint of the subinterval for each z_i.

_____

2. Find the exact value of the definite integral $\int_{-2}^{0} 7\sqrt{4 - x^2}\, dx$.

2.

3. Express the area of the shaded region as an integral.

3. _____

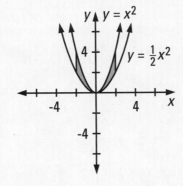

4. *True or False*. Justify your answer.

$$\int_{0}^{1} x^2 dx = \left(\int_{0}^{1} x\, dx\right)^2$$

_____

5. Find the distance traveled over the 2-hour period by a train with the velocity-time graph below.

5. _____

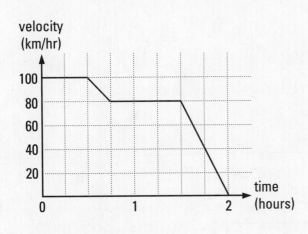

6. The velocity (in ft/sec) of an object at t seconds is $t^2 - 3t + 2$. Find the distance traveled by the object from $t = 6$ to $t = 10$ seconds to the nearest foot.

6. _____

7. Give an integral expressing the volume of the right circular cone generated by revolving the shaded region about the x-axis. Then find the value of the integral.

7. _____

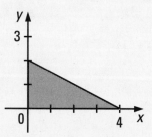

8. Consider the region bounded by the x-axis and the lines $x = -1$, $x = 1$, and $y = -x^2 + 4$.

   a. Sketch the region.

   b. Set up and evaluate an integral that describes the area of this region.

8. a.

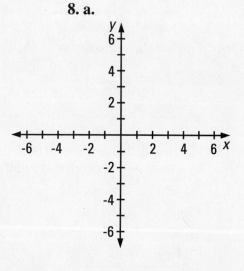

   b. _____

9. A parabolic plastic bowl which is 5 inches deep and has a radius of 10 inches can be generated by rotating the graph of $y = \sqrt{20x}$ from 0 to 5 about the x-axis. What is the volume of this bowl?

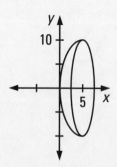

9. _____

Precalculus and Discrete Mathematics © Scott Foresman Addison Wesley

▶ **CHAPTER 13 TEST, Form B** *page 3*

10. a. Rewrite the following expression as a single integral.

$$\int_{-2}^{3} (8x - 7)dx + \int_{-2}^{3} (-6x + 9)dx$$

b. Evaluate your answer to part **a**.

10. a. _____

b. _____

CHAPTER 13 TEST, Form C

1. Consider the function f with $f(x) = -x^2 + 144$ over the interval $[0, 12]$. Evaluate $\sum_{i=1}^{n} f(z_i)\Delta x$ for appropriate interpretations of n and z_i. Be sure to specify the meanings of n, z_i and Δx.

2. Choose one property of definite integrals that you studied in Chapter 13.

   a. Describe the property in your own words.

   b. Give a formal statement of the property.

   c. Give an example to illustrate the property.

3. Kami said, "The graph at the right shows *without calculation* that $\int_0^6 10x\,dx > \int_0^6 x^2\,dx$."

   a. Explain why Kami's statement is true.

   b. Perform the calculations that support the statement.

   c. Find a value of n for which $\int_0^n 10x\,dx < \int_0^n x^2\,dx$ and justify your answer.

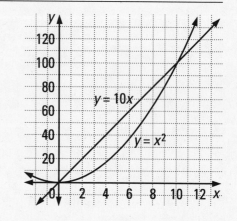

4. The equation below gives the velocity of $v(t)$ of a car in feet per second as a function of the time t in seconds, from $t = 0$ to $t = 8$. State as many facts as you can about the situation.

$$v(t) = -.875(t - 8)^2 + 56$$

5. Your friend was absent from class one day and now finds it hard to understand how the plane figure at the right could be related to volumes and integrals. Explain how.

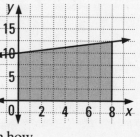

CHAPTER 13 TEST, Form D

At the right is a sketch of a vase. The part of the vase that holds the water or other contents, called the *bowl*, rests on a solid base.

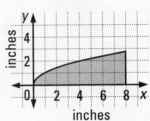

Below the sketch, half the "silhouette" of the bowl has been drawn on a coordinate plane. The region bounded by the y-axis, the line $f(x) = \sqrt{x}$, and the line $y = 8$ generates the bowl of the vase when it is rotated around the x-axis.

a. Show how to use integrals to find the volume of the bowl of this vase in cubic inches.

b. One gallon of water occupies bout 231 cubic inches. What is the capacity of the bowl of this vase in fluid ounces?

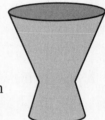

c. Suppose the region on the coordinate plane were bounded by $y = 4$ instead of $y = 8$, so that the height of the bowl is 4 inches rather than 8 inches. What effect would this have on the capacity of the bowl?

The second vase sketched at the right appears to have two sections, each of which is shaped like a part of a cone called a *frustum*. In this vase, the two sections together form a single bowl.

d. On the coordinate plane, the region bounded by the x- and y-axes, the line $f(x) = .5x + 2$, and the line $y = 2$ generates the bottom section of the vase when it is rotated around the x-axis. Show how to use integrals to find the volume of this part of the vase in cubic inches.

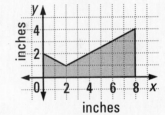

e. The top section of the vase is generated when the region bounded by the x-axis, the line line $f(x) = .5x$, and the lines $y = 2$ and $y = 8$ is rotated around the x-axis. Show how to use integrals to find the volume of this part of the vase in cubic inches.

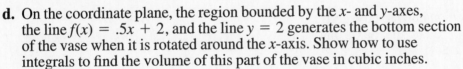

f. What is the total volume of this vase in cubic inches?

g. What is the capacity of this vase in fluid ounces?

h. Suppose that a friend is planning to start a business making and selling pottery. Your fiend has asked for help in designing a set of three pottery vases that have the following capacities.

- between 8 fluid ounces and 16 fluid ounces
- between 16 fluid ounces and 32 fluid ounces
- between 32 fluid ounces and 48 fluid ounces

Create three vase designs that are different from those shown above. Each design should be generated by rotating a plane region around the x-axis. You may work with the ideas shown at the right, or you may create your own original designs. For each design, sketch a "silhouette" on a coordinating plane, as was done above. Then show how to use integrals to find the capacity of the vase. Summarize your results in a description to your friend.

Precalculus and Discrete Mathematics © Scott Foresman Addison Wesley

CHAPTER 13 TEST, Cumulative Form

1. A car accelerates from 0 to 64 ft/sec with a speed given by $g(x) = -4(x - 4)^2 + 64$ ft/sec after x seconds. Estimate the distance the car travels in 4 seconds by splitting the interval up into 8 subintervals and letting z_i = the right endpoint of each subinterval.

1. _____

2. Graph the region described by $\int_2^4 \sqrt{16 - x^2}\,dx$.

2.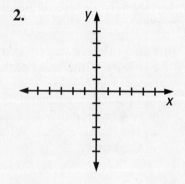

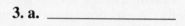

3. **a.** Compute $\int_0^4 (-x + 2)\,dx$.

3. a. _____

b. Sketch the region between the graph of $f(x) = -x + 2$ and the x-axis on the interval $0 \le x \le 4$.

b.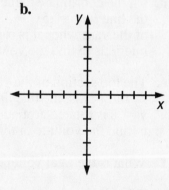

c. What is the area of the region sketched in part **b**?

c. _____

d. Why are the answers to parts **a** and **c** different?

Precalculus and Discrete Mathematics © Scott Foresman Addison Wesley

4. Suppose g is a continuous function such that
$\int_{-5}^{-2} g(x)dx = -3$, $\int_{-5}^{0} g(x)dx = -5$, and $\int_{0}^{5} g(x)dx = 4$. Find each.

   a. $\int_{-5}^{5} g(x)dx$ 4. a. _____

   b. $\int_{-2}^{0} g(x)dx$ b. _____

5. Find an Euler circuit, if it exists.   5. _____

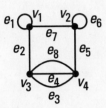

6. A vector equation of a line is $(x - 2, y + 5) = t(3, 4)$.

   a. Give parametric equations for this line.   6. a. _____

   b. Graph the line.   b.

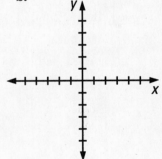

7. For what value of k is $\int_{3}^{k} 2x^2 dx = 126$?   7. _____

8. **a.** Sketch a graph of the region bounded by
     the graphs of $f(x) = 2\sqrt{x}$ and $x = 3$, and
     the x-axis.   8. a.

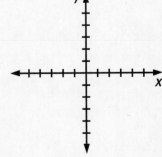

   b. Calculate the volume of the solid   b. _____
     generated when this region is revolved
     about the x-axis.

9. Find x so that the vectors $\vec{u} = (-5, 2, 3)$ and $\vec{v} = (x, -2, -1)$ are orthogonal.

9. _____

10. **a.** Sketch the vector $\vec{v}$ from the point $(3, 5)$ to the point $(-2, 3)$.

   10. a.

   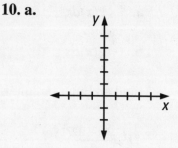

   b. Find the component representation of $\vec{v}$.

   b. _____

   c. Find the polar representation of $\vec{v}$.

   c. _____

11. Sketch a graph with the following adjacency matrix.

    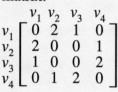

    $$\begin{array}{c} \\ v_1 \\ v_2 \\ v_3 \\ v_4 \end{array} \begin{array}{cccc} v_1 & v_2 & v_3 & v_4 \\ \left[\begin{array}{cccc} 0 & 2 & 1 & 0 \\ 2 & 0 & 0 & 1 \\ 1 & 0 & 0 & 2 \\ 0 & 1 & 2 & 0 \end{array}\right] \end{array}$$

    11.

Precalculus and Discrete Mathematics © Scott Foresman Addison Wesley

COMPREHENSIVE TEST, CHAPTERS 1-13

1. Find the negation of the statement.
All classes that reach chapter 13 move quickly.

1. _____

(a) *All classes that do not reach chapter 13 do not move quickly.*

(b) *All classes that reach chapter 13 do not move quickly.*

(c) *Some class that reaches chapter 13 does not move quickly.*

(d) *Some class that does not reach chapter 13 moves quickly.*

2. What statement is equivalent to $\sim (p \ or \ q)$?

2. _____

(a) $(\sim p)$ and $(\sim q)$ (b) $\sim (p$ and $q)$

(c) $\sim p$ or $\sim q$ (d) p and q

3. Which of the following is the contrapositive of
the statement below?
*If an employee's performance review is positive,
then the employee receives a raise.*

3. _____

(a) *There is an employee whose performance review was negative and received a raise.*

(b) *If an employee's performance review is negative, then the employee does not receive a raise.*

(c) *If an employee receives a raise, then the employee's performance review is positive.*

(d) *If an employee does not receive a raise, then the employee's performance review is negative.*

4. The argument $p \Rightarrow q$
$$\sim q$$
$$\therefore \sim p$$
is an example of what type of reasoning?

4. _____

(a) converse error   (b) inverse error

(c) Law of Indirect Reasoning   (d) Law of Transitivity

5. The domain of a function f is $(-\infty, 100]$ and
the range is $[-4, 5]$. What is the maximum value of f?

5. _____

(a) 100   (b) 5

(c) -4   (d) $-\infty$

6. Which equation describes a function which
is neither an increasing nor a decreasing function?

6. _____

(a) $f(x) = \log x$ (b) $g(x) = x^3$

(c) $h(x) = x^2 - 1$ (d) $k(x) = e^x - 1$

Precalculus and Discrete Mathematics © Scott Foresman Addison Wesley

7. The parametric equations below represent the path of a baseball after it is hit, where y is the height and x is the horizontal distance traveled.

$$\begin{cases} x(t) = 80t \\ y(t) = -16t^2 + 30t + 4 \end{cases}$$

What does the 4 represent?　　　　　　　　　　　　　7. _____

(a) the distance the ball is hit in front of the plate

(b) the height at which the ball is hit

(c) the speed of the ball

(d) the value of gravitational acceleration

8. Which equation describes a function that is continuous over the interval $[1, 3]$?　　　　8. _____

(a) $f(x) \lfloor \frac{1}{-3} x \rfloor$ 　　　　　　(b) $g(x) = \lfloor x + 4 \rfloor$

(c) $h(x) = 7 \lfloor x \rfloor$ 　　　　　　　　(d) $k(x) = \lfloor 2x \rfloor$

9. If $g(x) = x^2 + 2x + 1$ and $h(x) = \sqrt{x}$, what is an equation for $h(g(x))$?　　　　　　9. _____

(a) $h(g(x)) = x + 2\sqrt{x} + 1$ 　　(b) $h(g(x)) = |x| + 2\sqrt{x} + 1$

(c) $h(g(x)) = |x + 1|$ 　　　　　　(d) $h(g(x)) = |x| + 1$

10. Use the Intermediate Value Theorem to find the interval which contains a solution to $x^3 - 3x^2 - 4x + 5 = 0$.　　　　　　　　　　10. _____

(a) $[1, 3]$ 　　　　　　　　　(b) $[-1, 0]$

(c) $(2, 3)$ 　　　　　　　　　(d) $(3, 4)$

11. Solve the inequality $x^2 - 2x - 24 \geq 0$.　　　　　　　　11. _____

(a) $x \leq -4$ or $x \geq 6$ 　　　　(b) $-4 \leq x \leq 6$

(c) $x \leq -3$ or $x \leq 8$ 　　　　(d) $-3 \leq x \leq 8$

12. If the transformation $T: (x, y) \to (3x + 2, 2y + 1)$ is applied to the graphs of the parametric equations　　　　12. _____

$$\begin{cases} x(t) = t^2 + 2t + 1 \\ y(t) = 3t + 1 \end{cases},$$

what equations describe the graph of the image?

(a) $\begin{cases} x(t) = \frac{t^2 + 2t + 1}{3} - 2 \\ y(t) = \frac{3t + 1}{2} - 1 \end{cases}$ 　　(b) $\begin{cases} x(t) = 3t^2 + 6t + 5 \\ y(t) = 6t + 3 \end{cases}$

(c) $\begin{cases} x(t) = \frac{t^2 + 2t + 1}{3} - 2 \\ y(t) = 6t + 3 \end{cases}$ 　　(d) $\begin{cases} x(t) = 3t^2 + 6t + 5 \\ y(t) = \frac{3t + 1}{2} - 1 \end{cases}$

13. What is the remainder when
$p(x) = 5x^3 + 2x^2 + 3x + 1$
is divided by $q(x) = x^2 - 3$?

(a) $5x + 2$ (b) 163

(c) $18x + 7$ (d) $5x^2 + 17x + 54$

13. _____

14. If each cake has y pieces and a caterer is
serving a party with x guests, each of which
receives at least 1 piece of cake, how many cakes
must be made?

(a) $\frac{x}{y}$ (b) $\frac{y}{x}$

(c) $\lfloor \frac{x}{y} \rfloor$ (d) $\lceil \frac{x}{y} \rceil$

14. _____

15. Which of the following is equivalent to 3 mod 7?

(a) 183 mod 7 (b) 66 mod 7

(c) 92 mod 7 (d) 121 mod 7

15. _____

16. Which statement would you make to begin a
proof by contradiction of the statement below?
*There are infinitely many rational numbers
between 1 and 2.*

(a) Suppose there are finitely many rational numbers between 1 and 2.

(b) Suppose there are infinitely many imaginary numbers between 1 and 2.

(c) Suppose there exists a number between 1 and 2 which is not rational.

(d) Suppose there are infinitely many real numbers between 1 and 2.

16. _____

17. Which of the following rational expressions is
in lowest terms?

(a) $\dfrac{x^2 - \frac{3}{2}x - 1}{2x^2 + 5x + 2}$ (b) $\dfrac{x^2 + 2x + 5}{x - 1}$

(c) $\dfrac{x^2 + 2x - 3}{x - 1}$ (d) $\dfrac{x^2 - 3x - 28}{x^2 + x - 56}$

17. _____

18. Find the oblique asymptote of the function f with
$f(x) = \dfrac{7x^3 + 4x^2 + 3x + 3}{13x^2 + 2}$.

(a) $y = \frac{7}{13}$ (b) $y = 0$

(c) $y = \frac{7}{13}x + \frac{4}{13}$ (d) $y = 25x + 31$

18. _____

19. Rationalize the denominator of $\dfrac{3}{\sqrt{2}+7}$.

19. _____

(a) $\dfrac{3\sqrt{2}+21x}{47}$

(b) $\dfrac{3\sqrt{2}-21}{47}$

(c) $\dfrac{-3\sqrt{2}-21}{47}$

(d) $\dfrac{-3\sqrt{2}+21}{47}$

20. A trucker drives from Nashville to Atlanta and back. On the way to Atlanta, the truck drives 60 mph. If the distance from Nashville to Atlanta is d miles, and the trucker averaged A mph, which equation relates A, d, and the rate returning to Nashville r?

20. _____

(a) $\dfrac{2d}{60+r}=A$

(b) $\dfrac{120r}{60+r}=A$

(c) $\dfrac{60+r}{A}=d$

(d) $\dfrac{2}{60+r}=A$

21. Determine which of the following is an identity.

21. _____

(a) $2\cos\theta=2\sin\theta\cos\theta$

(b) $\sin(x^2)-\cos(x^2)=1$

(c) $1+\tan^2 x=\sec^2 x$

(d) $\cos(\alpha+\beta)=\sin\alpha\sin\beta-\cos\alpha\cos\beta$

22. Determine the amplitude of $h\colon x\to 7\cos 3x$.

22. _____

(a) $\dfrac{1}{7}$

(b) 7

(c) $\dfrac{2\pi}{3}$

(d) 6π

23. Which of the following equals $\cos(a-b)$ for all a and b?

23. _____

(a) $\sin a\cos b-\cos a\sin b$

(b) $\sin a\cos b+\cos a\sin b$

(c) $\sin b\cos a-\sin a\cos b$

(d) $\sin a\sin b+\cos a\cos b$

24. A golf ball travels a horizontal distance d according to the equation $\dfrac{v^2\sin(2\theta)}{9.8\text{ m/sec}^2}=d$, where v is the velocity of the ball in m/sec and θ is the angle at which the ball leaves the ground. Which of the following expresses the distance using the double angle identity?

24. _____

(a) $d=\dfrac{v^2(\cos^2\theta-\sin^2\theta)}{9.81\text{ m/sec}^2}$

(b) $d=\dfrac{v^2(2\cos\theta\sin\theta)}{9.81\text{ m/sec}^2}$

(c) $d=\dfrac{v^2(1-2\sin^2\theta)}{9.81\text{ m/sec}^2}$

(d) $d=\dfrac{v^2(1+\cos^2 2\theta)}{9.81\text{ m/sec}^2}$

Precalculus and Discrete Mathematics © Scott Foresman Addison Wesley

25. A sequence has an initial condition 3 and a constant difference of 4. Which is an explicit formula for the sequence?

    (a) $a_n = 3(4^n)$ (b) $a_n = 3n + 4$

    (c) $a_n = 4n - 1$ (d) $a_n = 3n + 1$

25. _____

26. Which correctly represents the series $1^3 - 2^3 + 3^3 - 4^3 + 5^3 - 6^3$?

    (a) $\sum\limits_{i=1}^{6} (-1)^{i+1}(i)^3$ (b) $\sum\limits_{i=1}^{6} -i^3$

    (c) $-\sum\limits_{i=1}^{6} i^3$ (d) $\sum\limits_{i=1}^{6} (-i)^3$

26. _____

27. Determine the value of $\sum\limits_{i=1}^{15} 3(4)^i$.

    (a) 357913941   (b) 4294967292

    (c) 1073741823   (d) 28697812

27. _____

28. To prove $\sum\limits_{n=1}^{n} \dfrac{i}{(i-1)(i-2)} = \dfrac{n-2}{2n}$ using mathematical induction, which is the correct basis step?

    (a) $S(1)$ is true   (b) $S(3)$ is true

    (c) $S(k) \Rightarrow S(k+1)$ (d) $S(k+1) \Rightarrow S(k)$

28. _____

29. The current I in an AC circuit is 7 amps and the impedance Z is $-4 + 6i$. Determine the voltage V, if $V = IZ$.

    (a) $V = -28 + 42i$ (b) $V = -\frac{4}{7} + \frac{6}{7}i$

    (c) $V = 3 + 6i$ (d) $V = -11 + 6i$

29. _____

30. Convert the polar coordinates $[5, 30°]$ to rectangular coordinates.

    (a) $\left(\frac{\sqrt{3}}{2}, \frac{1}{2}\right)$ (b) $\left(\frac{1}{2}, \frac{\sqrt{3}}{2}\right)$

    (c) $\left(\frac{5}{2}, \frac{5\sqrt{3}}{2}\right)$ (d) $\left(\frac{5\sqrt{3}}{2}, \frac{5}{2}\right)$

30. _____

31. A polynomial with real coefficients and a degree of 6 has a complex zero of $1 - 2i$. Which of the following is a possible set of zeros for the polynomial?

    (a) 5 real, 1 non-real   (b) 3 real, 3 non-real

    (c) 1 real, 5 non-real   (d) 2 real, 4 non-real

31. _____

32. Suppose a town's population is 24,000 and is growing continuously at an annual rate of 3%. About what will the population's average rate of change be over 10 years?

    (a) 840/yr   (b) 1250/yr

    (c) 720/yr   (d) 1520/yr

32. _____

33. Given the graph of the function k' below, which is true of the function k?

    (a) k is increasing on the interval $(0, 3)$.

    (b) k is decreasing on the interval $(-2, 2)$.

    (c) k has a relative maximum at $y = -3$.

    (d) k has a relative minimum at $y = -2$.

33. _____

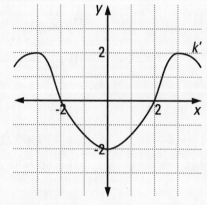

In 34 and 35, a toy rocket is launched from a 4-ft platform. The height of the rocket in feet is given by $h(t) = -16t^2 + 60t + 4$, where t is measured in seconds.

34. What maximum height does the rocket achieve?

    (a) $60\frac{1}{4}$ ft   (b) $\frac{15}{8}$ ft

    (c) 80 ft   (d) 50 ft

34. _____

35. What is the velocity of the rocket at $t = 1$?

    (a) 60 ft/sec   (b) 28 ft/sec

    (c) 48 ft/sec   (d) 32 ft/sec

35. _____

36. How many different 3-element subsets can be made from a 15-element set?

    (a) 3375   (b) 2730

    (c) 455   (d) 680

36. _____

37. Suppose 3% of a company's yo-yos are delivered with tangled strings. If a store receives a shipment of 20 yo-yos, what is the probability that more than 3 have tangled strings?

    (a) $\approx .018$ (b) $\approx .997$

    (c) $\approx .003$ (d) $\approx .982$

37. _____

38. An employee is sent to the store to buy prizes for the company picnic. If the employee needs to buy 15 prizes and there are 4 types of prizes that can be bought, how many different collections of prizes are there?

(a) 1365   (b) 3060

(c) 32760   (d) 816

38. _____

In 39–41, use the graph at the right.

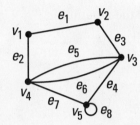

39. Determine the degree of v_5.

(a) 3   (b) 5

(c) 4   (d) 2

39. _____

40. Find all the edges which are adjacent to e_4.

(a) e_3, e_5, e_6 (b) e_3, e_5, e_6, e_7

(c) e_5, e_6, e_7 (d) e_3, e_5, e_6, e_7, e_8

40. _____

41. Which of the following is an Euler circuit?

(a) $e_1 \, e_3 \, e_4 \, e_8 \, e_7 \, e_6 \, e_5 \, e_2$ (b) $e_5 \, e_6 \, e_2 \, e_1 \, e_3 \, e_6 \, e_7 \, e_8 \, e_2$

(c) $e_4 \, e_7 \, e_6 \, e_5 \, e_2 \, e_1 \, e_3$ (d) No Euler circuit exists.

41. _____

42. Suppose in a certain city, if it snows on any given day, the probability that it will snow on the following day is .3 and if it doesn't snow on any given day the probability is .8 that it doesn't snow on the following day. What is the approximate probability that it will snow on any given day?

(a) .63   (b) .47

(c) .22   (d) .08

42. _____

43. Estimate the measure of the angle between the vectors $\vec{u} = (3, 2)$ and $\vec{v} = (-2, 5)$.

(a) 136°   (b) 78°

(c) 12°   (d) 164°

43. _____

44. Find the value of x such that $\vec{s} = (7, 2)$ is orthogonal to $\vec{t} = (x, -2)$.

(a) $x = -7$ (b) $x = \frac{4}{7}$

(c) $x = 7$ (d) $x = -\frac{4}{7}$

44. _____

45. Which is an equation for the plane perpendicular to the vector $(-3, 6, 2)$ and passing through the point $(1, 0, 3)$?

45. _____

(a) $x + 3z = 1$ (b) $-3x + 6y + 2z = 7$

(c) $-6x + 12y + 4z = 6$ (d) $2x - y + 12z = 38$

46. Two forces are applied to an object as shown in the diagram below. Estimate the magnitude of the resultant force.

46. _____

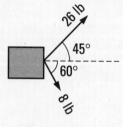

(a) 25 lb (b) 34 lb

(c) 18 lb (d) 29 lb

47. Calculate the Riemann sum of $g(x) = 2^x$ over the interval $[0, 3]$, letting $\Delta x = .5$ and $z_i = $ the right endpoint of the ith subinterval.

47. _____

(a) 8.4 (b) 11.9

(c) 10.1 (d) 14.3

48. Find the exact value of the definite integral $\int_{1}^{7} (x^2 + 3)\, dx$.

48. _____

(a) $135\frac{1}{3}$ (b) 109

(c) 157 (d) 132

49. A bicycle decelerates from 44 ft/sec to 14 ft/sec in 15 seconds. How far did the bicycle travel in the 15 seconds? (Assume the deceleration is constant.)

49. _____

(a) 14 ft (b) 400 ft

(c) 435 ft (d) 30 ft

50. Find the volume of the solid generated when the region bounded by $h(x) = \sqrt{x}$, $x = 3$, and the x-axis is revolved about the x-axis.

50. _____

(a) $\frac{9\pi}{2}$ (b) 9π

(c) 8π (d) $\frac{234\pi}{5}$

Precalculus and Discrete Mathematics © Scott Foresman Addison Wesley

Answers and Evaluation Guides*

Quiz — Lessons 1-1 Through 1-4

1. a. Sample: There is at least one number x such that x^2 is less than the opposite of x.

   b. True

2. (c)

3. p and q

4. a. $\sim(p \text{ and } q) \text{ or } (q \text{ and } r)$
   b. 1

5. a. $\exists$ a real number x such that $\frac{1}{x} = x$.

   b. negation

6. The sentence $x^2 + x^2 \geq 2xy$ holds for all real numbers x and y. Hence, in particular, it holds when $x = \sqrt{k}$ and $y = \frac{1}{\sqrt{k}}$, since $\sqrt{k}$ and $\frac{1}{\sqrt{k}}$ are real numbers if $k > 0$. Substituting $\sqrt{k}$ for x and $\frac{1}{\sqrt{k}}$ for y yields $k + \frac{1}{k} \geq 2$.

Quiz — Lessons 1-5 Through 1-7

1.

p	q	$p \Rightarrow q$
T	T	T
T	F	F
F	T	T
F	F	T

2. a. $\forall x, |x| < 5 \Rightarrow x < 5$
   b. converse

3. (d)

4. $\exists$ real numbers a and b such that $a^2 = b$ and $b - a \leq 0$.

5. No, the argument is not valid. The argument is an example of inverse error.

6. a. 961 is not prime
   b. Modus Tollens

Chapter 1 Test, Form A

1. (c) 2. (d)

3. Let $x = n^{100}$. Since for all real numbers n, n^{100} is a nonzero real number, $(n^{100})^2 = n^{200} > 0$.

4. (c); valid

5. (d); invalid

6. True

7. $\exists$ a real number x such that $|x| - x < 0$.

8. If the inverse of a function f is itself a function, then no horizontal line intersects the graph of f in more than one point. If no horizontal line intersects the graph of f in more than one point, then the inverse of f is itself a function.

9. (b)

10. $k > 0$ or $k = 0$ and $k < 100$

11. (b)

12. $\sim(p \text{ or } q) \text{ or } \sim q$

13. 0   14. See below.

15. False; Sample: If $x = -1$ and $y = -1$, then $xy > 0$ but $x < 0$ and $y < 0$.

16. Invalid: the argument applies the inverse error

17. True   18. False

19. False

20. $\forall a$ and b, $ab = 0 \Rightarrow a = 0$ or $b = 0$

Chapter 1 Test, Form B

1. (b) 2. (a)

3. Let $a = x$ and $b = -y$. Then $a^3 + b^3 = x^3 + (-y^3) = (x^3 - y^3) = (x + (-y))(x^2 - x(-y)) + (-y^2)) = (x - y)(x^2 + xy + y^2)$

4. (e); invalid

5. (a); valid

6. False

7. $\exists$ a real number x such that $x^2 - |x| < 0$

8. If two lines are perpendicular, then the product of their slopes is -1.

9. (c)

10. $k > -10$ and $k < 5$

11. (b)

12. $\sim(p \text{ and } q) \text{ or } \sim q$

13. 1   14. See below.

15. False; Sample counterexample: If $x = 0$ and $y = 2$, then $0 \cdot 2 = 0$ (the antecedent is true) but $y = 2$ (the consequent is false).

16. Valid; the argument applies the Law of Indirect Reasoning followed by the Law of Detachment.

17. False   18. False

19. True

20. $\forall a$ and b, $a = b \Rightarrow a + c = b + c$

Test Form A

14.

p	q	$\sim q$	$p \Rightarrow \sim q$	$\sim(p \Rightarrow \sim q)$	p and q
T	T	F	F	T	T
T	F	T	T	F	F
F	T	F	T	F	F
F	F	T	T	F	F

Test Form B

14.

p	q	$\sim q$	$\sim p \Rightarrow q$	p or q
T	T	F	T	T
T	F	F	T	T
F	T	T	T	T
F	F	T	F	F

*Evaluation Guides for Chapter Test, Forms C and D, are on pages 191–216.

Quiz — Lessons 2-1 Through 2-4

1. domain: $(-\infty, 9]$; range: $[2, \infty)$
2. a. $[5, 9]$
   b. 50
3. No; Sample: 13.6 volts is mapped to two different currents (15.5 and -15.5 milliamps)
4. a. -7
   b. $y = -7$
5. a. $I = \frac{250}{x^2}$
   b. $S = 4x^2 = \frac{1500}{x}$
   c. $x \approx 5.7$ cm

Quiz — Lessons 2-5 Through 2-7

1. At $t = 0$, $(-6, 5)$; at $t = 2$, $(2, 11)$
2. No. At 15 ft from the server (when $x(t) = 15$), the ball is only 8.25 ft high.
3. $\frac{8\pi}{9}$
4. a. max: 9; min: -5
   b. $\frac{2\pi}{3}$
5. a. domain: $(-\infty, \infty)$;
   b. range: $(0, \infty)$
6. a. $15,791
   b. $5,751

Chapter 2 Test, Form A

1. a. $(3, \infty)$
   b. $(-\infty, 0)$
2. $x = 24$
3. a. increasing on $[.3, \infty)$; decreasing on $(-\infty, .3]$
   b. minimum: -2.45
4. a. $(-\infty, -1]$, $[1, \infty)$
   b. rel. max: 1; rel. min: -1
   c. odd
5. a. $r(p) = 23{,}000p - 1123p^2$
   b. $10.22
   c. $118,000
6. -13
7. a. $\lim\limits_{t \to -\infty} k(t) = -\infty$, $\lim\limits_{t \to \infty} k(t) = 2$
   b. $y = 2$
8. a. $A_n = 0.3A_{n-1} + 750$
   b. ≈ 1070 mg
9. a. $x(t) = 90t$ $y(t) = -16t^2 + 20t + 45$
   b. 130 ft
10. a. $\left\{ y \colon \frac{9}{2} \le y \le \frac{11}{2} \right\}$
    b. $\frac{2\pi}{3}$
11. a. $P(t) = 200\left(\frac{1}{2}\right)^{\frac{t}{5.26}}$
    b. ≈ 9 years

Chapter 2 Test, Form B

1. a. $(-\infty, 4)$
   b. $(-\infty, 0)$
2. $x = 45$
3. a. increasing on $(-\infty, 1]$; decreasing on $[1, \infty)$
   b. maximum: 5
4. a. increasing on $(-\infty, -2]$; decreasing on $[-2, \infty)$
   b. maximum: 4
   c. neither
5. a. $r(N) = 23{,}000N - 1123N^2$
   b. 1700
   c. $7,225
6. 4
7. a. $\lim\limits_{x \to -\infty} h(x) = 0$, $\lim\limits_{x \to \infty} h(x) = 0$
   b. $y = 0$
8. a. $P_{n+1} = 1.1P_n$
   b. $P_{n+1} = 1.1P_n - \frac{.1}{2000}P_n^2$
9. a. $x(t) = 29.6t$ $y(t) = -4.9t^2 + 9.8t + 1.5$
   b. 63.4 m
10. a. $\{y \colon -8 \le y \le -2\}$
    b. 4π
11. a. $P(t) = 20e^{-0.326t}$
    b. 2003

Chapter 2 Test, Cumulative Form

1. $\frac{73}{8}$

2. $\lim\limits_{x\to-\infty} f(x) = 7$, $\lim\limits_{x\to\infty} f(x) = 7$

3. Sample: $\sim p \Rightarrow \sim q$
$$\frac{\sim q}{\therefore \sim p}$$

4. a. [0, 4]
   b. $(-\infty, 0]$
   c. rel. min: 0,
   rel. max: 6
   on interval $[4, \infty)$

5. a. 0
   b. 0

6. False; let $x = 1$ and $y = -1$.
   Then $|-1 + 1| = 0 < |-1| + |1| = 2$.

7. $\frac{11}{36}\pi$

8. ≈ 3.6 million people

9. a. $V_n = 2(0.6)^n$
   b. 2, 1.2, .72, .432
   c. 0

10. Sample: For all governments g, g is inefficient.

11. Sample: For all states s, s has at least one lake.

12. Sample: There exists a president who was born in Wisconsin.

13. 23 feet, 5 inches

14. domain: $(-\infty, 81]$;
    range: $[0, \infty)$

Quiz — Lessons 3-1 Through 3-4

1. $\frac{f}{g}(x) = \log\frac{x}{x^2 - 1}$
   domain $\{x: x > 0, x \neq 1\}$

2. $f \circ g(x) = \log(x^2 - 1)$
   domain: $\{x: x > 1$ or $x < -1\}$

3. No; Sample: h is not a 1-1 function, since $h(1) = h(-1)$.

4. $t = 2.5$

5. Since f is continuous over the interval $(-\infty, \infty)$, it is continuous over the interval [2, 3]. Then, by the Intermediate Value Theorem, since 0 is between -7 and 5, there is at least one real number c between 2 and 3 such that $f(c) = 0$. Since f is 1-1, $\forall x$, $x \neq c \Rightarrow f(x) \neq f(c)$. 4 is not between 2 and 3 so $f(4) \neq 0$.

Quiz — Lessons 3-5 Through 3-8

1. $\{x: x < -.5 \ln 2 \approx -.347\}$
2. $\{m: -4 < m < 2\}$
3. $\left\{x: x = 2n\pi \text{ or} \right.$
   $x = \frac{2\pi}{3} + 2n\pi$ or
   $\left. x = \frac{4\pi}{3} + 2n\pi\right\}$
4. a. $\left(\frac{x+7}{3}\right)^2 + \left(\frac{y-2}{4}\right)^2 = 1$
   b. $(-7, 2)$
5. $x = \frac{\sqrt{3}-5}{2}$, $x = \frac{-\sqrt{3}-5}{2}$,
   $x = -3$
6. $y = 5\sin\left(\frac{3(x-1)}{2}\right) + 4$

Chapter 3 Test, Form A

1. $r \circ v(x) = e^{\frac{x}{2}}$
   domain: set of all real numbers

2. $\frac{r}{v}(x) = \frac{\sqrt{x}}{e^x}$
   domain: $\{x: x \geq 0\}$

3.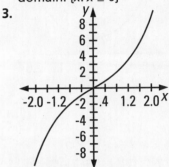

4. $x = 2$ or $x = 10^7$

5. Yes, it is a function.
   $f^{-1}(x) = \log_4 x$.

6. $\frac{y-4}{2} = 3(5x)^2 - 2(5x) + 5$
   or $y = 150x^2 - 20x + 14$

7. $\{z: 16 < z < 32\}$

8. True

9. False

10. (a)

11. $r = 6$

12. (d)

13. Sample: [1.17, 1.19], [2.40, 2.42]

14. ≈ 55.5 hrs

15. $v = \frac{3c}{5}$

16. a. $C(S(p)) = 187,500 - 38,700p$
    b. the cost to produce the number of light bulbs sold at the price p
    c. $R(p) = 250,000p - 86,000p^2$
    d. $F(p) = -86,000p^2 + 288,700p - 187,500$
    e. the profit generated from the light bulbs sold at price p

ANSWERS

Chapter 3 Test, Form B

1. $v \circ r(x) = \ln\sqrt{x}$
   domain: $\{x: x > 0\}$
2. $r \circ v(x) = \sqrt{\ln x}$
   domain: $\{x: x \geq 1\}$
3.

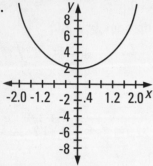

4. $k = 1$ or $k = \sqrt[3]{-7}$
5. No, it is not a function.
   $f(1) = e = f(-1)$, so f is not 1-1.
6. $y - 6 = \left|\frac{3}{2}(x + 2)\right|$
7. $\left\{x: -2 < x < 0 \text{ or } x > \frac{1}{2}\right\}$
8. True
9. True
10. (d)
11. $r = 3$
12. (c)
13. Sample: $[.51, .53]$, $[-1.30, -1.28]$
14. ≈ 31 years
15. $v = \frac{5c}{13}$
16. a. $C(S(p)) = 40{,}000 - 3125p$
    b. the cost to produce the number of thermometers sold at the price p
    c. $R(p) = 8000p - 2500p^2$
    d. $F(p) = -2500p^2 + 11{,}125p - 40{,}000$
    e. the profit generated from the thermometers sold at price p

Chapter 3 Test, Cumulative Form

1. False
2. True
3. $\lim\limits_{x \to \infty} g(x) = 0$, $\lim\limits_{x \to -\infty} g(x) = \infty$
4. No; if f is even, then $f(-x) = f(x)$ for all x and therefore $f(2) = f(-2)$. But $2 \neq -2$, so f is not 1-1. If f is not 1-1, then the inverse of f is not a function.
5. (a)
6. $\{x: -3 < x < 0 \text{ or } 0 < x < 2\}$
7. $r = 5$
8. a. $\exists$ a real number x such that $\ln(e^x) \neq x$
   b. the statement of part a
9. (b)
10. a. increasing $(-\infty, -.5]$, $[.5, \infty)$; On no intervals is h decreasing.
    b. relative max: $-.5$; relative min: $.5$
11. a. $T: (x, y) \to \left(5x - 6, \frac{y}{3} + 2\right)$
    b. $\frac{(x + 6)^2}{25} + 9(y - 2)^2 = 1$
    c. $(-6, 2)$
12. The function k is not continuous on the interval $[10, 20]$.
13. ≈ 1.364
14. a. $\left(\frac{a}{b}\right)_n = \frac{2n}{5}$, integers $n \geq 1$
    b. arithmetic
15. The Bulls did not beat the Nets, or the Hawks did not beat the Hornets in the first round.
16. a. $|c - 28.3| \leq .5$
    b. $27.8 \leq c \leq 28.8$
17. ≈ 3.1 years
18. $13.65

Comprehensive Test, Chapters 1–3

1. (b)
2. (a)
3. (d)
4. (d)
5. (a)
6. (d)
7. (a)
8. (c)
9. (d)
10. (a)
11. (d)
12. (d)
13. (c)
14. (a)
15. (a)
16. (c)
17. (d)
18. (b)
19. (b)
20. (c)
21. (d)
22. (c)
23. (d)
24. (b)
25. (b)

Quiz — Lessons 4-1 Through 4-4

1. a. 8
   b. 3
2. -49
3. Sample: $n = 151, d = 8$
4. Yes; $165 = 23 \cdot 7 + 4$
5. $q(x) = 2x^2 + 5x + 1,$
   $r(x) = 2x + 1$
6. $x + a$ is a factor of $f(x) = x^n + a^n$ if $f(-a) = 0$.
   When n is odd $f(-a) = (-a)^n + a^n = -a^n + a^n = 0$
7. False. Sample: 3 and 6 are factors of 12, but 18 is not.
8. -1, 5, 12

Quiz — Lessons 4-5 Through 4-7

1. 12
2. 3
3. $2^2 \cdot 3 \cdot 5 \cdot 11$
4. 219
5. 3,473
6. 10001000_2
7. a. 13
   b. No. $243 = 3 \cdot 81$
8. $(x - 1)(x - \sqrt{3})(x + \sqrt{3})$
9. 607
10. If $x - 2$ is a factor of $f(x)$, then $f(2) = 0$. But $f(2) = 2^5 - 2 \cdot 2^4 + 3 \cdot 2^3 - 4 \cdot 2^2 - 5 \cdot 2 + 3 = 1 \neq 0$, so $x - 2$ is not a factor of $f(x)$.

Chapter 4 Test, Form A

1. a. 1666
   b. 8
   c. $20,000 = 1666 \cdot 12 + 8$
2. 101011_2
3. $q(x) = 3x^2 - 4x + 6,$
   $r(x) = -3$
4. Sample: Because $a - b$ is divisible by c, $-(a - b)$ is also divisible by c. Therefore, $a + [-(a - b)] = b$ is divisible by c, by the Factor of an Integer Sum Theorem.
5. 11000_2
6. $-2\sqrt{2}, 2\sqrt{2},$ and 2
7. Let $f(x) = 2x^4 - 3x^3 + x^2 - 4x + 9$. $f(-3) = 2 \cdot (-3)^4 - 3 \cdot (-3)^3 + (-3)^2 - 4 \cdot (-3) + 9 = 273 \neq 0$. Therefore, $x + 3$ is not a factor of $f(x)$.
8. 9
9. $a - b$ is divisible by c.
10. False, because it is clear from the graph that for a certain value k, $f(x) - k$ has 5 zeroes, more than 4. This violates the Number of Zeros of a Polynomial Theorem.
11. $2 \cdot 3^2 \cdot 11 \cdot 47$
12. 7225
13. $x^2(x - 5)(x + 2)$
14. 7776
15. True
16. a. There is a polynomial of largest degree
    b. Let $f(x)$ be a polynomial of largest degree, and let its degree be n. Then $x \cdot f(x)$ is a polynomial of degree $n + 1$, contradicting the assumption that $f(x)$ has largest degree. Therefore, there is no polynomial that has largest degree.

Chapter 4 Test, Form B

1. a. 833
   b. b
   c. $10,000 = 833 \cdot 12 + 4$
2. 111011_2
3. $q(x) = -2x^2 - 9x - 20,$
   $r(x) = -62x + 26$
4. Because n and m are odd, both $n - m$ and $n + m$ are even. So $n - m = 2p$ and $n + m = 2q$ for some integers p and q, and $(n - m)(n + m) = 4pq$. That is, $n^2 - m^2$ is divisible by 4.
5. 101100_2
6. $-1, 1,$ and $\frac{3}{2}$
7. Let $f(x) = x^4 - 3x^3 + 2x^2 - 5x + 8$. Then $f(2) = (2)^4 - 3 \cdot (2)^3 + 2 \cdot (2)^2 - 5 \cdot (2) + 8 = -2 \neq 0$. So, $x - 2$ is not a factor of $f(x)$.
8. 5
9. $p + q$ is divisible by 5
10. Wrong. The graph crosses the x-axis at four points, implying the polynomial has four real zeroes, but should cross any horizontal line at most 3 times by the Number of Zeroes of a Polynomial Theorem.
11. $2 \cdot 3^2 \cdot 11 \cdot 17$
12. 10,233
13. $2x^2(x - 1)(x + 7)$
14. 6,979
15. False
16. a. There is a largest odd integer.
    b. Assume n is the largest odd integer. Then $n + 2$ is also an odd integer. But $n + 2 > n$, contradicting the initial assumption that n is the largest odd integer. Therefore, there is no largest odd integer.

Chapter 4 Test
Cumulative Form

1. a. valid
   b. invalid
2. 10
3. $|N - 19{,}982| \leq 3\%(19982)$
4. 1101011_2
5. -3, -2, 1, 2, 3
6. b
7. The semicircle with center at the origin and radius 1 laying above the x-axis.
8. a. decreasing
   b. increasing
9. 29
10. a. 10
    b. 16
11. $-\frac{1}{2}$
12. a. $(x + 1)^2 + (y - 1)^2 = 36$
    b. circle with center $(-1, 1)$; radius $= 6$
13. $n \equiv 0 \pmod 7$
14. If c and d are odd, then then $c = 2m + 1$ and $d = 2n + 1$, for some integers m and n. So $3c + 3d = 3(2m + 1) + 3(2n + 1) = 6m + 3 + 6n + 3 = 6(m + n + 1)$. $\therefore 3c + 3d$ is divisible by 6.
15. $x < -1$ or $x > 4$
16. a. 416
    b. 16
    c. $10{,}000 = 24 \times 416 + 16$
17. 7
18. $x(x - 3)(x + 3)(x^2 + 9)$

Quiz   Lessons 5-1 Through 5-4

1. Yes, $\dfrac{m + 1}{m} - \dfrac{m}{m - 1}$

   $= \dfrac{(m + 1)(m - 1)}{m(m - 1)} - \dfrac{m(m)}{m(m - 1)}$

   $= \dfrac{m^2 - 1}{m(m - 1)} - \dfrac{m^2}{m(m - 1)}$

   $= \dfrac{-1}{m(m - 1)}$;

   $\{m: m \neq 0, m \neq 1\}$

2. $\dfrac{x + 8}{x + 7}$; $x \neq -7$, $x \neq \dfrac{3}{5}$

3. a. domain $\{x: x \neq 8\}$
      range $\{y: y > 0\}$

   b. horizontal: $y = 0$;
      vertical: $x = 8$

   c. $\displaystyle\lim_{x \to 8^+} f(x) = \infty$,
      $\displaystyle\lim_{x \to 8^-} f(x) = \infty$

4. a. $x = 4, x = -2, x = 0$
   b. $x = -2$, and $x = 0$

5. $S(u) = 1{,}000{,}000 \cdot \left(\dfrac{.12}{u} - \dfrac{.12}{u + k}\right)$

6. $\$3692.31 \approx \$3700$

Quiz   Lessons 5-5 Through 5-7

1. $\displaystyle\lim_{x \to \infty} f(x) = \frac{3}{4}$, $\displaystyle\lim_{x \to -\infty} f(x) = \frac{3}{4}$

2. oblique: $y = \frac{1}{2}x - 4$;
   vertical: $x = -2$

3. $\dfrac{5798}{990}$

4. $\dfrac{7\sqrt{3} + 21}{6}$

5. Irrational. The denominator is irrational because $\sqrt{2}$ is irrational and the sum of a rational number an an irrational number is irrational. Since a nonzero rational number divided by an irrational number is irrational, the fraction is irrational.

6. We need to show that for all x, sec$(-x) = $ sec x.
   $\sec(-x) = \dfrac{1}{\cos(-x)} = \dfrac{1}{\cos x}$
   $= \sec x$, for all x in its domain. So the secant function is an even function.

7. a. $\cot \alpha = \dfrac{y}{x}$
   b. $\sec \theta = \dfrac{\sqrt{x^2 + y^2}}{x}$

8. a. $\{\theta: \theta \neq n\pi, n$ an integer$\}$
   b. $\left\{\theta: \theta \neq \dfrac{(2k + 1)\pi}{2}, k$ an integer$\right\}$

Precalculus and Discrete Mathematics © Scott Foresman Addison Wesley

Chapter 5 Test, Form A

1. a. $\frac{z - 5}{5z - 3}$

   b. $z \neq -6,\ z \neq \frac{3}{5}$

2. a. $\frac{1}{6 - y}$

   b. $y \neq 4,\ y \neq 6$

3. $\frac{12\sqrt{13} + 9}{13}$

4. rational; $\left\{x: x \neq -\frac{1}{4}\right\}$

5. rational

6. not rational

7. rational; $\frac{159{,}323}{10{,}000}$

8. irrational

9. rational; $\frac{514}{99}$

10. irrational

11. $x = \frac{2 \pm \sqrt{139}}{5}$

12. False. Sample: Suppose $q = \sqrt{3}$ and $p = 2$. Then $q^p = (\sqrt{3})^2$, which is rational.

13. a. $\lim\limits_{x \to -3^+} k(x) = -\infty$

    b. $\lim\limits_{x \to -3^-} k(x) = \infty$

    c. $\lim\limits_{x \to \infty} k(x) = 3;$
       $\lim\limits_{x \to -\infty} k(x) = 3$

14. $c(x) = \frac{x - 3}{x^2 - 8x + 15}$

15. a. $x = 0,\ x = 1$

    b. $\lim\limits_{x \to 1^+} j(x) = 1,$
       $\lim\limits_{x \to 1^-} j(x) = 1$

    c. $\lim\limits_{x \to \infty} j(x) = 0$
       $\lim\limits_{x \to -\infty} j(x) = 0$

16. x-intercepts: $\frac{-5 \pm \sqrt{17}}{2}$;
    y-intercept: $\frac{1}{2}$

17. vertical: $x = -4$;
    oblique: $y = x + 1$

18. $\frac{13\sqrt{153}}{4}$ or $\frac{3\sqrt{17}}{4}$

19. $x = n\pi$ for any integer n;
    all vertical

20. a. $\frac{90A}{A + 45}$ mph

    b. 56.25 mph

Chapter 5 Test, Form B

1. a. $\frac{-4}{x^2 - 3x - 10}$

   b. $x \neq 5,\ -2$

2. a. $\frac{2y + 1}{2y - 1}$

   b. $y \neq -1,\ 0,\ \frac{1}{2}$

3. $-4\sqrt{5} - 8$

4. rational

5. rational, $\left\{n: n \neq -\frac{5}{3}\right\}$

6. not rational

7. irrational

8. rational; $\frac{9}{1}$

9. irrational

10. rational; $\frac{4}{3}$

11. $x = 4 \pm \sqrt{71}$

12. True. $p + p = 2p$; a nonzero rational number times an irrational number is irrational.

13. a. $\lim\limits_{x \to -5^+} f(x) = -\infty$

    b. $\lim\limits_{x \to -5^-} f(x) = \infty$

    c. $\lim\limits_{x \to \infty} f(x) = 1$
       $\lim\limits_{x \to -\infty} f(x) = 1$

14. Sample:
    $d(x) = \frac{x - 5}{x^3 + 3x^2 - 40x}$

15. a. $x = -1,\ x = 3$

    b. $\lim\limits_{x \to -1^+} m(x) = \infty$
       $\lim\limits_{x \to -1^-} m(x) = -\infty$

    c. $\lim\limits_{x \to \infty} m(x) = \infty$
       $\lim\limits_{x \to -\infty} m(x) = -\infty$

16. x-intercepts: $\sqrt[3]{-3}$
    y-intercepts: -3

17. vertical: $x = 1,\ x = -1$;
    oblique: $y = x$

18. $\frac{2\sqrt{3}}{3}$

19. $x = n\pi$ for any integer n,
    all vertical

20. a. $\frac{20B}{B + 10}$ mph

    b. 30 mph

Chapter 5 Test Cumulative Form

1. No; this is an example of inverse error.

2. $\frac{5\sqrt{7} - 5\sqrt{3}}{4}$

3. $\left\{n: -\frac{2}{5} < n < 2\right\}$

4. $x = \pm\sqrt{3}$

5. -20

6. $\frac{5277}{9990} = \frac{1759}{3330}$

7. a. 149

   b. $d(m(x)) = \frac{3}{4}(3x + 5)^3$

8. a. $(-\infty, .9],\ [2.1, \infty)$

   b. $[.9, 2.1]$

9. 196

10. quotient: $x^2 + 4x + 6$,
    remainder: 7

11. a. $x = 2,\ x = -8$

    b. $x = -8$

12. a. 14

    b. 8 points

13. 12

14. $\frac{z^2 + 4z - 12}{z^2 + 2z - 35}$

15. $y = 5x - 2$

16. $\lim\limits_{x \to \infty} g(x) = 2;$
    $\lim\limits_{x \to -\infty} g(x) = -2$

17. $\{x: x = 2k\pi,\ k$ an integer$\}$

18. 8 ft²/gal

Quiz **Lessons 6-1 Through 6-3**

1. a. $y = -4.2 \sin (3x + 1.2) + 6$
   b. amplitude: 4.2
      period: $\frac{2\pi}{3}$
2. a. 44 volts
   b. 32 volts
   c. .5 seconds
3. Not an identity; sample counterexample when:
   $x = \frac{\pi}{6}$, $\csc^2 x = \frac{1}{\sin^2 x} = 4$
   but $\frac{1}{2} \cdot \frac{2}{\sqrt{3}} \neq 4$.
4. See below

Quiz **Lessons 6-4 Through 6-6**

1. a. $\frac{\sqrt{6} + \sqrt{2}}{4}$
2. $-2 - \sqrt{3}$
3. $\frac{3\sqrt{13} - 24}{35}$
4. $-\frac{1}{9}$
5. $\theta = \tan^{-1} \frac{x}{4}$
6. Sample proof:

$$\begin{array}{c|c}
\cos 2x & 2 \sin \left(x + \frac{\pi}{4}\right) \cos \left(x + \frac{\pi}{4}\right) \\
= \cos^2 x - \sin^2 x & = 2\left(\frac{\sqrt{2}}{2} \sin x + \frac{\sqrt{2}}{2} \cos x\right)\left(\frac{\sqrt{2}}{2} \cos x - \frac{\sqrt{2}}{2} \sin x\right) \\
 & = \cos^2 x - \sin^2 x
\end{array}$$

So for all x, $\cos 2x = 2 \sin \left(x + \frac{\pi}{4}\right) \cos \left(x + \frac{\pi}{4}\right)$

Chapter 6 Test, Form A

1. $2 - \sqrt{3}$
2. $\frac{-\sqrt{6} - \sqrt{2}}{4}$
3. -1
4. $-\sqrt{.84}$
5. $\theta = \frac{-\pi}{3}$, $\theta = \frac{2\pi}{3}$
6. a. $x = \frac{\pi}{2}$, $x = \frac{2\pi}{3}$, or $x = \frac{4\pi}{3}$
   b. $\left\{x: x = \frac{\pi}{2} + 2n\pi, \right.$
      $x = \frac{2\pi}{3} + 2n\pi$, or
      $x = \frac{4\pi}{3} + 2n\pi$, n an
      $\left. \text{integer}\right\}$
7. 2.0, 5.9
8. a. $T(x, y) = (2x, 2y + 2)$
   b. $y = 2 \sin \frac{x}{2} + 2$
9. $\theta = \cos^{-1}\left(\frac{6 - h}{5}\right)$
10. $.30 \leq t \leq .70$
11. identity; domain $\{\theta: \theta \neq n\pi, n$ an integer$\}$

12. Sample:
    Left side: $2 \cos^2 \alpha$
    Right side:
    $(1 + \sec 2\alpha) \cos 2\alpha$
    $= \cos 2\alpha + \sec 2\alpha \cos 2\alpha$
    (Distributive Property)
    $= \cos 2\alpha + 1$
    (Definition of secant)
    $= 2 \cos^2 \alpha - 1 + 1$
    (Identity for cos 2x)
    $= 2 \cos^2 \alpha$ (addition)
13. Sample: Left side:
    $\sin 2x = 2 \sin x \cos x$
    (Identity for sin 2x)
    Right side:
    $2 \sin^2 \left(x + \frac{\pi}{4}\right) - 1$
    $= 2\left(\frac{\sqrt{2}}{2} \sin x + \right.$
    $\left. \frac{\sqrt{2}}{2} \cos x\right)^2 - 1$
    (Sine of a Sum Theorem)
    $= 2\left(\frac{1}{2} \sin^2 x + \frac{1}{2} \cos^2 x + \right.$
    $\left. \sin x \cos x\right)$
    (Distributive Property)
    $= \sin^2 x + \cos^2 x +$
    $2 \sin x \cos x - 1$
    (Distributive Property)
    $= 1 + 2 \sin x \cos x - 1$
    (Pythagorean Identity)
    $= 2 \sin x \cos x$
    (addition)

Quiz **Lessons 6-1 Through 6-3**

4. identity; domain: $\left\{x: x \neq \frac{(2n + 1)\pi}{2}, n \text{ any integer}\right\}$

$$\begin{array}{c|c}
\sec^2 x - \tan^2 x & \cos^2 x + \sin^2 x \\
\hline
\text{definition of} \quad = \frac{1}{\cos^2 x} - \frac{\sin^2 x}{\cos^2 x} & = 1 \begin{array}{l} \text{Pythagorean} \\ \text{Identity} \end{array} \\
\text{sec and tan} \\
\text{addition of} \quad = \frac{1 - \sin^2 x}{\cos^2 x} \\
\text{fractions} \\
\text{Pythagorean} \quad = \frac{\cos^2 x}{\cos^2 x} \\
\text{Identity} \\
\text{Inverse Prop.} \quad = 1 \\
\text{of Multiplication.}
\end{array}$$

So $\sec^2 x - \tan^2 x = \cos^2 x + \sin^2 x$ for all x.

Precalculus and Discrete Mathematics © Scott Foresman Addison Wesley

1. $\dfrac{\sqrt{2} - \sqrt{6}}{4}$

2. $-2 + \sqrt{3}$

3. $\dfrac{\sqrt{2}}{2}$

4. $\dfrac{-4\sqrt{6}}{25}$

5. $x = -\dfrac{5\pi}{6}, x = \dfrac{5\pi}{6}$

6. **a.** $x = \dfrac{\pi}{2}, x = \dfrac{3\pi}{2}, x = \dfrac{\pi}{4}$,
   $x = \dfrac{7\pi}{4}$

   b. $\left\{ x: x = \dfrac{(2n + 1)\pi}{2}, \right.$
   $x = \dfrac{\pi}{4} + 2n\pi$, or
   $x = \dfrac{7\pi}{4} + 2n\pi$,
   $\left. n \text{ an integer} \right\}$

7. 1.2, 3.8, 4.1

8. **a.** $T:(x, y) = \dfrac{1}{2}x + \dfrac{\pi}{2}$,
   $2y - 1)$

   b. $y = 2 \cos (2x - \pi) - 1$

9. $\theta = \tan^{-1} \left(\dfrac{20,000}{d} \right)$

10. 102 days

11. not an identity;
    counterexample: $\theta = \dfrac{3\pi}{2}$

12. See below

13. See below

1. rational; $\dfrac{\sqrt{50}}{\sqrt{32}}$ can be
   expressed as a ratio of
   two integers: $\dfrac{5}{4}$

2. **a.** $x = -6, x = -\dfrac{2}{5}$

   b. $x = -\dfrac{2}{5}$

3. $\dfrac{\sqrt{2} - \sqrt{2}}{2}$

4. $-\dfrac{3\sqrt{5}}{7}$

5. $\dfrac{-x - 3}{5x^2 + x}$

6. Sample: $\tan \left(x - \dfrac{\pi}{4} \right) = \dfrac{\tan x - 1}{\tan x + 1}$;

   domain: $\left\{ x: x \neq \dfrac{3\pi}{4} + n\pi, n \text{ an integer} \right\}$

   $\tan \left(x - \dfrac{\pi}{4} \right) = \dfrac{\tan x - \tan \left(\dfrac{\pi}{4} \right)}{1 + \tan x \tan \left(\dfrac{\pi}{4} \right)}$ Tangent of a Difference Theorem

   $= \dfrac{\tan x - 1}{\tan x + 1}$ $\tan \left(\dfrac{\pi}{4} \right) = 1$

11. $\sin (\alpha + \beta) - \sin (\alpha - \beta)$
    $= \sin \alpha \cos \beta + \cos \alpha \sin \beta - (\sin \alpha \cos \beta - \cos \alpha \sin \beta)$
    $= \sin \alpha \cos \beta + \cos \alpha \sin \beta - \sin \alpha \cos \beta + \cos \alpha \sin \beta$
    $= 2 \cos \alpha \sin \beta$
    domain: set of real numbers.

7. $t = \ln 2$ or $t = \ln 5$

8. -6

9. **a.** $y = 3 \cos \dfrac{x - \pi}{-2} - 2$

   b. period: 4π;
   phase shift: π

10. $x = \dfrac{\pi}{2}, x = \dfrac{3\pi}{2}, x = \dfrac{2\pi}{3}$

11. See below

12. $\lim\limits_{x \to .5^+} g(x) = \infty$;
    $\lim\limits_{x \to .5^-} g(x) = -\infty$

13. 8

14. Sample: $\theta = 2 \tan^{-1} \left(\dfrac{3.25}{d} \right)$

12. Sample proof

	$\sin \alpha + \cot \alpha \cos \alpha$		$\csc \alpha$	
Definition of cotangent	$= \sin \alpha + \dfrac{\cos \alpha}{\sin \alpha} \cdot \cos \alpha$		$= \dfrac{1}{\sin \alpha}$	Definition of cosecant
multiplication	$= \sin \alpha + \dfrac{\cos^2 \alpha}{\sin \alpha}$			
addition of fractions	$= \dfrac{\sin^2 \alpha + \cos^2 \alpha}{\sin \alpha}$			
Pythagorean Identity	$= \dfrac{1}{\sin \alpha}$			

domain: $\{ \alpha: \alpha \neq n\pi, n \text{ an integer} \}$

13. Sample proof:

	$\dfrac{2}{\sin 2x}$	$\tan x + \cot x$	
Identity for $\sin 2x$	$= \dfrac{2}{2 \sin x \cos x}$	$= \dfrac{\sin x}{\cos x} + \dfrac{\cos x}{\sin x}$	Definition of tan. and cot
	$= \dfrac{1}{\sin x \cos x}$	$= \dfrac{\sin^2 x + \cos^2 x}{\sin x \cos x}$	addition of fractions
		$= \dfrac{1}{\sin x \cos x}$	Pythagorean Identity

domain: $\left\{ x: x \neq \dfrac{n\pi}{2}, n \text{ an integer} \right\}$

Precalculus and Discrete Mathematics © Scott Foresman Addison Wesley

Chapters 1-6, Comprehensive Test

1. (b)
2. (c)
3. (b)
4. (d)
5. (a)
6. (c)
7. (c)
8. (a)
9. (b)
10. (d)
11. (c)
12. (d)
13. (b)
14. (c)
15. (d)
16. (a)
17. (c)
18. (b)
19. (c)
20. (a)
21. (b)
22. (b)
23. (a)
24. (b)

Quiz Lessons 7-1 Through 7-4

1. $\begin{cases} b_1 = 6 \\ b_{n+1} = b_n + (8n + 4) \end{cases}$
   for $n \geq 1$

2. a. $\sum_{j=2}^{n} j \cdot (j + 2)$

   b. $\left(\sum_{j=2}^{k} j \cdot (j + 2) \right) +$
   $(k + 1)(k + 3)$

3. Basis step:
   $c_1 = 7^1 - 1 = 6$.
   Inductive step: Assume
   that $c_k = 7^k - 1$. Then
   $c_{k+1} = 7c_k + 6$
   $= 7(7^k - 1) + 6$
   $= 7^{k+1} - 7 + 6$
   $= 7^{k+1} - 1$. Thus, the
   formula is valid for all
   positive integers n, by the
   Principle of Mathematical
   Induction.

4. Basis step: 3 is clearly a
   factor of $1^3 + 3 \cdot 1^2 +$
   $2 \cdot 1 = 6$. Inductive step:
   Assume that 3 is a factor
   of $k^3 + 3k^2 + 2k$.
   Then $(k + 1)^3 +$
   $3(k + 1)^2 + 2(k + 1)$
   $= k^3 + 3k^2 + 3k + 1 +$
   $\quad 3(k^2 + 2k + 1) +$
   $\quad 2(k + 1)$
   $= (k^3 + 3k^2 + 2k) +$
   $\quad 3(k^2 + 3k + 2)$.
   3 is a factor of $k^3 + 3k^2 +$
   $2k$ by the inductive
   hypothesis and 3 is a
   factor of $3(k^2 + 3k + 2)$.
   $\therefore$ 3 is a factor of
   $(k + 1)^3 + 3(k + 1)^2 +$
   $2(k + 1)$ by the Factor of
   an Integer Sum Theorem.
   Thus, 3 is a factor of the
   expression for all positive
   integers n, by the Principle
   of Mathematical
   Induction.

Quiz Lessons 7-5 Through 7-7

1. 8
2. $r \geq 1$ or $r \leq -1$
3. a. $S = \sum_{j=0}^{25} 3 \cdot 2^j$

   b. 201,326,589

4. Basis step: $a_1 = 6 = 2 \cdot 3$.
   $a_2 = 18 = 6 \cdot 3$. So a_n
   is divisible by 3 for
   $n = 1$ and $n = 2$. Inductive
   step: Assume that a_j is
   divisible by 3 for all $j \leq k$.
   Then $a_k = 3b$ and
   $a_{k-1} = 3c$ for some
   integers b and c. So
   $a_{k+1} = 3a_k + 9a_{k-1}$
   $= 3 \cdot 3b + 9 \cdot 3c$.
   $= 3(3b + 9c)$. Since b and c
   are integers, $3b + 9c$ is an
   integer by closure. Thus, 3
   is a factor of a_{k+1} by the
   Factor of an Integer Sum
   Theorem. So the
   statement, a_n is divisible
   by 3 for all $n \geq 1$, is true
   by the Strong Form of
   Mathematical Induction.

Chapter 7 Test, Form A

1. 1, 3, 4, 6, 7
2. **a.** 3, 6, 9, 12, 15
   b. $a_n = 3n$
3. $\displaystyle\sum_{k=-2}^{n} k(k+1)$
4. $\displaystyle\sum_{j=1}^{2k} j^2 + (2k+1)^2$
5. 4,304,672   **6.** 14
7. Basis step: When $n = 1$,
   $a_n = \frac{3}{2} \cdot 1 \cdot (1+1) = 3$
   $= a_1$.
   Inductive step: Assume
   that $a_k = \frac{3}{2} k(k+1)$. Then
   $a_{k+1} = a_k + 3(k+1)$
   $= \frac{3}{2} k(k+1) + 3(k+1)$
   $= \frac{3}{2}(k+1)(k+2)$
   $= \frac{3}{2}((k+1)+1)(k+1)$.
   Thus, a_n satisfies the
   formula for all $n \geq 1$ by
   the Principle of
   Mathematical Induction.
8. **a.** 2, 3, 5, 9, 17
   b. $c_1 = 2$; $c_{k+1} =$
       $2c_k - 1$ for $k \geq 1$
9. Basis step: When $n = 1$,
   $n^3 - n = 1^3 - 1 = 0$, and
   3 is a factor of 0.
   Inductive step: Assume
   that 3 is a factor of $k^3 - k$.
   Then
   $(k+1)^3 - (k+1)$
   $= k^3 + 3k^2 + 2k$
   $= k^3 - k + 3k^2 + 3k$
   $= k^3 - k + 3(k^2 + k)$
   By the inductive
   assumption, 3 is a factor
   of $k^3 - k$, and since 3 is a
   factor of $3(k^2 + k)$, by the
   Factor of a Sum Theorem,
   3 is a factor of $k^3 - k +$
   $3(k^2 + k)$. Thus by the
   Principle of Mathematical
   Induction, 3 is a factor of
   $n^3 - n$ for all integers
   $n \geq 1$.
10.
5	5	5	5	5
2	2	2	4	4
3	3	4	2	3
-1	4	3	3	2
4	-1	-1	-1	-1
11. $S_1 = 10$,
    $S_{k+1} = S_k + 10 \cdot \frac{1}{5^k}$,
    for $k \geq 1$

Chapter 7 Test, Form B

1. 0, 0, 1, 1, 2
2. **a.** 3, 9, 27, 81, 243
   b. $b_n = 3^n$
3. $\displaystyle\sum_{j=-10}^{7} (j^3 - j)$
4. $\displaystyle\sum_{k=1}^{2n-1} (-x)^k + (-x)^{2k}$
5. 9,973.770   **6.** 22
7. Basis step: When $n = 1$,
   $c_n = \frac{-5 \cdot 1(1+1)}{2} = -5 = c_1$.
   Inductive step:
   Assume that
   $c_k = \frac{-5k(k+1)}{2}$. Then
   $c_{k+1} = c_k - 5(k+1)$
   $= \frac{-5k(k+1)}{2} - 5(k+1)$
   $= \frac{-5}{2}(k+1)(k+2)$
   $= \frac{-5((k+1)+1)(k+1)}{2}$
   Thus, c_n satisfies the
   formula for all $n \geq 1$ by
   the Principle of
   Mathematical Induction.
8. **a.** 2, 5, 11, 23, 47
   b. $c_1 = 2$; $c_{k+1} =$
       $2c_k + 1$ for $k \geq 1$
9. Basis step: When $n = 2$,
   $s_2 = 1 - \frac{1}{4} = \frac{3}{4} = \frac{2+1}{2 \cdot 2}$.
   Inductive step: Assume
   that $s_k = \frac{k+1}{2k}$. Then
   $s_{k+1} = \left(1 - \frac{1}{4}\right) \cdots$
   $\left(1 - \frac{1}{k^2}\right)\left(1 - \frac{1}{(k+1)^2}\right)$
   $= s_k\left(1 - \frac{1}{(k+1)^2}\right)$
   $= \frac{k+1}{2k} \cdot \frac{(k+1)^2 - 1}{(k+1)^2}$
   $= \frac{(k+1)^2 - 1}{2k(k+1)}$
   $= \frac{k^2 + 2k}{2k(k+1)} = \frac{k+2}{2(k+1)}$
   $= \frac{(k+1)+1}{2(k=1)}$.
   Thus, the formula is valid
   for all integers $n \geq 2$ by
   the Principle of
   Mathematical Induction.
10. $L = 8, 3, 1, 11, 9$

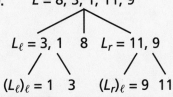

    $L_\ell = 3, 1$ 8 $L_r = 11, 9$

    $(L_\ell)_\ell = 1$ 3 $(L_r)_\ell = 9$ 11
11. $S_1 = 2$; $S_{k+1} = k +$
    $2\left(\frac{1}{3}\right)^k$, $k \geq 1$

Chapter 7 Test, Cumulative Form

1. ((not p) and (not q)) or q
2. $\sec x - \cos x$
   $= \frac{1}{\cos x} - \cos x$
   $= \frac{1 - \cos^2 x}{\cos x} = \frac{\sin^2 x}{\cos x}$
   $= \sin x \left(\frac{\sin x}{\cos x}\right)$
   $= \sin x \tan x$.
   domain:
   $\left\{x : x \neq \frac{(2n+1)\pi}{2}\right\}$
3. $t_n = (\pi)^{2^{n-1}}$
4. $\displaystyle\sum_{k=1}^{27} 3k$
5. $\displaystyle\lim_{x \to \infty} f(x) = -2$,
   $\displaystyle\lim_{x \to -\infty} f(x) = -2$
6. $T: (x, y) \to$
   $(8x - 2, 6y + 1)$
7. $x = \ln 3$
8. $\frac{\sqrt{6} + \sqrt{2}}{4}$
9. $\frac{2^5 - 1}{\sqrt{2} - 1} = \frac{31}{\sqrt{2} - 1}$ or
   $31(1 + \sqrt{2})$
10. 1
11. 4
12. Basis step: When $n = 3$,
    $2^3 = 8 > 7 = 2 \cdot 3 + 1$.
    Inductive step: Assume
    for arbitrary $k \geq 3$ that
    $2^k > 2k + 1$ is true.
    Then $2^{k+1} = 2 \cdot 2^k >$
    $2(2k + 1) = 4k + 2 =$
    $2k + 2k + 2 =$
    $2(k+1) + 2k$.
    Since $k \geq 3$, $2k > 1$.
    So, $2(k+1) + 2k >$
    $2(k+1) + 1$. Then by
    transitivity of inequalities,
    $2^{k+1} > 2(k+1) + 1$. Thus,
    the formula $2^n \geq 2n + 1$ is
    true for all $n \geq 3$ Principle
    of Mathematical
    Induction.

ANSWERS

Quiz — Lessons 8-1 Through 8-4

1. a. $12 - 5i$
b. $-39 + 23i$

2. $\frac{4}{5} - \frac{8}{5}i$

3. a. $(-6, -6)$
b. $\left[6\sqrt{2}, \frac{5\pi}{4}\right]$
c. $6\sqrt{2}\left(\cos\frac{5\pi}{4} + i\sin\frac{5\pi}{4}\right)$

4.

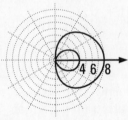

5.

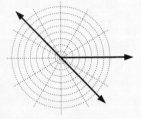

6.

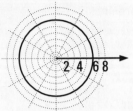

Quiz — Lessons 8-5 Through 8-8

1. $64\left(\cos\frac{9\pi}{8} + i\sin\frac{9\pi}{8}\right)$

2. a. $[2, 30°], [2, 120°],$
$[2, 210°], [2, 300°]$

b.

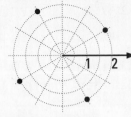

3. regular pentagon

4. a. $3(\cos 150° + i\sin 150°)$
$3(\cos 270° + i\sin 270°)$
b. $27i$

5. a. 1
b. 2
c. 2
d. 6

6.

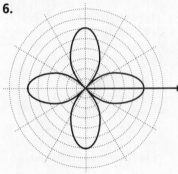

Chapter 8 Test, Form A

1. a. $(0, -4)$
b. 4
c. $\frac{3\pi}{2}$
d. $\left[4, \frac{3\pi}{2}\right]$

2. a. $-18 - 23i$
b. $-\frac{41}{53} - \frac{11}{53}i$

3. $|z - \bar{z}| =$
$|a + bi - (a - bi)| =$
$|2bi| = \sqrt{(2bi)(-2bi)}$
$= \sqrt{4b^2} = 2|b|.$

4. $x = -5, r = 10$

5. $4 + 2i$

6. $3\left(\cos\frac{\pi}{8} + i\sin\frac{\pi}{8}\right),$
$3\left(\cos\frac{5\pi}{8} + i\sin\frac{5\pi}{8}\right)$
$3\left(\cos\frac{9\pi}{8} + i\sin\frac{9\pi}{8}\right),$
$3\left(\cos\frac{13\pi}{8} + i\sin\frac{13\pi}{8}\right)$

7. a. $[.64, , 90°],$
$[.512, 135°],$
$[.4096, 180°]$

b.

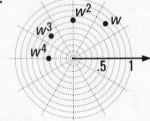

8. rose curve

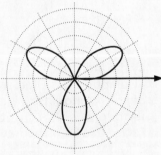

9. limaçon

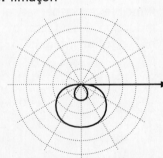

10. $x = -1$, multiplicity 2;
$x = \sqrt{3}\,i$, $x = -\sqrt{3}\,i$,
simple zeros

11. a. 2
  b. 2
  c. 4
  d. 6

12. a. parallelogram
  b. imaginary

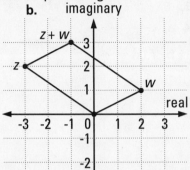

Chapter 8 Test, Form B

1. a. $(-2\sqrt{3}, 2)$
  b. 4
  c. $\frac{5\pi}{6}$
  d. $\left[4, \frac{5\pi}{6}\right]$

2. a. $-24 - 30i$
  b. $-\frac{3}{26} - \frac{15}{26}i$

3. $|z| = \left|\dfrac{a + bi}{\sqrt{a^2 + b^2}}\right|$

$= \sqrt{\dfrac{a + bi}{\sqrt{a^2 + b^2}} \cdot \dfrac{a - bi}{\sqrt{a^2 + b^2}}}$

$= \sqrt{\dfrac{a^2 + b^2}{a^2 + b^2}} = \sqrt{1} = 1$

4. $(-1, \sqrt{3})$

5. $\frac{9}{5} - \frac{3}{5}i$ amps

6. $\frac{\sqrt{3}}{2} + \frac{1}{2}i$, $-\frac{1}{2} + \frac{\sqrt{3}}{2}i$,
$-\frac{\sqrt{3}}{2} - \frac{1}{2}i$, $\frac{1}{2} - \frac{\sqrt{3}}{2}i$

7. a. $[2.25, 60°]$,
$[3.375, 90°]$,
$[5.0625, 120°]$
  b.

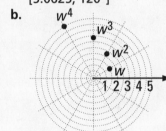

8. circle

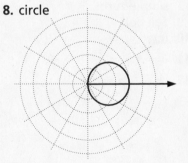

9. limaçon

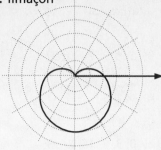

10. simple zeros: $x = -7$
$x = 2 + 3i$, $x = 2 - 3i$

11. a. 2
  b. 5
  c. 5
  d. 7

12. a, b. imaginary

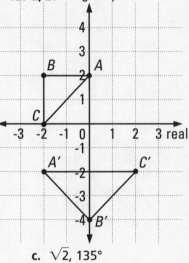

  c. $\sqrt{2}$, 135°

ANSWERS

Chapter 8 Test
Cumulative Form

1. $\frac{1}{5} + \frac{3}{5}i$

2. $3(\cos 97° + i \sin 97°)$

3. a. $\sum\limits_{i=0}^{\infty} \frac{2}{3^i}$
   b. Yes, 3.

4. $\left[2, \frac{2\pi}{3}\right], \left[-2, \frac{5\pi}{3}\right]$

5. a. 0, 3, 8, 15, 24, 35
   b. Let $S(n)$ be the sentence:
   $a_n = n^2 - 1$. When $n = 1$, $1^2 + 1 = 0$. This agrees with the recursive definition of the sequence. Hence, $S(1)$ is true. Assume $S(k)$ is true for some arbitrary integer $k \geq 1$. Then $a_k = k^2 - 1$.
   $a_{k+1} = (k+1)^2 - 1$
   $= k^2 + 2k + 1 - 1$
   $= k^2 - 1 + 2k + 1$
   $= a_k + 2k + 1$ (by the inductive assumption). So $S(k+1)$ is true. Thus, by the Principle of Mathematical Induction, $S(n)$ is true for all integers $n \geq 1$.

6. a. $x + y = 4$
   b.
   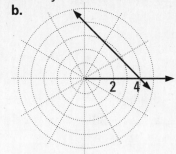

7. a. square
   b. $1 + \sqrt{3}i, -\sqrt{3} + i,$
   $-1 - \sqrt{3}i, \sqrt{3} - i$
   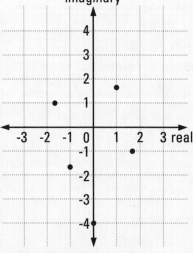

8. $x = 0$, multiplicity 4;
   $x = \frac{5}{2} + \frac{\sqrt{7}}{2}i,$
   $x = \frac{5}{2} - \frac{\sqrt{7}}{2}i,$
   simple zeros

9. See below.

10. (c)

11. $\theta = \pi, \theta = \frac{2\pi}{3}, \theta = -\frac{2\pi}{3}$

12. $\frac{-x^2 + 3}{2}, x \neq \pm 1$

Quiz
Lessons 9-1 Through 9-3

1. a. -25 cm
   b. $-\frac{25}{3}$ cm/sec
   c. The motion was toward its starting point.

2. $\frac{1}{5}$

3. .5

4. a. $\frac{-1}{x^2 + x\Delta x}$
   b. $f'(x) = -\frac{1}{x^2}$

9.
$$L = 4, 3, 9, 7, 1, 2$$
$f = 4$
$L_\ell = 3, 1, 2 \qquad L_r = 9, 7$
$f = 3 \qquad\qquad f = 9$
$(L_\ell)_\ell = 1, 2 \quad (L_\ell)_r = \varnothing$
$(L_r)_\ell = 7 \quad (L_r)_r = \varnothing$

Precalculus and Discrete Mathematics © Scott Foresman Addison Wesley

Chapter 9 Test, Form A

1. a. 15.775 cents
   per gal/year
 b. -.0875 cents
   per gal/year
 c. The average price of
   gasoline fell from 1980
   to 1996

2. a. $-32 - 8\Delta x$
 b. -32.4

3. (a)

4. (a)

5. a. $\frac{2}{5}$
 b. (b)

6. a. $\left(\frac{4}{3}, \infty\right)$ or $(-\infty, 0)$
 b. $\left(0, \frac{4}{3}\right)$

7. a. $(-\infty, -2), (-2, 2), (5, \infty)$
 b. $(2, 5)$
 c. $x = -2, x = 2, x = 5$

8. a. $\frac{\ln(3 + \Delta x) - \ln 3}{\Delta x}$
 b. .333

9. a. -10 m/sec
 b. -10m/sec^2
 c. 35 m
 d. 0 m/sec

Chapter 9 Test, Form B

1. a. -8,719.75
   complaints/year
 b. -369.25
   complaints/year
 c. positive

2. a. $24 + 4\Delta x$
 b. 26

3. (d)

4. (c)

5. a. 1
 b. (a)

6. a. $\left(-\infty, -\frac{1}{3}\right), (1, \infty)$
 b. $\left(-\frac{1}{3}, 1\right)$

7. a. $(3, \infty)$
 b. $(-\infty, 3)$
 c. $x = 3$

8. a. $\frac{\tan\left(\frac{\pi}{4} + \Delta x\right) - \tan\frac{\pi}{4}}{\Delta x}$
 b. 2.00

9. a. 20 m/sec
 b. -10 m/sec^2
 c. 65 m
 d. 0 m/sec

Chapter 9 Test, Cumulative Form

1. a. $\lim\limits_{\Delta x \to 0} \dfrac{\cos\left(\frac{\pi}{6} + \Delta x\right) - \cos\left(\frac{\pi}{6}\right)}{\Delta x}$
 b. -.500

2. (b)

3. a. $(-12, -12)$
 b. $\left[12\sqrt{2}, \frac{5\pi}{4}\right]$
 c. $12\sqrt{2}\left(\cos\frac{5\pi}{4} + i\sin\frac{5\pi}{4}\right)$

4. a. $\left(-\infty, -\frac{4}{3}\right), (2, \infty)$
 b. $x = -\frac{4}{3}, x = 2$
 c. -8

5. $x^3 - 4x^2 + 6x - 4$

6. a. $v(t) = 160 - 32t$
 b. 32 ft/sec
 c. 400 ft

7. a. 64
 b. $4, -2, -2\sqrt{3}\,i$
 c.

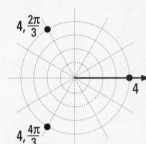

8. $\begin{cases} s_1 = 0 \\ s_{n+1} = s_n + 2n, \end{cases}$
  $\forall\, n \geq 1$

9. a. $\lim\limits_{u \to 2^+} h(u) = 7,$
  $\lim\limits_{u \to 2^-} h(u) = 7$
 b. removable

10. $\cos(\alpha + \beta)\cos(\alpha - \beta)$
  $= (\cos\alpha\cos\beta -$
  $\sin\alpha\sin\beta)\cdot$
  $(\cos\alpha\cos\beta +$
  $\sin\alpha\sin\beta)$
  $= \cos^2\alpha\cos^2\beta -$
  $\sin^2\alpha\sin^2\beta$
  $= \cos^2\alpha(1 - \sin^2\beta) -$
  $(1 - \cos^2\alpha)\sin^2\beta$
  $= \cos^2\alpha - \cos^2\alpha\sin^2\beta -$
  $\sin^2\beta + \sin^2\beta\cos^2\alpha$
  $= \cos^2\alpha - \sin^2\beta$

ANSWERS

Chapters 1-9
Comprehensive Test

1. (b)
2. (d)
3. (c)
4. (c)
5. (a)
6. (b)
7. (d)
8. (a)
9. (c)
10. (a)
11. (b)
12. (d)
13. (b)
14. (d)
15. (a)
16. (c)
17. (c)
18. (c)
19. (d)
20. (a)
21. (b)
22. (c)
23. (b)
24. (d)
25. (c)

Quiz Lessons 10-1 Through 10-3

1. a. ordered, with repetition.
   b. $26^{10} \approx 1.4 \cdot 10^{14}$
2. a. ordered, without repetition
   b. 1320
3. a. Ordered, without repetition
   b. 967,680

4.

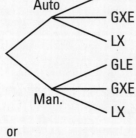

or

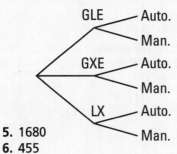

5. 1680
6. 455
7. 4

Quiz Lessons 10-4 Through 10-6

1. a. unordered, without repetition
   b. 70
2. $r = 5$
3. 792,792
4. 3432
5. 4096
6. 29
7. $\approx .043$

Precalculus and Discrete Mathematics © Scott Foresman Addison Wesley

Chapter 10 Test, Form A

1. 30,240
2. 220
3. $-336{,}798a^6b^5$
4. $\binom{17}{7}$
5. a. ordered, repetition not allowed
   b. $P(6, 4) = 360$
6. a. ordered, repetition allowed
   b. $62^6 \approx 5.68 \times 10^{10}$
7. a. unordered, repetition not allowed
   b. $\binom{228}{7} \cdot \binom{206}{5} \approx 1.7 \times 10^{22}$
8. a. unordered, repetition allowed
   b. $\binom{16 + 5 - 1}{16} = 4{,}845$
9. $\approx .87$
10. $\approx .022$
11.

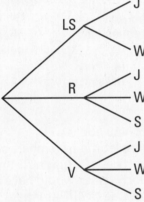

12. 8375
13. 165
14. $\binom{r + (n - 1)}{r}$
    $= \dfrac{(r + n - 1)!}{(r + n - 1 - r)!r!}$
    $= \dfrac{(r + n - 1)!}{(n - 1)!r!}$
    $= \dfrac{(n + r - 1)!}{(n - 1)!(n - 1 + r - (n - 1))!}$
    $= \binom{n + r - 1}{n - 1}$

Chapter 10 Test, Form B

1. 7920
2. 78
3. $673{,}596a^6b^6$
4. $\binom{16}{5}$
5. a. unordered, repetition not allowed
   b. $\binom{75}{10} \approx 8.3 \times 10^{11}$
6. a. ordered, repetition allowed
   b. $3^{12} = 531{,}441$
7. a. ordered, repetition not allowed
   b. $P(7, 5) = 2520$
8. a. unordered, repetition allowed
   b. $\binom{50 + 4 - 1}{50} \approx 23{,}426$
9. $\approx .03$
10. $\approx .006$
11.

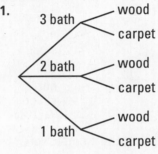

or

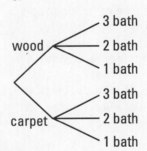

12. 792
13. 4368
14. $r! \cdot C(n, n - r)$
    $= \dfrac{r!n!}{(n - r)!(n - (n - r))}$
    $= \dfrac{r!n!}{(n - r)!r!}$
    $= \dfrac{n!}{(n - r)!} = P(n, r)$

Chapter 10 Test, Cumulative Form

1. 990
2. 4096
3. $x = -3, 3, -3i, 3i$
4. a. $g'(x) = 6x + 4$
   b. 34
5. 130
6. 11
7. $4^{20} \approx 1.1 \times 10^{12}$
8. $y = 4 \sin (3x + 2)$
9. $y = 3x + 4$
10. 15 mph/sec
11. $(-4, 0)$
12. a. unordered, repetition allowed
    b. $\binom{59}{40} \approx 1.4 \cdot 10^{15}$
13. a. $\begin{cases} a_1 = 5 \\ a_{n+1} = a_n + 7 \end{cases}$
    b. $a_n = 7n - 2$
14. $\approx .82$
15. $x = -\dfrac{\sqrt{2}}{6}$
16. $\binom{50}{10} \approx 1.03 \cdot 10^{10}$
17. $64k^6 - 192k^5 + 240k^4 - 160k^3 + 60k^2 - 12k + 1$

1. a.

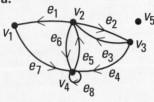

Favor-able .65
- .80 Democrat
- .18 Republican
- .02 Independent

Not Favor-able .35
- .25 Democrat
- .74 Republican
- .01 Independent

b. 60.75%

c. ≈.144

2. a.

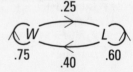

b. No, v_4 has a loop and there are parallel edges.

c. v_5

d. v_1: 2, v_2: 5, v_3: 3, v_4: 6, v_5: 0

e. 16

3. No; the six computers in the network would each be a vertex of odd degree (3) and the printer would be a vertex of odd degree (5). So the graph would have an odd number of vertices of odd degree, which is impossible.

4. a. yes

b. Sample: $f g g e$

c. Sample: $f g h e$

d. Sample: $f g h e c a$

e. No, remove c; Sample: $a b d e h g f$

Chapter 11 Test, Form A

1.

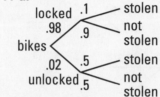

2. a. v_1, v_5

b. e_1 and e_3, e_7 and e_8

c. No; sample: remove e_3, e_7

d. 6   **e.** 18

3. (b)   **4.** (a)

5. add e_7: {v_1, v_5} Euler circuit: v_1 e_1 v_2 e_2 v_5 e_6 v_4 e_3 v_3 e_4 v_6 e_5 v_5 e_7 v_1

6. No, there cannot be a graph with an odd total degree. Here, $0 + 1 + 3 + 2 + 1 = 7$.

7. a.

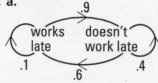

bikes
- locked .98
  - stolen .1
  - not stolen .9
- unlocked .02
  - stolen .5
  - not stolen .5

b. 1,080 bikes

8. No; let the 11 members be vertices of a graph. Then each would have a degree of 5. The graph would have an odd number of vertices with odd degree, which is impossible.

9. No. Not all the vertices are of even degree, so there is no Euler Circuit.

10. a.

works late ⟷ doesn't work late
.9, .1, .6, .4

b.

	late	not late
late	.1	.9
not late	.6	.4

c. .5

11.

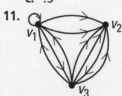

12. 8

Chapter 11 Test, Form B

1.

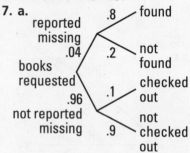

2. a. v_3, v_2

b. v_7

c. No; remove e_5

d. 4   **e.** 12

3. (c)   **4.** (d)

5. add e_7: {v_1, v_2}; Sample: v_1 e_1 v_2 e_2 v_3 e_3 v_6 e_6 v_5 e_5 v_4 e_4 v_2 e_7 v_1

6. No, there cannot be a graph with an odd total degree. Here, $1 + 3 + 3 + 5 = 9$.

7. a.

books requested .04
- reported missing .8
  - found .8
  - not found .2
- not reported missing .96
  - checked out .1
  - not checked out .9

b. 480 books

8. Yes; let the 7 members be vertices of a graph. Then each vertex would have a degree of 4. Thus, the graph has an odd number of vertices each of even degree, which gives the graph a total degree which is even.

9. Yes. All the vertices are of even degree and the graph is connected.

10. a.

W ⟷ L
.25, .75, .40, .60

b.

	won	lost
won	.75	.25
lost	.40	.60

c. 49

11. $\begin{bmatrix} 1 & 1 & 0 \\ 0 & 2 & 0 \\ 1 & 1 & 1 \end{bmatrix}$

12. 3

Chapter 11 Test, Cumulative Form

1. a. e_1, e_2, e_4
   b. No, there are parallel edges
   c. 2
   d. 14
2. No; there are vertices of odd degree.
3. 560
4. -9
5. $x = 3 - i, x = 2, x = 3$
6. a. $\begin{bmatrix} 0 & 2 & 1 \\ 2 & 0 & 0 \\ 1 & 0 & 1 \end{bmatrix}$
   b. 33
7. a. ordered, repetitions not allowed
   b. 358,800
8. a. not ordered, repetitions not allowed
   b. 14,950
9. a. $\begin{matrix} 1 & 0 \\ 1 \\ 0 \end{matrix} \begin{bmatrix} .50 & .50 \\ .75 & .25 \end{bmatrix}$
   b. 60
10. $\lim_{x \to 2^+} f(x) = \infty;$
   $\lim_{x \to 2^-} f(x) = -\infty$
11. [5, 210°]
13. No, this situation is equivalent to a graph with an odd number of vertices of odd degree, which is impossible.
14. a.

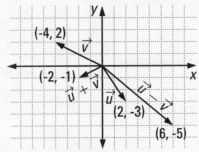

   b. $\approx 71.4\%$
15. 252
16. No, the graph has two vertices which are of odd degree; therefore there is no Euler circuit.

Quiz   Lessons 12-1 Through 12-3

1. a. (-3, -3)
   b. $\left[3\sqrt{2}, \frac{5\pi}{4}\right]$ or $[3\sqrt{2}, 225°]$
2.

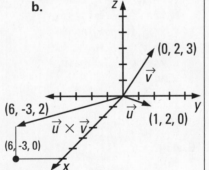

3. $(3 + 2\sqrt{3}, 1)$
4. $(x - 4, y + 7) = t(2,1)$
5. a. $\frac{1}{2}(200 + 400\sqrt{3}) \approx$ 446 km
   b. 200 km

Quiz   Lessons 12-4 Through 12-6

1. $120° = \frac{2\pi}{3}$ radians
2. $45° = \frac{\pi}{4}$ radians
3. -15
4. a. (6, -3, 2)
   b.

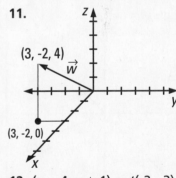

5. center: (-3, 4, -5)
   radius: 10

Chapter 12 Test, Form A

1. magnitude: 10, angle: $\tan^{-1}\left(\frac{4}{3}\right) \approx 307.7°$ or 5.36 rad
2. $\approx$ [15.7, 104°] or (-3.9, 16.2)
3. 14
4. $\left|r\vec{u}\right| = |r(x, y, z)| = |(rx, ry, rz)| = \sqrt{(rx)^2 + (ry)^2 + (rz)^2} = \sqrt{r^2(x^2 + y^2 + z^2)} = \sqrt{r^2} + \sqrt{x^2 + y^2 + z^2} = |r||\vec{u}|.$
5. $\approx 62.5°$
6. parallel
7. a. 10.1 m/sec
   b. 6.8 m/sec
8. speed $\approx 330 \frac{mi}{hr}$; heading $\approx$ 16° north of east
9. $(-2, -2\sqrt{3})$
10.

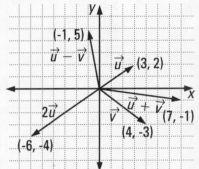

11.

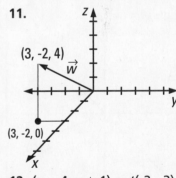

12. $(x - 4, y + 1) = t(-2, -3)$
13. Sample: $5x - 4y + z = 15$
14. (b)

Chapter 12 Test, Form B

1. magnitude 13, direction:
$\tan^{-1}\left(-\frac{5}{12}\right) \approx 157°$ or
2.75 rad

2. [3.2, 344°] or (3.1, -.90)

3. $6\sqrt{3}$

4. $(r\vec{u}) \cdot (s\vec{v}) =$
$(r(u_1, u_2, u_3)) \cdot (s(v_1, v_2, v_3)) = (ru_1, ru_2, ru_3) \cdot (sv_1, sv_2, sv_3) =$
$(ru_1)(sv_1) + (ru_2)(sv_2) + (ru_3)(sv_3) = (rs)(uv_1 + uv_2 + uv_3) =$
$(rs)(\vec{u} \cdot \vec{v})$

5. $\approx 76°$

6. orthogonal

7. a. 19.7 pounds
   b. 15.4 pounds

8. air speed ≈ 206 mph; heading $\approx 14°$ south of west

9. $\approx [5, 127°]$ or [5, 2.2]

10.

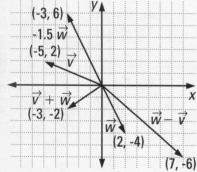

11.

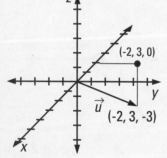

12. $\begin{cases} x = -3 + 7t \\ y = 5 - 2t \end{cases}$

13. Sample: $x + y - z = 4$

14. Sample: (-5, -6, 8)

Chapter 12 Test, Cumulative Form

1. q or ((not p) and (not q))

2. No. If the 9 teams are represented as vertices of a graph and the games as edges joining the opposing teams, the total degree of the graph would be odd, which is impossible.

3. a. $\left[5, \sin^{-1}\frac{3}{5}\right] \approx$
   $[5, 36.9°] \approx [5, .64]$
   b.

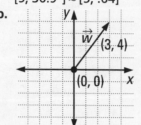

4. $\approx [\sqrt{821}, 19°]$

5. Let $\vec{u} = (u_1, u_2, u_3)$, $\vec{v} = (v_1, v_2, v_3)$, and $\vec{w} = (w_1, w_2, w_3)$.
   If $\vec{u} \perp \vec{w}$ and $\vec{v} \perp \vec{w}$,
   then $\vec{u} \cdot \vec{w} = \vec{v} \cdot \vec{w} = 0$.
   So $(\vec{u} + \vec{v}) \cdot \vec{w} =$
   $(u_1 + v_1, u_2 + v_2, u_3 + v_3) \cdot (w_1, w_2, w_3) = (u_1 + v_1)w_1 + (u_2 + v_2)w_2 + (u_3 + v_3)w_3 = (u_1 w_1 + u_2 w_2 + u_3 w_3) + (v_1 w_1 + v_2 w_2 + v_3 w_3) =$
   $(\vec{u} \cdot \vec{w}) + (\vec{v} \cdot \vec{w}) = 0 + 0 = 0 \Rightarrow (\vec{u} + \vec{v}) \perp \vec{w}$.

6. 45 mph

7. (b)

8. $(\sqrt{20}, \sqrt{5}), (-\sqrt{20}, -\sqrt{5})$

9. $3x - y + z = 7$

10. -2, $1 + \sqrt{3}i$, $1 - \sqrt{3}i$

11. $\dfrac{\binom{20}{10}}{2^{20}} \approx .176$

12. $\begin{cases} x = t - 1 \\ y = -2t \\ z = -t + 2 \end{cases}$

13. $\sin^{-1}\left(\frac{2500}{4000}\right) \approx 38.7°$

14. (3, -2, 1)

15. a. $\begin{bmatrix} 0 & 1 & 1 & 1 \\ 1 & 0 & 1 & 1 \\ 1 & 1 & 0 & 1 \\ 1 & 1 & 1 & 0 \end{bmatrix}$

    b. 61

Quiz Lessons 13-1 Through 13-3

1. 54 kilowatt-hours

2. 20

3. a. $\frac{1}{4} \times \frac{1}{64} + \frac{1}{4} \times \frac{1}{8} + \frac{1}{4} \times \frac{27}{64} + \frac{1}{4} \times 1 = \frac{25}{64}$
   b. $\frac{1}{4} \times 0 + \frac{1}{4} \times \frac{1}{64} + \frac{1}{4} \times \frac{1}{8} + \frac{1}{4} \times \frac{27}{64} = \frac{9}{64}$
   c. $\frac{9}{64}, \frac{25}{64}$

4. a. $6 + 8 = 14$
   b. $8 - 5 = 3$

5. $\int_0^3 (\sqrt{9 - x^2} + x - 3)\, dx$

Precalculus and Discrete Mathematics © Scott Foresman Addison Wesley

1. $2 \times 8 + 2 \times 32 + 2 \times 72 + 2 \times 128 + 2 \times 200 = 2(440) = 880$

2. 50π

3. $\int_0^2 (-2x^2 + 8)\, dx$

4. No. Sample: Right side should be
$$\int_2^4 \frac{1}{x-1}\, dx - \int_3^4 \frac{1}{x-1}\, dx.$$

5. 172.5 km

6. 690 ft

7. $\int_0^4 \pi \left(\frac{3}{4}x\right)^2 dx = 12\pi$ cubic units

8. a.

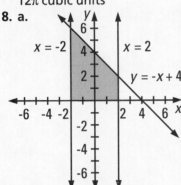

$x = -2$ $x = 2$ $y = -x + 4$

b. $\int_{-2}^{2} (-x + 4)\, dx = 16$ square units

9. minimum: 62.6 gallons; maximum: 71.6 gallons

10. a. $\int_2^6 x\, dx$

d. 16

1. $2 \times 12 + 2 \times 48 + 2 \times 108 + 2 \times 192 = 2(360) = 720$

2. 7π

3. $\int_{-2}^{2} \frac{1}{2}x^2\, dx$

4. False; $\int_0^1 x^2\, dx = \frac{1}{3}$,
$$\left(\int_0^1 x\, dx\right)^2 = \left(\frac{1}{2}\right)^2 = \frac{1}{4}$$

5. 152.5 km

6. 173 ft

7. $\int_0^4 \pi \left(-\frac{1}{2}x + 2\right)^2 dx = \frac{16\pi}{3} \approx 17.552$ cubic units.

8. a.

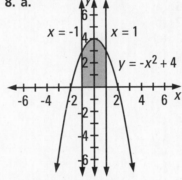

$x = -1$ $x = 1$ $y = -x^2 + 4$

b. $\int_{-1}^{1} (-x^2 + 4)\, dx = \frac{22}{3}$ square units.

9. 250π in³

10. a. $\int_{-2}^{3} (2x + 2)\, dx$

b. 15

1. 186 ft

2.

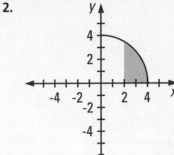

3. a. 0

b.

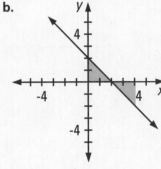

c. 4

d. The area of the region sketched in part **c** is greater than the value of the integral in part **a** because the integral is negative over the interval [2, 4], while the area of the region is positive.

4. a. $-5 + 4 = -1$

b. $-5 - (-3) = -2$

5. Sample: starting v_1: e_1, e_7, e_6, e_5, e_8, e_4, e_3, e_2.

6. a. Sample: $\begin{cases} x = 2 + 3t \\ y = -5 + 4t \end{cases}$

b.

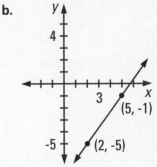

(5, -1)

(2, -5)

7. $k = 6$

ANSWERS

8. a.

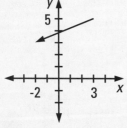

b. $\int_0^3 \pi(2\sqrt{x})^2\,dx = 18\pi$

9. $x = -\frac{7}{5}$

10. a.

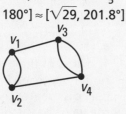

b. $(-5, -2)$

c. Sample: $[29, \tan^{-1}\frac{2}{5} + 180°] \approx [\sqrt{29}, 201.8°]$

11.

v_1 v_3
v_2 v_4

Chapters 1-13
Comprehensive Test

1. (c)
2. (a)
3. (d)
4. (c)
5. (b)
6. (c)
7. (b)
8. (a)
9. (c)
10. (d)
11. (a)
12. (b)
13. (c)
14. (d)
15. (b)
16. (a)
17. (b)
18. (c)
19. (d)
20. (b)
21. (c)
22. (b)
23. (d)
24. (b)
25. (c)
26. (a)
27. (b)
28. (b)
29. (a)
30. (d)
31. (d)
32. (a)
33. (b)
34. (a)
35. (b)
36. (c)
37. (c)
38. (d)
39. (c)
40. (d)
41. (a)
42. (c)
43. (b)
44. (b)
45. (c)
46. (a)
47. (b)
48. (d)
49. (c)
50. (a)

ANSWERS

Precalculus and Discrete Mathematics © Scott Foresman Addison Wesley

1. a. Write a statement that relates to algebra for each of the following.

    i. a true universal statement.
    ii. a false existential statement.
    iii. neither true nor false.

b. For each statement in part **a**, write a negation if possible. If it is not possible to write a negation, explain.

c. Identify each negation you wrote in part **b** as either true or false.

Objectives A, C, D, E

☐ Can identify forms of logical statements.
☐ Can write the negation of a logical statement.
☐ Can determine the truth value of a logical statement.
☐ Can identify properties of logical statements.
☐ Writes three appropriate statements.
☐ Writes correct negations for statements **i** and **ii**.
☐ Explains why statement **iii** cannot be negated.
☐ Identifies negation **i** as false and **ii** as true.

2. Clare's parents made two firm statements:

If you finish your homework, then you may go to the movies.

If you do not finish your homework, then you may not go to the movies.

Clare knows the statements are both true, so she reasons that the second statement is logically equivalent to the first. Use truth tables to explain why her reasoning is incorrect. Then write a statement that *is* logically equivalent to the first.

Objectives B, I, L

☐ Can determine the truth of quantified statements outside of mathematics.
☐ Can write truth tables for logical expressions.
☐ Can write equivalent forms of logical statements.
☐ Creates correct truth tables for both statements.
☐ Logically explains why they are not equivalent.
☐ Writes an equivalent statement. (Sample: *If you may not go to the movies, then you did not finish your homework.*)

3. Below you are given the beginning of a logical argument.

If z = 5, then z + 6 > 10.

    _____?_____

∴ _____?_____

a. Show two different ways to fill in the blanks to create a valid argument. Identify the form of each argument.

b. Show two different ways to fill in the blanks to illustrate an invalid argument. Identify the type of each argument error.

Objective G

☐ Can determine whether arguments are valid or invalid.
☐ Completes two valid arguments and correctly identifies the argument form. (Samples: 1. $z = 5$; ∴ $z + 6 > 10$ [Law of Detachment] 2. $z + 6 \not> 10$; ∴ $z \neq 5$ [Law of Indirect Reasoning])
☐ Completes two invalid arguments and identifies the argument error. (Samples: 1. $z + 6 > 10$; ∴ $z = 5$ [Converse Error] 2. $z \neq 5$; ∴ $z + 6 \not> 10$ [Inverse Error])

4. Below are the "mixed-up" steps of a direct proof of a theorem from algebra.

(i) $-(-x) + (-x + x) = [-(-x) + -x] + x$
(ii) $-(-x) = -(-x) + 0$
(iii) $0 + x = x$
(iv) $[-(-x) + -x] + x = 0 + x$
(v) $-(-x) + 0 = -(-x) + (-x + x)$

Rearrange the steps in the correct order to create the direct proof. Give a justification for each step. Then write a universal statement of the theorem.

Objectives A, H

☐ Can use logic to prove or disprove statements.
☐ Can identify forms of logical statements.
☐ Gives the correct order for the steps. (ii, v, i, iv, iii)
☐ Gives a correct justification for each step. (ii: Additive Identity Property of Zero; v: Additive Inverse Property; i: Associative Property of Addition; iv: Additive Inverse Property; iii: Additive Identity Property of Zero)
☐ Gives a correct universal statement of the theorem. (Sample: ∀ x in R, $-(-x) = x$.)

Precalculus and Discrete Mathematics © Scott Foresman Addison Wesley

Teacher Notes

Objectives A, B, C, E, G

Concepts and Skills This activity requires students to:
- identify forms of logical statements and write equivalent forms and negations.
- identify properties of logical statements.
- determine whether arguments are valid or invalid.
- play a logic game and expand its scope.

Guiding Questions
- How do you know if two statements are logically equivalent?
- Why is *If a figure has three sides, then it is a rectangle* inconsistent with the other statements? [It contradicts the statements *No figure with three sides is a parallelogram,* and *If a figure is not a parallelogram, then it is not a rectangle.*]
- Can you devise a systematic way to check that any new statement you write is consistent with all the others? [organized listing, Venn diagrams]

Answers
a. *If a figure is a rectangle, then it is a parallelogram.*; *If a figure is not a parallelogram, then it is not a rectangle.*; The statements are contrapositives.
b. **i.** existential statement; **ii.** There exists a parallelogram that is a rectangle. **iii.** No. Sample statements of a negation are *All parallelograms are not rectangles,* and *If a figure is a parallelogram, then it is not a rectangle.* There is no statement like these among those listed.
c. *Figure I is not a quadrilateral.*; Law of Indirect Reasoning.
d. No. That conclusion results from the invalid argument form called Inverse Error.
e. Sample: *If a figure is a parallelogram, then it is a quadrilateral. If a figure is a quadrilateral, then it is not a triangle.*; Conclusion: *If a figure is a parallelogram, then it is not a triangle.*
f. *If a figure is not a paralleogram, then it is not a rectangle. Figure B is not a parallelogram.*; Law of Detachment.
g, h. Answers will vary. Check students' work.

Extension
Have students create an original logic game that can assess understanding of truth values of logical statements and De Morgan's Laws.

Evaluation

Level	Standard to be achieved for performance at specified level
5	The student demonstrates an in-depth understanding of logical statements and logical arguments. Responses to all questions are accurate and complete. The student plays the game thoughtfully and creates a logically consistent set of additional statements. The student may put forth additional effort to analyze the game, such as preparing a list of all possible valid arguments.
4	The student demonstrates a clear understanding of forms of logical statements and logical arguments. Responses to all questions are reasonable, but may contain some minor errors. The student creates an appropriate set of additional statements, but may overlook a minor logical inconsistency.
3	The student demonstrates a fundamental understanding of forms of logical statements and logical arguments, but may need some assistance in applying the concepts to the logic game. The student answers all the questions posed, but may make one or more major errors. The additional statements are relevant and correct in form, but there may be one or more major inconsistencies with those given.
2	The student demonstrates some understanding of forms of logical statements and logical arguments, but needs considerable assistance in understanding their use in the logic game. Even with help, the student may make several major errors in responding to the questions posed. The student prepares additional statements that are relevant, but they may not be of the proper form, and many may be logically inconsistent with those given.
1	The student demonstrates little if any understanding of forms of logical statements and logical arguments. Even with assistance, any attempts to respond to the questions posed are irrelevant or trite. Instead of writing a reasonable set of additional statements, the student may simply write nonsense sentences.

1. Peter says that, no matter what the value of n, you need a calculator to evaluate $\log_3 n$. But Pam says that you *cannot* use a calculator to evaluate $\log_3 n$, because calculators only have keys for common logarithms and natural logarithms. Do you agree with Peter, with Pam, or with neither? Justify your answer.

Objective A

☐ Is able to rewrite logarithmic expressions.

☐ Recognizes that Peter's statement is incorrect, and gives an appropriate justification. (Sample: If n is a simple power of 3 – such as 1, 3, 9, 27, 81, ... or 1/3, 1/9, 1/27, 1/81, ... – you should only need to apply the definition of logarithm.)

☐ Recognizes that Pam's statement is incorrrect, and gives an appropriate justification. (Sample: You can evaluate any expression of this form by entering either $\log n \div \log 3$ or $\ln n \div \ln 3$.)

2. The equations below represent the location at time t of a projectile fired from a cannon like the one shown at the right.

Graph the equations. Then write a detailed description of the motion of the projectile.

$$\begin{cases} x = 33.9t + 1.9 \\ y = -4.9t^2 + 19.6t + 1.1 \end{cases} \quad 0 \le t \le T$$

Objective H

☐ Can analyze and graph parametric equations.

☐ Draws a correct graph of the equations.

☐ Writes an appropriate description. (Sample: Its constant horizontal speed is 33.9 m/s. Its initial vertical speed is 19.6 m/s. It is released at a point 1.1 m above and 1.9 m forward of the rear rest of the cannon. Its maximum height is 20.7 m, at $t = 2$ s. It hits the ground at $T \approx 4.1$ s.)

3. Your parents have k feet of fencing, and they want to use it to enclose a rectangular garden. Explain how a function can help determine the dimensions of the garden that will give it the greatest possible area.

Objective F

☐ Is able to solve max-min problems.

☐ Gives a logical explanation. (Sample: f such that $f(x) = \dfrac{kx}{2} - x^2$ gives the area in ft² for a width of x ft. The maximum value of f is the greatest area. The value of x at the maximum is the desired width, and $\left(\dfrac{k}{2} - x\right)$ is the length.)

4. Write a real-life problem that can be solved by evaluating the nth term of a sequence. Then show how to solve your problem using either an explicit or recursive formula for the sequence.

Objective E

☐ Demonstrates an ability to use a sequence as a model of a real-life situation.

☐ Writes an appropriate problem.

☐ Writes a correct formula for the sequence.

☐ Writes a correct solution of the problem.

5. Compare the characteristics of functions f and g graphed at the right. How are the functions alike? How are they different? State as many likenesses and differences as you can.

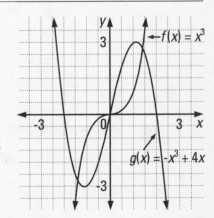

Objectives A, C, D, G

☐ Can determine relative maxima and minima of a function and intervals on which it is increasing or decreasing.

☐ Can give the domain, range, and maximum/minimum values of a function.

☐ Can determine the end behavior of a function.

☐ Can analyze a function from its graph.

☐ States several likenesses. (Sample: The domain of each is R.)

☐ States several differences. (Sample: g has a relative maximum at $x \approx 1.15$, a relative minimum at $x \approx -1.15$; f has no relative maxima or minima.)

Teacher Notes

Objectives A, C, D, G

Concepts and Skills This activity requires students to:
- identify key characteristics of a function, such as maxima, mnima, intervals on which it is increasing or decreasing, and end bahavior.
- use functions to model real-life phenomena.
- recognize errors in a given analysis of a function.
- create a complete original analysis of a function.

Guiding Questions
- If the equation of a parabola is $y = ax^2 + bx + c$, what is the equation of its axis of symmetry? $[x = \frac{-b}{2a}]$
- How can you tell from its equation if a parabola opens upward or downward? [If $a > 0$, it opens upward. If $a < 0$, it opens downward.]

Answers
a. Add "$a \neq 0$." If $a = 0$, the function is linear.
b. No. The parabolas that open "sideways" are not functions because many elements of the domain correspond to two elements of the range.
c. No. The domain *always* is the set of all real numbers. The range *never* is the set of all real numbers: if $a > 0$, the range is all real numbers $\geq \frac{-b}{2a}$, if $a < 0$, all real numbers $\leq \frac{-b}{2a}$.
d. Sample: The maximum (or minimum) is the value of y when $x = \frac{-b}{2a}$. If $a > 0$, this is a minimum; if $a > 0$: it is a maximum.
e. Samples: **i.** if $a > 0$: decreasing over $(-\infty, \frac{-b}{2a}]$; increasing over $[\frac{-b}{2a}, \infty)$; if $a < 0$: increasing over $(\infty, \frac{-b}{2a}]$, decreasing over $[\frac{-b}{2a}, \infty)$
  ii. if $a > 0$: $\lim_{x \to -\infty} f(x) = \infty$, $\lim_{x \to \infty} f(x) = \infty$; if $a < 0$: $\lim_{x \to \infty} f(x) = -\infty$, $\lim_{x \to -\infty} f(x) = -\infty$
f. Sample: Graph a specific equation and show how to use the equation and graph to find the maximum height and when the ball hits the ground.
g. Sample: maximizing a rectangular area for a given perimeter.
h, i. Answers will vary. Check students' work.

Extension
Have students write similar articles for all other types of elementary functions and arrange all their articles into an elementary function "scrapbook."

Evaluation

Level	Standard to be achieved for performance at specified level
5	The student demonstrates an in-depth understanding of elementary functions and their applications. All analyses of the functions and all graphs are accurate and complete. The student may use an imaginative original approach in rewriting the given article and in creating an original article, and may offer insights beyond those solicited.
4	The student demonstrates a clear understanding of elementary functions and their applications. The student analyzes all functions thoughtfully and prepares appropriate graphs, but the work may contain minor errors. Both the rewritten and original articles are well-organized and easy to read, but they may lack in some detail.
3	The student demonstrates a fundamental understanding of elementary functions and their applications, but may need assistance in some aspect of analyzing functions. There may be one or more major errors or omissions in the student's statements or graphs. The rewritten and original articles are essentially complete, but they may be somewhat disorganized.
2	The student demonstrates some understanding of elementary functions and their applications, but needs considerable assistance in preparing an analysis of a function. Even with help, the student may make several major misstatements or may create inappropriate graphs. The student attempts to rewrite the given article and to create an original one, but the results are jumbled and incomplete.
1	The student demonstrates little if any understanding of elementary functions and their applications. Even with assistance, any attempts to analyze the functions are trivial or irrelevant. Instead of writing articles in the suggested format, or creating an original format, the student may simply copy statements verbatim from the textbook.

1. **a.** $\forall x$, let $f(x) = x^2$ and let $g(x) = \frac{1}{x}$.
   Show that $f \circ g = g \circ f$.
   b. Identify a third function h for which
   $f \circ h \neq h \circ f$. Give simplified formulas
   for $f \circ h$ and $h \circ f$.

Objective B

☐ Is able to describe a composite of functions.
☐ Correctly demonstrates that $f \circ g = g \circ f$.
☐ Gives a rule for an appropriate function h.
(Sample: $h(x) = x + 1$)
☐ Gives correct rules for $f \circ h$ and $h \circ f$.
(Sample: When $h(x) = x + 1$, $(f \circ h)(x) =$
$x^2 + 2x + 1$ and $(h \circ f)(x) = x^2 + 1$.)

2. Your friend was absent when the class
studied equation-solving and has asked
you this question: Why is it that taking the
logarithm of each side of an exponential
equation is reversible, while taking the
square root of each side of a quadratic
equation is nonreversible? Write an
explanation for your friend. Be sure to
give examples.

Objectives A, E

☐ Is able to solve equations by applying a
function to each side.
☐ Is able to analyze reversibility of steps.
☐ Writes an appropriate explanation.

3. Write a real-life problem that can be solved
using an inequality of the form $|x - a| \leq b$.
Write a step-by-step algebraic solution of
the inequality. Use the solution of the
inequality to solve your problem.

Objectives D, J

☐ Is able to solve inequalities algebraically.
☐ Can use inequalities to solve real-life
problems.
☐ Writes an appropriate problem.
☐ Shows a correct solution to the inequality.
☐ Gives a correct solution to the problem.

4. Write two equations *of different types* that
can be solved by placing each ■ in the
following equation with the same
expression.

$$■^2 + 3■ = 4$$

Then find all real solutions of each
equation.

Objective C

☐ Can find zeros using factoring and chunking.
☐ Writes two appropriate equations (Samples:
1. $(\log x)^2 + 3 \log x = 4$ 2. $(n^2)^2 + 3n^2 = 4$)
☐ Gives correct solutions. (Samples:
1. $x = 0.0001$ or $x = 10$ 2. $n = 1$ or $n = -1$)

5. Suppose a function f is continuous on the
interval [-4, 4], with values as given below.

x	-4	-2	0	2	4
$f(x)$	-39	11	5	-9	17

Write a brief paragraph in which you
describe what you know about f as a result
of the Intermediate Value Theorem.

Objective G

☐ Demonstrates an understanding of the
Intermediate Value Theorem.
☐ Writes an appropriate paragraph. (Sample:
In the interval [-4, 2], the function f takes on
all values from -39 to 11; in [-2, 0], all values
from 11 to 5; in [0, 2], all values from 5 to -9;
and in [2, 4], all values from -9 to 17. So one
zero of f lies between -4 and -2, another
between 0 and 2, and another between 2
and 4.)

6. Identify transformations T and S for
which $T \circ S$ maps the unit circle onto an
ellipse that is not centered at the origin.
Graph the ellipse on a sheet of grid paper.
Then show how to represent the ellipse by
the following:

   a. a pair of parametric equations
   b. a single equation in x and y

Objective L

☐ Is able to find an equation of a graph after
a transformation.
☐ Identifies two appropriate transformations.
(Sample: $T: (x, y) \rightarrow (x + 5, y - 2)$ and
$S: (x, y) \rightarrow (4x, 3y)$)
☐ Correctly graphs the ellipse.
☐ Gives correct parametric equations. (For T
and S given: $x = 4 \cos t + 5$, $y = 3 \sin t - 2$),
$0 \leq t < 2\pi$
☐ Gives a correct equation in x and y. (For T and
S given: $\left(\frac{x-5}{4}\right)^2 + \left(\frac{y+2}{3}\right)^2 = 1$)

Precalculus and Discrete Mathematics © Scott Foresman Addison Wesley

EVALUATION GUIDES

Teacher Notes

Objectives H, L

Concepts and Skills This activity requires students to:
- find an equation of a graph after a transformation.
- analyze given designs to determine their equations.
- write equations that will generate original designs.

Guiding Questions
- Why is it necessary to restrict the domain of the equation for the cubic curves? Why is it *not* necessary to place any restrictions on the equations of the ellipses?
- Which designs in the right column seem to involve equations that are quadratic? [2, 11] cubic? [9] quadratic? [3, 8] logarithmic or exponential? [1, 10, 12] absolute-value equations? [4, 6, 7, 11] Which seem to involve floor or ceiling functions? [1] circles? [7, 10] ellipses? [5] hyperbolas? [5, 6]

Answers
a. i. $x = 4 \cos t, y = 3 \sin t, 0 \le t < 2\pi$
    ii. $\left(\frac{x}{4}\right)^2 + \left(\frac{y}{3}\right)^2 = 1$
b. centered at (8, 0); **i.** $x = 4 \cos t + 8, y = 3 \sin t, 0 \le t < 2\pi$ **ii.** $\left(\frac{x-8}{4}\right)^2 + \left(\frac{y}{3}\right)^2 = 1$; centered at (-16, 0); **i.** $x = 4 \cos t - 16, y = 3 \sin t, 0 \le t < 2\pi$ **ii.** $\left(\frac{x+16}{4}\right)^2 + \left(\frac{y}{3}\right)^2 = 1$
c. i. $x = 4 \cos t + 8n, y = 3 \sin t, 0 \le t < 2\pi$
    ii. $\left(\frac{x+8n}{4}\right)^2 + \left(\frac{y}{3}\right)^2 = 1$
d. equation: $y = .125(x-8)^3 - 2(x-8)$, $4 \le x < 12$; zeros: 4, 8, 12
e. $y = .125(x+8n)^2 - 2(x+8n)$, $(8n-4) \le x \le (8n+4)$, for all integers n; zeros: $8n-4, 8n, 8n+4$
f, g. Answers will vary. Check students' work.

Extension
Have students create designs generated by inequalities and systems of inequalities in the coordinate plane.

Evaluation

Level	Standard to be achieved for performance at specified level
5	The student demonstrates an in-depth understanding of equations, equation-solving, and graphs of equations. All equations and graphs are accurate and complete. The given designs are analyzed thoughtfully, and the original designs may be complex and imaginative. The student may offer additional insights.
4	The student demonstrates a clear understanding of equations, equation-solving, and graphs of equations. The student is able to discern appropriate models to generate the given designs, but may make minor errors in writing the equations. The original designs are well-planned and attractive, but the equations or graphs may contain minor inaccuracies.
3	The student demonstrates a fundamental understanding of equations, equation-solving, and graphs of equations, but may need some assistance in applying the concepts to the given situation. There may be one or more major errors or omissions in the student's equations or graphs. The presentation of original designs is essentially complete, but it may be somewhat disorganized.
2	The student demonstrates some understanding of equations, equation-solving, and graphs of equations, but needs considerable assistance in understanding their application to the given situation. Even with help, the student may make several major errors in writing equations or drawing graphs, or may omit one or more major steps of the process. The student attempts to create original designs, but the presentation is jumbled and incomplete.
1	The student demonstrates little if any understanding of equations, equation-solving, or graphs of equations. Even with assistance, any attempts to write appropriate equations or draw graphs are trivial or irrelevant. Rather than create original designs, the student may simply copy one or more of the given designs.

Precalculus and Discrete Mathematics © Scott Foresman Addison Wesley

EVALUATION GUIDES

1. a. Explain how you know that the following statement is incorrect.

$$179 \equiv 4 \ (\text{mod } 16)$$

Show how to make the statement true by:

b. replacing 179 with a number other than 4.

c. replacing 4 with a number other than 179.

d. replacing 16 with a different number.

Objective C

☐ Is able to determine congruence of integers in a given modulus.

☐ Gives a logical explanation why the statement is false.

☐ Identifies three correct ways to make a true statement. (Samples: **a.** $180 \equiv 4 \ (\text{mod } 16)$ **b.** $179 \equiv 3 \ (\text{mod } 16)$ **c.** $179 \equiv 4 \ (\text{mod } 25)$

2. Let $p(x) = 2x^3 + 5x^2 - x - 6$. Choose a first-degree polynomial $d(x)$ and find $q(x)$ and $r(x)$ such that $p(x) = q(x) \cdot d(x) + r(x)$. Is $d(x)$ a factor of $p(x)$? Explain why or why not.

Objectives A, B, D

☐ Is able to find quotients and remainders using the Quotient-Remainder Theorem for Polynomials.

☐ Is able to divide polynomials.

☐ Understands the concept of factoring polynomials over the reals.

☐ Gives a correct $q(x)$ and $r(x)$. (Sample: For $d(x) = x + 1$, $q(x) = 2x^2 + 3x - 4$ and $r(x) = -2$.)

☐ Correctly determines if $d(x)$ is a factor of $p(x)$. (Sample: For $d(x) = x + 1$, $d(x)$ is not a factor. The factors are $(x + 2)$, $(x - 1)$, and $(2x - 3)$.)

☐ Gives a logical explanation.

3. For $f(x) = 2x^4 + 9x^3 - 4x^2 - 36x - 16$, Tran says that the real zeros of f are -4, -2, 1, and 2. Do you agree or disagree? Explain your reasoning. If you disagree, make a corrected list of all the real zeros.

Objective E

☐ Is able to use factoring or the Factor Theorem to solve polynomial equations.

☐ Recognizes that Tran's statement is incorrect.

☐ Gives a logical explanation.

☐ Gives a corrected list of the zeros. $\left(-\frac{1}{2}, -4, -2, 2\right)$

4. Suppose a number k is written in a base other than base 10. Relate the polynomial $5x^3 + x^2 + 7$ to the process of finding the base 10 representation of k. Give a specific example to illustrate your answer.

Objective M

☐ Demonstrates an understanding of the process of writing numbers in bases other than 10.

☐ Gives a logical explanation.

☐ Gives an appropriate example. (Sample: $5107_8 = 5 \cdot 8^3 + 1 \cdot 8^2 + 0 \cdot 8^1 + 7 \cdot 8^0 = 2631$.)

5. Write an original real-life problem that can be solved by applying the Quotient-Remainder Theorem for Integers. Show how to use the theorem to solve your problem. Be sure to provide a meaning for both the quotient and the remainder in the context of your problem.

Objective K

☐ Is able to use the Quotient-Remainder Theorem to solve problems.

☐ Writes an appropriate problem.

☐ Gives a correct solution to the problem.

☐ Gives a correct interpretation of the quotient and remainder in the context of the problem.

6. Consider the interval $2000 \le n \le 3000$.

a. Find an integer n in this interval that is not prime. Give its standard prime factorization.

b. Find an integer n in this interval that *is* prime. Justify your answer.

Objective J

☐ Can use the Fundamental Theorem of Arithmetic and the Factor Search Theorem in determining prime numbers and prime factorizations.

☐ Correctly identifies a number in this interval that is not prime. (Sample: 2500)

☐ Gives a correct standard prime factorization. (Sample: $2500 = 2^2 \cdot 5^4$)

☐ Correctly identifies a number in this interval that is prime. (Sample: 2003)

☐ Logically explains why the number is prime.

Teacher Notes

Objectives A, B, D, F, H, J

Concepts and Skills This activity requires students to:
- exemplify properties of integers and polynomials.
- compare and contrast properties of integers and polynomials.
- write a convincing argument to support a point of view.

Guiding Questions
- Does the value of an integer ever vary? Does the value of a polynomial ever vary?
- What is a factor of an integer? of a polynomial?
- When is an integer prime? When is a polynomial prime?
- How is polynomial division like integer division? How is it different?

Answers
a. **i.** Sample: An integer is a specific number, with a single value. If a polynomial involves a variable, its value will vary. **ii.** Sample: A polynomial p looks like an integer when it is the constant function $p(x) = k$, for k a nonzero integer.

b. **i.** Sample: 7 is a factor of both 35 and 56, so 7 is a factor of $35 + 56$, or 91. **ii.** Sample: $x + 1$ is a factor of both $x^3 + 1$ and $x^2 - 1$, so $x + 1$ is a factor of $(x^3 + 1) + (x^2 - 1)$, or $x^3 + x^2$.

c. Answers will vary. Samples of companion theorems students might choose are: Transitive Property of Integer Factors/Transitive Property of Polynomial Factors; Quotient-Remainder Theorem for Integers/Quotient-Remainder Theorem for Polynomials; Fundamental Theorem of Arithmetic/Unique Factorization Theorem for Polynomials. Check students' examples.

d. Answers will vary. Sample: Integers are a type of *number*. Polynomials are a type of *function*.

e. Sample: Factor Search Theorem. Check students' examples.

f. Sample: Factor Theorem. Check students' examples.

g. Answers will vary. Check students' work.

Extension
Have students make a list of conjectures about similarities between rational number division and rational expression division.

Evaluation

Level	Standard to be achieved for performance at specified level
5	The student demonstrates an in-depth understanding of integers and polynomials. Responses to all questions are accurate and complete. The student prepares a comprehensive, well-organized argument that convincingly supports the chosen position, and it may be presented imaginatively. The student may offer several significant insights beyond those covered in the text.
4	The student demonstrates a clear understanding of integers and polynomials. Responses to all questions are reasonable, but they may contain minor errors. The argument supporting the chosen position is well-organized and easy to read, but it may lack in some detail.
3	The student demonstrates a fundamental understanding of integers and polynomials, but may need some assistance in determining appropriate responses to the questions posed. There may be one or more major logical errors or omissions in the examples the student chooses to illustrate the theorems. The argument essentially supports the chosen position, but it may be somewhat disorganized and lacking in depth.
2	The student demonstrates some understanding of integers and polynomials, but needs considerable assistance in responding to the questions posed. Even with help, the student may make several major logical errors in presenting examples to illustrate the theorems. The student attempts to prepare a convincing argument, but it is jumbled and incomplete.
1	The student demonstrates little if any understanding of integers and polynomials. Even with assistance, any attempts to answer the questions posed are trivial or irrelevant. Instead of choosing a position and writing a logical, well-planned argument, the student may simply write definitions and theorems at random.

1. a. Give an example of an infinite decimal that represents a rational number. Explain how you know it is rational.
  b. Give an example of an infinite decimal that represents an irrational number. Explain how you know it is irrational.

Objectives B, F

☐ Can identify numbers as rational or irrational.
☐ Is able to prove properties of rational and irrational numbers.
☐ Names a rational number. (Sample: $.\overline{05}$)
☐ Names an irrational number. (Sample: .05005000500005000005. . .)
☐ Explains why the first number is rational.
☐ Explains why the second number is irrational.

2. Compare the process of simplifying expression (i) to simplifying expression (ii).

(i) $\dfrac{r^2 - 2r - 3}{r^2 - r - 2} \cdot \dfrac{r - 2}{r + 1}$

(ii) $\dfrac{r^2 - 2r - 3}{r^2 - r - 2} + \dfrac{r - 2}{r + 1}$

State as many similarities and differences as you can. Be sure to give the simplified form of each expression.

Objective A

☐ Can simplify rational expressions.
☐ States two or more similarities.   (i) $\dfrac{r - 3}{r + 1}$
☐ States two or more differences.
☐ Simplifies each expression correctly. (Answers at right.) (ii) $\dfrac{2r^2 - 6r + 1}{r^2 - r - 2}$

---

3. In each part, fill in the blank at the right, so that f is a rational function with the given characteristic.
  a. no discontinuities
  b. one removable discontinuity
  c. two essential discontinuities

$$f(x) = \dfrac{x^2 - 2x - 3}{\rule{2cm}{0.4pt}}$$

Objective D, H

☐ Is able to identify rational functions.
☐ Is able to classify discontinuities.
☐ Fills in the blanks appropriately.
(Samples: **a.** 5 **b.** $x - 3$ **c.** $x^2 - 4x - 3$)

4. Give an example to show how conjugates can be used to rationalize the denominator of a fraction.

Objective C

☐ Is able to simplify expressions involving radicals.
☐ Chooses an appropriate fraction. (See below.)
☐ Correctly rationalizes the denominator of the chosen fraction.
(Sample: $\dfrac{2}{3 + \sqrt{5}} = \dfrac{2}{3 + \sqrt{5}} \cdot \dfrac{3 - \sqrt{5}}{3 - \sqrt{5}} = \dfrac{3 - \sqrt{5}}{2}$)

---

5. Write a step-by-step description of the method you would use to solve a rational equation of the following form.

$$\dfrac{\blacksquare}{x^2 + 3x} + \dfrac{\blacktriangle}{x + 3} = \dfrac{\bullet}{x}$$

Objective E

☐ Is able to solve rational equations.
☐ Describes an appropriate method.
(Sample:
1. Factor $x^2 + 3x$ as $x(x + 3)$.
2. Multiply both sides of the equation by the LCM of the denominators, which is $x(x + 3)$.
3. Solve $\blacksquare + \blacktriangle x = \bullet(x + 3)$.
4. Eliminate any solutions of this equation that are restricted from the original equation.)

6. State as many facts as you can about the rational function g graphed below.

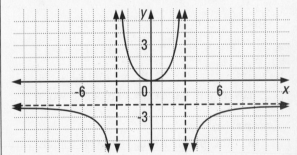

Objective K

☐ Is able to relate the limit of a function to its graph.
☐ Is able to identify equations of asymptotes.
☐ States two or more significant facts.
(Samples: $\lim\limits_{x \to \infty} g(x) = \lim\limits_{x \to -\infty} g(x) = -2$; discontinuities at -3, 3)

Teacher Notes

Objectives A, E, I

Concepts and Skills This activity requires students to:
- write rational expressions.
- solve rational equations.
- apply rational expressions and equations.
- make decisions based on real-life experiences.
- summarize results in a written report.

Guiding Questions
- If two copies are available, what is the greatest time that might be required for a 100-page run? the least time? [$\approx$ 3 min 19 s; 1 min]
- How can you check that your estimate of the time required for any two copiers working simultaneously is reasonable? [Sample: It should be greater than the time required if both copiers worked at the faster rate, and less than the time required if both worked at the slower rate.]
- How can you adjust your work in part **a** through **f** for 1000 copies? [Multiply the times required for 100 copies by 10.]

Answers

a. i. $\frac{1}{500}$ ii. $\frac{1}{330}$ iii. $\frac{1}{230}$ iv. $\frac{1}{215}$ v. $\frac{1}{150}$ vi. $\frac{1}{110}$

b. i. $\frac{1}{x}$ ii. $\frac{60}{x}$

c. i. $\frac{1}{500} + \frac{1}{100} = \frac{3}{250}$ ii. $\frac{180}{250} = \frac{18}{25}$ iii. $\frac{18m}{25}$

d. i. $\frac{1}{x} + \frac{1}{y} = \frac{x + y}{xy}$ ii. $\frac{60(x + y)}{xy} = \frac{60x + 60y}{xy}$

  iii. $\frac{m(60x + 60y)}{xy} = \frac{60mx + 60my}{xy}$

e. i. $\frac{18m}{25} = 1$ ii. $m = \frac{25}{18}$; ≈ 1 min 23 s

f. i. $\frac{60mx + 60my}{xy} = 1$ ii. ≈ 1 min 43 s

g. Answers will vary. Check students' work.

Extension
Consider this problem: Suppose a customer comes to the copy center and wants a large number of copies made within a specific amount of time. Have students devise a method an employee can use to determine if the customer's job can be done with the machines available at the time.

Evaluation

Level	Standard to be achieved for performance at specified level
5	The student demonstrates an in-depth understanding of rational expressions, rational equations, and their application to the given situation. Answers to all questions are accurate and complete. The student makes a reasonable recommendation for a time to make the copies and prepares a thoughtful, well-organized report to justify it.
4	The student demonstrates a clear understanding of rational expressions, rational equations, and their application to the given situation. The student answers all questions in an appropriate manner, but the responses may contain minor errors. The recommendation for a time to make the copies is reasonable, but the report may lack in some detail.
3	The student demonstrates a fundamental understanding of rational expressions and rational equations, but may need assistance in applying the concepts. The student may make a major error in writing an expression, or may omit a major step in solving an equation . The student makes a reasonable recommendation for a time to make the copies, but the report may be somewhat disorganized.
2	The student demonstrates some understanding of expressions and rational equations, but needs considerable assistance in applying the concepts. Even with help, the student may make several major errors in writing the expressions or solving the equations. The recommendation for a time to make the copies may be somewhat unreasonable, and the report may be discorded and incomplete.
1	The student demonstrates little if any understanding of rational expressions, rational equations, and their application to the given situation. Even with assistance, any attempts to write expressions or solve equations are trivial or irrelevant. Instead of making a recommendation and writing a report, the student may simply copy given information.

Precalculus and Discrete Mathematics © Scott Foresman Addison Wesley

1. Show algebraically that
$$\frac{\sec x}{\cos x} - 1 = \frac{\cot x}{\tan x}$$
is *not* an identity. Show two different ways to create an identity by changing the right side. Identify the domain of each identity.

Objective D

☐ Can prove trigonometric identities.
☐ Explains why the equation is not an identity.
☐ Gives two correct ways to make an identity. (Samples: 1. $= \tan^2 x$ 2. $= \frac{(\tan x)}{(\cot x)}$)
☐ Gives correct domains. (Samples, for the identities given: 1. $x \neq \frac{\pi n}{2}$, n an integer 2. $x \neq \pi n$ and $x \neq \frac{\pi n}{2}$, n an integer)

2. Explain how to find sin $2x$ if you know cos x and the quadrant in which x lies. Give an example to illustrate your method.

Objective A

☐ Can use trigonometric identities to express trigonometric functions in terms of rational numbers and radicals, without using a calculator.
☐ Gives a logical explanation. (Sample:
   1. Use the Pythagorean Identity to determine a value n such that $\sin x = \pm n$
   2. Use the information about the quadrant to determine whether $\sin x = n$ or $\sin x = -n$.
   3. Apply the identity $\sin 2x = 2 \sin x \cos x$)
☐ Gives an appropriate example. (Sample: Let $\cos x = -\frac{4}{5}$ $\left(\frac{\pi}{2} < x < \pi\right)$ 1. $\sin x = \pm\frac{3}{5}$
   2. $\sin x = \frac{3}{5}$ 3. $\sin 2x = 2\left(-\frac{4}{5}\right)\left(\frac{3}{5}\right) = -\frac{24}{25}$)

3. At the right, a ladder is shown resting against a building. Write a problem about the situation that can be solved by evaluating an inverse trigonometric function. Show how to solve the problem.

Objective B, E

☐ Can evaluate inverse trigonometric functions.
☐ Can apply inverse trigonometric functions.
☐ Writes a suitable problem. (Sample: When the base of the ladder is 3 ft from the wall, what is θ?)
☐ Gives a correct solution. (Sample, for the problem given: θ = cos^{-1} .25 ≈ 76°)

4. Jerry wrote the following.
$$\sin x = \frac{1}{2} \text{ or } \sin x = -1$$
What trigonometric equation might he have been solving? Give two possible equations, one involving just the sine function, the other involving both the sine and cosine functions. Then solve each equation over the set of real numbers.

Objective C

☐ Can solve trigonometric equations algebraically.
☐ Gives two possible equations. (Samples: $2 \sin^2 x + \sin x = 1$; $2 \cos^2 x - \sin x = 1$)
☐ Gives a correct solution. $x = \frac{\pi}{2} + 2\pi n$ or $x = \frac{\pi}{6} + 2\pi n$ or $x = \frac{5\pi}{6} + 2\pi n$, for all integers n)

5. Create a rubberband transformation T that can be applied to a circular function:
$$T(x, y) = (\rule{1cm}{0.15cm} , \rule{1cm}{0.15cm})$$
On the axes at the right, graph the image of the graph of $y = \sin x$ under your transformation T. Find an equation for the image. Then state its amplitude, period, phase shift, and vertical shift.

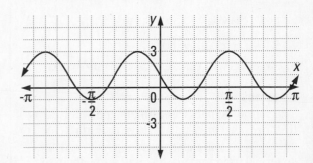

Objective G

☐ Is able to find an equation for the image of a graph under a transformation.
☐ Creates an appropriate transformation. (Sample: $T(x, y) = \left(\frac{1}{3}x + \frac{\pi}{3}, 2y + 1\right)$)
☐ Draws a correct graph of the image. (See figure for the graph of T given above.)
☐ Gives a correct equation for the image. (Sample, for T given above: $y = 2 \sin(3x - \pi) + 1$)
☐ Correctly identifies the required characteristics of the function. (Sample, for T given above: amplitude = 2; period = $\frac{2\pi}{3}$; phase shift = $\frac{\pi}{3}$; vertical shift = 1)

Teacher Notes

Objectives B, E

Concepts and Skills This activity requires students to:
- read information from text and graphics.
- evaluate and apply trigonometric functions and inverse trigonometric functions.
- create a set of rules that define a procedure.

Guiding Questions
- What is a great circle of a sphere? [the intersection of the sphere with a plane that contains its center]
- If the buoy lies due north, how far east of the ship is it? [0 miles] If the buoy lies due east, how far north of the ship is it? [0 miles]
- In part **d,** where is the buoy relative to the ship? [northeast] How many minutes north is it? [2'] How many minutes east? [5']
- What distance is spanned by one *minute* of latitude? [≈ 1.15 miles] A latitude $x°$, what distance is spanned by one minute of longitude? [≈ 1.15 (cos x)] miles]
- Why do your formulas apply only when the buoy is relatively close? [At small distances, the curvature of Earth's surface is negligible, so you can use plane trigonometry. At regular distances, you must begin to consider the curvature of the surface.]

Answers
a. **i.** ≈ 8.6 mi. **ii.** ≈ 36°

b. **i.** $d = \sqrt{N^2 + E^2}$ **ii.** If $N \neq 0$,
$b = \tan^{-1}\left(\frac{E}{N}\right)$; if $N = 0, b = 90$.

c. **i.** $d = \sqrt{N^2 + W^2}$ **ii.** If $W \neq 0$,
$b = \tan^{-1}\left(\frac{N}{W}\right) + 270$; if $W = 0, b = 0$.

d. **i.** ≈ 4.6 mi **ii.** ≈ 60°

e. Answers will vary. Check students' work.

Extension
The formulas in this assessment apply only to distances that are small relative to Earth's surface. Have students research methods from spherical trigonometry that will allow them to find greater distances by calculating the great-circle distance between two points on Earth. Then have them develop formulas to calculate bearings within a large body of water, such as the North Atlantic Ocean.

Evaluation

Level	Standard to be achieved for performance at specified level
5	The student demonstrates an in-depth understanding of trigonometric functions, inverse trigonometric functions, and their application to the given situation. All calculations are accurate and complete. The student creates a thorough, well-organized set of formulas that accounts for all cases, and it may be presented imaginatively.
4	The student demonstrates a clear understanding of trigonometric and inverse trigonometric functions. The student takes a suitable approach to answering all questions, but the responses may contain minor errors. The set of formulas is well-organized and easy to read, but it may lack in some detail.
3	The student demonstrates a fundamental understanding of trigonometric and inverse trigonometric functions, but may need some assistance in applying the concepts to the given situation. There may be one or more major errors or omissions in the student's responses to the questions posed. The set of formulas is essentially complete, but it may be somewhat disorganized.
2	The student demonstrates some understanding of trigonometric and inverse trigonometric functions, but needs considerable assistance in understanding their application to the given situation. Even with help, the student may make several major errors in responding to the questions posed, or may omit one or more major steps of a process. The student attempts to prepare a set of formulas, but it is jumbled and incomplete.
1	The student demonstrates little if any understanding of trigonometric functions, inverse trigonometric functions, and their application to the given situation. Even with assistance, any attempts to respond to the questions posed are trivial or irrelevant. Instead of writing a set of formulas, the student may simply restate given information.

Precalculus and Discrete Mathematics © Scott Foresman Addison Wesley

1. Compare the computer programs at the right with respect to what you have seen in this chapter. How are the two programs alike? different?

	Program A	Program B
10	FOR N = 1 TO 8	TERM = 1
20	TERM = 4*N − 3	PRINT TERM
30	PRINT TERM	FOR N = 2 TO 8
40	NEXT N	PRINT TERM
50	END	TERM = TERM + 4
60		NEXT N
70		END

Objectives A, J

☐ Is able to determine terms of a sequence that is defined either explicitly or recursively.
☐ Is able to interpret computer programs that calculate terms of sequences.
☐ States at least one significant likeness. (Sample: Both programs will output the first eight terms of the sequence 1, 5, 9, 13, 17, 21, 25, 29. . . .)
☐ States at least one significant difference. (Sample: Program A calculates the terms using an explicit formula. Program B uses a recursive formula.)

---

2. Fill in the blanks to create two different examples of writing a sum recursively:

$$\sum_{i=1}^{6} \blacksquare = \sum_{i=1}^{5} \blacksquare + 41$$

For each example, write the sum in expanded form and find its value.

Objectives C, D

☐ Can use summation notation to write sums.
☐ Can rewrite sums recursively.
☐ Creates two suitable examples. (See below.)
☐ Writes the correct expanded form for each sum. (See below.)
☐ Gives the correct value for each sum. (Samples: 1. Place $i^2 + 5$ in each blank. Then $(1^2 + 5) + (2^2 + 5) + (3^2 + 5) + (4^2 + 5) + (5^2 + 5) + (6^2 + 5) = 121$. 2. Place $6i + 5$ in each blank. Then $[6(1) + 5] + [6(2) + 5] + [6(3) + 5] + [6(4) + 5] + [6(5) + 5] + [6(6) + 5] = 156$.)

3. Del's class proved the following statement.

$$\sum_{i=1}^{n} i = \frac{n(n + 1)}{2}$$

So Del made the following conjecture.

$$\sum_{i=1}^{n} (3i) = \frac{3n \cdot 3(n + 1)}{2}$$

Show that Del's conjecture is false. Correct it to make a true statement, and prove your new statement using mathematical induction.

Objective G

☐ Can write proofs using mathematical induction.
☐ Makes a logical argument that Del's conjecture is false. (Sample: It is false when $n = 1$.)
☐ Makes a correct conjecture. (Sample: Replace the right side of the equation with $\frac{3n(n + 1)}{2}$.)
☐ Writes a correct proof of the conjecture.

---

4. To evaluate an infinite geometric series, Ali wrote the expression $\frac{6}{1 - \frac{1}{5}}$ at the right. What series could Ali have been evaluating? Write the series using summation notation. Find the first four partial sums, then evaluate the series.

Objective E

☐ Can evaluate a finite or infinite geometric series.
☐ Writes a correct expression for the series. (See sample at right.) $\sum_{k=0}^{\infty} \frac{6}{5^k}$
☐ Correctly identifies the partial sums. ($S_0 = 6$, $S_1 = 7.2$, $S_2 = 7.44$, $S_3 = 7.488$)
☐ Correctly evaluates the series. ($S_\infty = 7.5$)

5. Explain the purpose of the Bubblesort and Quicksort Algorithms. Then create a list of five different numbers, choose one of the algorithms, and show how the algorithm can be applied to the list. Be sure to show intermediate results of each step.

Objective I

☐ Can execute algorithms on sets of numbers.
☐ Gives a suitable explanation. (Sample: These algorithms provide a way for a computer to sort large lists of items into a desired order.)
☐ Creates an appropriate set of numbers.
☐ Correctly applies one of the algorithms.

Precalculus and Discrete Mathematics © Scott Foresman Addison Wesley

EVALUATION GUIDES

Teacher Notes

Objectives A, E, H

Concepts and Skills
This activity requires students to:
- read information from text and graphics.
- investigate sequences defined explicitly and recursively.
- investigate partial sums of a geometric series.
- apply the concepts of sequences and series to the creation of a spreadsheet.
- summarize results in a written report.

Guiding Questions
- How do you think the numbers in column A of each spreadsheet were generated? [Sample: Enter 1 in cell A1. Enter $= A1+1$ in cell A2. Highlight cells A2 through A12 and choose "Fill Down."]
- Is the progression of increasing costs a sequence? [yes] the progression of increasing savings? [no]

Answers
a. explicitly; Explanations will vary. Sample: The entries in cells A1 through A12 are the natural numbers $1, 2, 3, \ldots, 12$. The entry in any cell Bn is given in terms of the entry in cell An.
b. $b_p = 4p + 21$
c. recursively; Explanations will vary. Sample: A specific value has been entered in cell B1. After that, the entry in each cell Bn is defined in terms of the entry in cell B$(n-1)$.
d. $c_{q+1} = c_q + 4$, for $q \geq 1$
e. Samples: For Sheet 1, enter $=1/(5\wedge(A1-3))$ in cell B1, then highlight cells B1 through B12 and choose "Fill Down." For Sheet 2, enter $=B1/5$ in cell B2, then highlight cells B2 through B12 and choose "Fill Down."
f. Sample: Use Sheet 1. Enter $=1/(5\wedge(A1-3))$ in cell B1. Enter $=1/(5\wedge(A2-3))+B1$ in cell B2. Highlight cells B2 through B12 and "Fill down."
g. Answers will vary. Check students' work.

Extension
If spreadsheet software is available, have students use it to make the spreadsheets they designed. Then have them research costs of several cars and current interest rates on savings accounts and certificates of deposit. Have them determine a reasonable amount for a down payment on each car they chose and devise specific plans to save each amount.

Evaluation

Level	Standard to be achieved for performance at specified level
5	The student demonstrates an in-depth understanding of explicit and recursive formulas and their application to spreadsheets. All formulas the student creates are appropriate, accurate, and complete. The student prepares a comprehensive, well-organized set of instructions, and it may be presented imaginatively.
4	The student demonstrates a clear understanding of explicit and recursive formulas and their application to spreadsheets. The student recognizes the types of formulas that are appropriate for the given situations, but may make minor errors in writing them. The set of instructions is well-organized and easy to read, but it may lack some detail.
3	The student demonstrates a fundamental understanding of explicit and recursive formulas, but may need some assistance in applying the concepts to spreadsheets. The student may make a major error in writing a formula, or may omit the part of a formula needed to fill a particular cell. The set of instructions is essentially complete, but it may be somewhat disorganized and hard to follow.
2	The student demonstrates some understanding of explicit and recursive formulas, but needs considerable assistance in understanding their application to spreadsheets. Even with help, the student may make several major errors in writing formulas, or may omit the formula needed to fill an entire set of cells. The student attempts to prepare a set of instructions, but it is jumbled and incomplete.
1	The student demonstrates little if any understanding of explicit and recursive formulas and their application to spreadsheets. Even with assistance, any attempts to write formulas are trivial or irrelevant. Instead of writing a set of instructions, the student may simply copy the graphic that appears on the page.

Precalculus and Discrete Mathematics © Scott Foresman Addison Wesley

1. Choose any two of the complex numbers below and find their product. Then write the product in each of the four forms shown.

   $(-3\sqrt{3}, -3)$ $-2\sqrt{3} + 2i$

   $[8, 60°]$ $12\left(\cos\frac{\pi}{6} + i\sin\frac{\pi}{6}\right)$

   Objectives A, B

   ☐ Can express complex numbers in various forms.
   ☐ Can perform operations with complex numbers.
   ☐ Correctly calculates the product.
   ☐ Correctly writes the product in each form.

2. Explain how this diagram can be related to complex numbers. Be as specific as possible.

   Objectives D, K

   ☐ Can find powers and roots of complex numbers.
   ☐ Can relate DeMoivre's Theorem to graphs.
   ☐ Gives a logical explanation. (Key points: Label the horizontal axis *real* and the vertical axis *imaginary*. Then the points represent the cube roots of $-8i$, which are $2i$, $-\sqrt{3} - i$, and $\sqrt{3} - i$.)

3. Explain the meaning of this statement in your own words.

   For a given point in the plane, the rectangular coordinate representation is unique, but the polar coordinate representation is not.

   Give an example to illustrate your response.

   Objective C

   ☐ Is able to convert between polar and rectangular representations of points.
   ☐ Gives a logical explanation. (Sample: Using rectangular coordinates, there is exactly one name for a point. Using polar coordinates, that same point has more than one name.)
   ☐ Gives an appropriate example.

4. Celia listed all the zeros of the polynomial $x^4 - 8x^3 + 23x^2 - 26x + 10$ as 1, $i - 3$ and $i + 3$. Explain how you know this list is incorrect.

   To help her correct the list, Celia's teacher gave her these clues.

   Two of the entries in the list *are* correct. One of these correct zeros has multiplicity 2.

   Show how to use the clues to correct the list.

   Objectives E, G

   ☐ Is able to use the properties of polynomials to find or describe their zeros.
   ☐ Is able to find all zeros of a given polynomial.
   ☐ Gives a logical explanation.
   ☐ Corrects the list. ($3 + i$; $3 - i$; 1 with multiplicity 2)

5. Shown at the right is a circle graphed in a polar coordinate system. Write a polar equation whose graph will be a circle in this position. Now, by modifying your circle equation, find an equation whose graph has the given shape and position. (*Note:* The graphs are not drawn to scale relative to one another.)

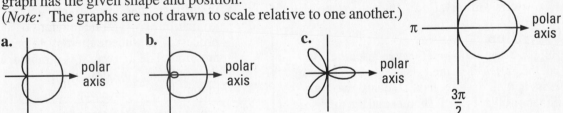

   a.   b.   c.

   Objective J

   ☐ Is able to sketch graphs of polar equations.
   ☐ Gives an appropriate equation for the circle. (Any equation of the form $r = a\cos\theta$, such as $r = 3\cos\theta$)
   ☐ Makes appropriate adjustments to obtain equations for the given shapes. (Samples [given $r = 3\cos\theta$ as the equation of the circle]: **a.** $r = 3 + 3\cos\theta$ **b.** $r = 2 + 3\cos\theta$ **c.** $r = 3\cos 3\theta$)

Teacher Notes

Objectives J, K

Concepts and Skills This activity requires students to:
- write a polar equation for a given graph.
- write polar equations and graph them.
- graph roots of complex numbers.
- create an original design in a polar coordinate system and write equations to describe it.

Guiding Questions
- What part of the equation of a rose curve determines its orientation? [the use of sine or cosine in the general form of the equation] the number of petals? [in $r = a \sin n\theta$ or $r = a \cos n\theta$, the value of n] the overall size? [the value of a]
- In a polar coordinate system, what is the general form of an equation of a circle? [$r = a$, $r = a \sin \theta$, or $r = a \cos \theta$] Why do you use $r = a$ in this design? [The circles are centered at [0, 0].]

Answers
a. Check students' work.
b. i. Each is a rose curve. **ii.** $A: r = a \cos n\theta$
$B: r = a \sin n\theta$ **iii.** A: $r = 10 \cos 2\theta$;
$B: r = 10 \sin 2\theta$ **iv.** Check students' graphs.
c., d. Equations are given. Check students' graphs.
c. $r = 10$ and $r = 12$
d. $r = 10 \sec \theta$, $r = -10 \sec \theta$, $r = 10 \csc \theta$, $r = -10 \csc \theta$, $r = 12 \sec \theta$, $r = -12 \sec \theta$, $r = 12 \csc \theta$, $r = -12 \csc \theta$
e. A point would be added near the center of each "petal" of graph A. Specifically, this would occur at the points [6, 0], $\left[6, \frac{\pi}{2}\right]$, $\left[6, \frac{3\pi}{2}\right]$, and [6, π].
f. Answers will vary. Check students' work.

Extension
Suppose that a computer-driven machine is to cut the pieces of stained glass. For each piece of glass in their designs, have students give the equations that form the border and the precise interval from the domain that would direct the machine to do no more cutting than necessary. For example, one piece of the design shown is bordered by $r = 10 \sin 2\theta$ in the interval $0 \le \theta \le \frac{\pi}{8}$ and $r = 10 \cos 2\theta$ in the interval $\frac{\pi}{8} \le \theta \le \frac{\pi}{4}$.

Evaluation

Level	Standard to be achieved for performance at specified level
5	The student demonstrates an in-depth understanding of polar equations, complex numbers, and their graphs. Answers to all questions are accurate and complete. The student creates an attractive original design that contains several distinct elements, and it may be presented imaginatively. The student may offer additional insights.
4	The student demonstrates a clear understanding of polar equations, complex numbers, and their graphs. The student is able to write equations of the appropriate form and to render suitable graphs, but the work may contain minor errors. The original design is well-planned and attractive, but the presentation may lack some detail.
3	The student demonstrates a fundamental understanding of polar equations, complex numbers and their graphs, but may need some assistance in applying them to the given situation. There may be one or more major errors or omissions in the student's equations or graphs. The original design and the accompanying description are essentially complete, but may be somewhat disorganized.
2	The student demonstrates some understanding of polar equations, complex numbers, and their graphs, but needs considerable assistance in understanding their application to the given situation. Even with help, the student may make several major errors in writing equations or rendering graphs, or may omit major steps of a process. The student attempts to prepare an original design, but it is jumbled, and the accompanying description is incomplete.
1	The student demonstrates little if any understanding of polar equations, complex numbers, and their graphs. Even with assistance, any attempts to write equations or render graphs are trivial or irrelevant. Instead of creating an original design, the student may simply copy the given design.

EVALUATION GUIDES

1. Refer to the function graphed at the right. **a.** Draw a secant line that passes through two named points and whose slope is positive. **b.** Draw a second secant line whose slope is negative. **c.** Draw a secant line whose slope is neither positive nor negative. Calculate the slope of each of your secant lines. Explain the meaning of each slope relative to the function.

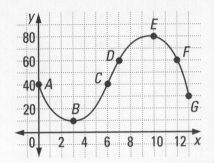

Objectives A, G

☐ Is able to compute average rates of change in functions.
☐ Is able to relate average rates of change to secant lines.
☐ Draws appropriate secant lines. (Samples: **a.** $\overleftrightarrow{BC}$ **b.** $\overleftrightarrow{EF}$ **c.** $\overleftrightarrow{AC}$).
☐ Correctly calculates and interprets the slope of each line. (Sample: The slope of $\overleftrightarrow{BC}$ is 10. This means that, from 3 to 6, the average rate of change of the function is 10.)

2. A student drew the graph at the right and arrived at this conclusion.

$$f'(3) = \frac{-3 - (-7)}{3 - .5} = \frac{4}{2.5} = 1.6$$

Do you agree or disagree? If you agree, justify your answer. If you disagree, show how to find a correct value for $f'(3)$ and describe what adjustment, if any, you would make to the graph.

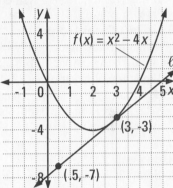

Objectives B, H

☐ Is able to estimate derivatives by finding slopes of tangent lines.
☐ Is able to use the definition of derivative to compute derivatives.
☐ Recognizes that the given conclusion is incorrect.
☐ Correctly computes $f'(3) = 2$ and shows work to support this conclusion.
☐ Explains how to correct the graph. (Sample: Redraw line ℓ so that it passes through (3, -3) and (1, -7).)

3. A projectile is shot upward so that its height in feet above the ground after t seconds is given by $h(t) = 16t^2 + 92t + 24$. Choose any time t during which the projectile is in motion and state as many facts as you can about its position and movement. Be as specific as possible, and justify each fact.

Objective E

☐ Is able to use derivatives to find the velocity and acceleration of a moving object.
☐ Chooses an appropriate time t. (The acceptable range is $0 < t < 6$.)
☐ States all pertinent facts for the chosen time t. (Sample: At $t = 4$, the projectile is 136 feet above the ground; its velocity is -36 ft/sec, meaning that it is moving at a speed of 35 ft/sec downward; and its acceleration is -32 ft/sec².)

4. Consider the functions f and g graphed below. Compare the functions f' and g'. How are they alike? How are they different?

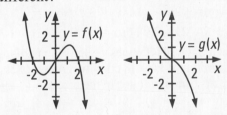

Objective I

☐ Is able to determine properties of derivatives from the graph of a function.
☐ States at least one significant likeness. (Sample: Both f' and g' are positive when $x < 1$ and when $x > 1$.)
☐ States at least one significant difference. (Sample: f' is negative when $-1 < x < 1$; g' is never negative.)

EVALUATION GUIDES

Teacher Notes

Objectives A, D, F, I

Concepts and Skills This activity requires students to:

- read information from text, graphs, and graphics.
- calculate average rates of change in functions and apply them to real situations.
- determine properties of derivatives from graphs.
- use derivatives to solve an optimization problem.
- extend their knowledge of derivatives to interpret and apply an unfamiliar theorem.
- make decisions based on real-life experiences.
- summarize results in a written report.

Guiding Questions

- What units are associated with the numerical rate of change in V? [cubic inches per inch]
- What type of function is V? How do you solve the equation? [quadratic; quadratic formula.]
- What is a reasonable depth for the flap on the cover of the box? [Answers will vary.]

Answers

a. Sample: **i.** $x < 3$ or $x > 9$ **ii.** $3 < x < 9$
   iii. $x = 3$ or $x = 9$
b. $0 < x < 8$; Sample explanation: $x < 0$ gives a negative height; $x = 0$ gives no height; $x \geq 8$ means the two cuts in the shorter side equal or exceed the length of the shorter side.
c. **i.** 192 **ii.** -96
d. Sample: From 0 in. to 2 in., the volume increases 192 in^3 for every one-inch increase in height. From 4 in. to 8 in., the volume decreases 96 in^3 for every one-inch increase in height.
e. Sample: $x \approx 3$; $V \approx 420$ in^3
f. $V'(x) = 12x^2 - 144x + 320$, so $x = 6 + \frac{2}{3}\sqrt{21} \approx 2.94$ or $x = 6 - \frac{2}{3}\sqrt{21} \approx 9.05$.
   Each of these identifies a relative maximum or minimum of $V(x)$. In this situation, $x < 8$, so the maximum volume of the box is $\approx V(2.94)$, or about 420 cubic inches.
g. Answers will vary. Check students' work.

Extension

Have students repeat the optimization problem for a box shaped like a right cylinder. Be sure they note that, when working with a non-square sheet of cardboard, they need to consider two layouts, as shown at the right.

Evaluation

Standard to be achieved for
Level performance at specified level

5 The student demonstrates an in-depth understanding of derivatives and their application to the situation. All questions are answered completely and accurately. The student prepares a thoughtful, well-organized report that describes a suitable set of boxes, and it may be presented imaginatively.

4 The student demonstrates a clear understanding of derivatives and their application to the situation. All questions are answered in an appropriate manner, but the responses may contain minor errors. The student describes a suitable set of boxes in a report that is well-organized and easy to read, but it may lack in some detail.

3 The student demonstrates a fundamental understanding of derivatives, but may need some assistance in applying the concept to the situation. There may be one or more major errors or omissions in the student's responses to the questions posed. The student devises a suitable set of boxes and describes them in a report that is essentially complete, though it may be somewhat disorganized.

2 The student demonstrates some understanding of derivatives, but needs considerable assistance in understanding their application to the situation. Even with help, the student may make several major errors in responding to the questions posed, or may omit one or more major steps of a process. The student attempts to devise a set of boxes, but the plan is flawed, and the report is jumbled and incomplete.

1 The student demonstrates little if any understanding of derivatives and their application to the situation. Even with assistance, any attempts to respond to the questions posed are trivial or irrelevant. Instead of planning a suitable set of boxes, the student may simply copy or restate the given dimensions.

Precalculus and Discrete Mathematics © Scott Foresman Addison Wesley

1. Write a paragraph that explains what is illustrated in the diagram at the right. Include a statement of a conclusion that can be drawn from the diagram.

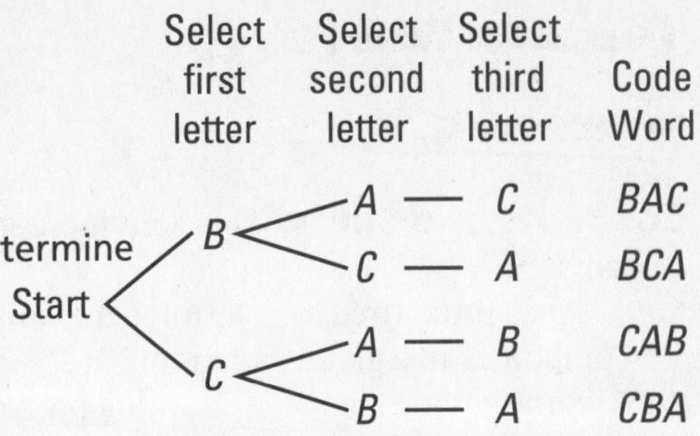

Select first letter	Select second letter	Select third letter	Code Word
B	A — C		BAC
	C — A		BCA
Start			
C	A — B		CAB
	B — A		CBA

Objective I

☐ Demonstrates an ability to use a possibility tree to determine the number of possible outcomes in a situation.

☐ Writes an appropriate description. (Sample: The diagram shows all the three-letter code words that can be made from A, B, and C if repetition is not allowed, and the first letter cannot be A.)

☐ States an appropriate conclusion. (Sample: There are four possible code words.)

---

2. Compare $_4P_3$ and $_4C_3$. How are they alike? How are they different? State as many likenesses and differences as you can.

Objective B

☐ Is able to evaluate expressions indicating permutations or combinations.

☐ States two or more significant likenesses. (Samples: Both relate to 3 elements taken from a set of 4 elements. Neither allows repetition.)

☐ States two or more significant differences. (Samples: The expression $_4P_3$ refers to permutations; the expression $_4C_3$ refers to combinations. With $_4P_3$, the 3 elements form an ordered string taken from the 4 elements; with $_4C_3$, the 3 elements form unordered subsets of the set of 4 elements. The value of $_4P_3$ is 24; the value of $_4C_3$ is 4.)

3. Identify a "counting situation." Write a problem about it that can be solved using:

a. permutations.   **b.** combinations.

Show how to solve each problem.

Objectives F, G

☐ Can use permutations to solve problems.

☐ Can use combinations to solve problems.

☐ Writes two appropriate problems. (Samples: **a.** In how many ways can four committee members be elected from a group of 7 students? **b.** In how many ways can a president, vice president, secretary, and treasurer be elected from a group of 7 students?

☐ Gives correct solutions to the problems. (Samples [for the problems given]: **a.** 35 **b.** 840)

---

4. In the past 0.3% of the microwave ovens manufactured at a certain factory have been defective. Assume this is the probability that an oven in a new shipment of 20 microwave ovens is defective. A student calculated the probability that this shipment contains at least one defective oven as shown below. Do you agree or disagree? If you agree, justify your answer. If you disagree, find a correct probability.

$$\binom{20}{1}(.997)^{19}(.003)^1 \approx .0567$$

Objective H

☐ Is able to find binomial probabilities in realistic situations.

☐ Recognizes that the student's work is incorrect. Give the correct probability. ($\binom{20}{0}(.003)^0(.997)^{20} \approx .0583$)

5. The expression $(x + y)^n$ is expanded for a certain value of n. One term in the expansion is $2024x^{21}y^3$. What is the next term? Explain your reasoning. (*Note:* Assume the terms are written as customary, with the exponents of x in decreasing order.)

Objective C

☐ Is able to apply the Binomial Theorem to expand binomials and find specified terms.

☐ Correctly identifies the next term. ($10,626x^{20}y^4$)

☐ Gives a logical explanation. (Sample: The value of n is 21 + 3, or 24. The given term is the 4th term of the expansion of $(x + y)^{24}$. The 5th term is $\binom{24}{4}x^{24-4}y^4$, or $10,626x^{20}y^4$.)

Precalculus and Discrete Mathematics © Scott Foresman Addison Wesley

Teacher Notes

Objectives G, I

Concepts and Skills This activity requires students to:
- use a possibility tree to determine the number of outcomes in a given situation.
- use combinations to solve counting problems.
- use real-life experience and mathematical investigation as the basis for creating a menu.
- write an argument to support a point of view.

Guiding Questions
- When identifying a "meal" in this context, is the order in which items are eaten important? [No]
- What multiplication gives the number of meals in the possibility tree in part **a**? [$1 \cdot 2 \cdot 3 \cdot 4 \cdot 2$]
- What multiplication gives the number of meals in the possibility tree in part **b**? [$1 \cdot 2 \cdot 3 \cdot 6 \cdot 2$]
- How is the number of meals in part **d** related to Pascal's triangle? [The total number of vegetable combinations is the sum of the elements in the fourth row of Pascal's triangle, or $2^4 = 16$.]

Answers
a. Check students' diagrams. There are 48 possible meals. (Consider pie with ice cream and pie without ice cream as two different choices.)

b. i. 6 ways; Sample: $_4C_2 = \dfrac{4!}{2!(4-2)!} = 6$

ii. Sample: Each node in the *Potatoes* category would have six branches into the *Vegetables* category, rather than four.

iii. There are 72 possible meals.

c. Sample: In part **a**, the number of choices in the *Vegetables* category is $_4C_1 = 4$. In Pascal's triangle, the values of the elements in each row are symmetric about the vertical axis. So $_4C_3 = {}_4C_1 = 4$. Therefore, just as in part **a**, there are 48 possible meals under these conditions.

d. 192

e. 4096

f. Answers will vary. Check students' work.

Extension
Have students work with menus from several local restaurants. Have them determine which of the restaurants offers the greatest number of possible meals.

Evaluation

Level	Standard to be achieved for performance at specified level
5	The student demonstrates an in-depth understanding of counting methods and their application to the given situation. All calculations and diagrams are accurate and complete. The student prepares a thoughtful response to the slogan, and creates an appropriate menu to support the response.
4	The student demonstrates a clear understanding of counting methods and their application to the given situation. All calculations and diagrams are suitable, but they may contain minor errors. The student prepares a logical response to the slogan and creates an appropriate menu, but one or both may lack in some detail.
3	The student demonstrates a fundamental understanding of counting methods, but may need some assistance in applying them to the given situation. There may be one or more major errors or omissions in the student's calculations or diagrams. The student's response to the slogan is reasonable, and the menu is essentially complete, but the presentation may be somewhat disjoint.
2	The student demonstrates some understanding of counting methods, but needs considerable assistance in applying them to the given situation. Even with help, there may be several major errors in the student's calculations or diagrams, or one or more major steps of a process may be omitted. The student attempts a response to the slogan, but its logical underpinnings may be weak. The student prepares a menu, but it is incomplete.
1	The student demonstrates little if any understanding of counting methods and their application to the given situation. Even with assistance, any attempts to perform calculations or create diagrams are trivial or irrelevant. Instead of preparing a response to the slogan or creating a menu, the student may simply copy given information.

EVALUATION GUIDES

1. Consider all that you have learned about graphs in Chapter 11. State five significant facts about the graph at the right.

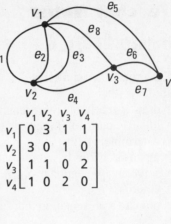

Objectives B, I

☐ Is able to identify parts and types of graphs.

☐ Is able to convert between the picture of a graph and its adjacency matrix.

☐ States five significant facts. Samples:
It has four vertices ($\{v_1, v_2, v_3, v_4\}$).
It has eight edges ($\{e_1, e_2, e_3, e_4, e_5, e_6, e_7, e_8\}$).
Its degree is 16.
Its edge-endpoint function is given in the table at the right.
The matrix at the far right is its adjacency matrix.

edge	endpoints
e_1	$\{v_1, v_2\}$
e_2	$\{v_1, v_2\}$
e_3	$\{v_1, v_2\}$
e_4	$\{v_2, v_3\}$
e_5	$\{v_1, v_4\}$
e_6	$\{v_3, v_4\}$
e_7	$\{v_3, v_4\}$
e_8	$\{v_1, v_3\}$

$$\begin{array}{c}\ \ \ \ v_1\ v_2\ v_3\ v_4\\ \begin{array}{c}v_1\\v_2\\v_3\\v_4\end{array}\left[\begin{array}{cccc}0&3&1&1\\3&0&1&0\\1&1&0&2\\1&0&2&0\end{array}\right]\end{array}$$

---

2. Consider this statement: A graph has 5 vertices of degree 3, 2, ▪, ▪, and ▪.

   a. Replace each ▪ with a number so that such a graph exists. Draw the graph.

   b. Replace each ▪ with a number so that no such graph exists. Justify your answer.

Objective C

☐ Is able to determine whether there exists a graph containing vertices with given degrees.

☐ Correctly lists degrees for a graph that exists. (Sample: 3, 2, 2)

☐ Correctly draws a graph with vertices of the chosen degrees. (See sample at right.)

☐ Correctly lists degrees so that no such graph exists. (Sample: 2, 2, 2)

☐ Gives a logical explanation. (Sample: The total degree of any graph must be an even positive integer; $3 + 2 + 2 + 2 + 2 = 11$, which is odd.)

---

3. a. Explain why the graph at the right below *does* have an Euler circuit.

   b. Write a real-life problem that can be solved by finding an Euler circuit in this graph. Show how to solve your problem.

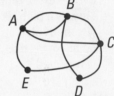

Objectives D, G

☐ Is able to determine if a graph has an Euler circuit.

☐ Is able to solve problems involving circuits.

☐ Gives a logical explanation. (Sample: It is connected, and every vertex has even degree).

☐ Writes an appropriate problem. (Sample: Can an airplane cover every route shown exactly once, returning to where it began?)

☐ Gives a correct solution to the problem. (Sample [for the problem given]: Yes. It can fly the route $A \to E \to C \to D \to B \to C \to A \to B \to A$.)

---

4. Matrix A at the right is the adjacency matrix for a graph. A student says it shows there are three walks of length 2 from v_2 to v_3 of the graph. Do you agree or disagree? Explain.

$$A = \begin{bmatrix} 1 & 0 & 1 \\ 0 & 2 & 3 \\ 1 & 3 & 0 \end{bmatrix}$$

Objective J

☐ Can use the powers of an adjacency matrix to find the number of walks of a given length.

☐ Recognizes that the student's statement is incorrect.

☐ Gives a logical explanation. (Sample: You must find entry $a_{2,3}$ of A^2. This number is 6.)

---

5. The matrix B at the right shows the probabilities that Sarah will go to the movies (M) or will not go (N) on consecutive Saturdays. Explain each entry. Then show how you can use this matrix to make a prediction.

$$B = \begin{array}{c}\ \ \ \ \ M\ \ N\\ \begin{array}{c}M\\N\end{array}\left[\begin{array}{cc}.4 & .6 \\ .8 & .2\end{array}\right]\end{array}$$

Objective H

☐ Can use stochastic matrices to make predictions.

☐ Gives an appropriate explanation of each entry.

☐ Makes an appropriate prediction. (Sample: Calculate B^8. The probability Sarah will go to the movies on any given Saturday is $\approx .57$.)

EVALUATION GUIDES

Teacher Notes

Objectives B, D, G

Concepts and Skills This activity requires students to:
- draw a graph that represents a real situation.
- identify parts of graphs and types of graphs.
- determine whether a graph has an Euler circuit.
- make decisions based on real-life experiences.
- solve an application problems involving circuits.
- prepare a presentation that summarizes results.

Guiding Questions
- In drawing a graph for the given map, must every exhibit be represented by a vertex? Must every vertex represent an exhibit? [yes; no]
- How is a path like a walk? How is it different? [Both involve an alternating sequence of adjacent vertices and edges. In a path, no edge is repeated.]

Answers
a. Sample:

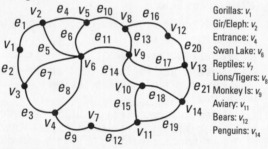

Gorillas: v_1
Gir/Eleph: v_2
Entrance: v_4
Swan Lake: v_6
Reptiles: v_7
Lions/Tigers: v_8
Monkey Is: v_9
Aviary: v_{11}
Bears: v_{12}
Penguins: v_{14}

b. The graph is simple and connected. Explanations will vary.

c. Samples (using the graph given for part **a**):
   i. $v_4\, e_9\, v_7\, e_{12}\, v_{11}\, e_{19}\, v_{14}\, e_{21}\, v_{13}\, e_{20}\, v_{12}$
   ii. $v_4\, e_8\, v_6\, e_6\, v_5\, e_4\, v_2\, e_5\, v_6\, e_6\, v_5\, e_{10}\, v_8\, e_{16}\, v_{12}$

d. Sample: The conditions require that the graph contain an Euler circuit. The graph has several vertices of odd degree, so this is impossible.

e. Answers will vary. Check students' work.

Extension
If students have access to a graphics calculator that features matrix operations, have them enter the adjacency matrix A for the graph they created and investigate A^n for several values of n. Have them obtain a map of a local zoo or of a popular zoo in another city, draw a graph for that zoo, and similarly investigate A^n for that graph. (Several maps of zoos are available through the Internet.)

Evaluation

Level	Standard to be achieved for performance at specified level
5	The student demonstrates an in-depth understanding of graphs and circuits and their application to the given situation. Answers to all questions are accurate and complete. The student carefully prepares a map that features a reasonable trail through the zoo, and it may be presented imaginatively. The student may offer additional insights.
4	The student demonstrates a clear understanding of graphs and circuits and their application to the given situation. The student responds appropriately to all the questions posed, but the responses may contain minor errors. The map is well-rendered and features an appropriate trail through the zoo, but it may lack in some detail.
3	The student demonstrates a fundamental understanding of graphs and circuits, but may need some assistance in applying the concepts to the given situation. There may be one or more major errors or omissions in the student's responses to the questions posed. The map is essentially complete, featuring an appropriate trail, but it may be somewhat disorganized and difficult to read.
2	The student demonstrates some understanding of graphs and circuits, but needs considerable assistance in applying the concepts to the given situation. Even with help, the student may make several major errors in responding to the questions posed, or may omit one or more major steps of a process. The student attempts to prepare a map with an appropriate trail, but it is jumbled and incomplete.
1	The student demonstrates little if any understanding of graphs and circuits and their application to the given situation. Even with assistance, any attempts to respond to the questions posed are irrelevant or trite. Instead of preparing a new map with an appropriate trail, the student may simply sketch a map with attractions and trails placed at random.

Precalculus and Discrete Mathematics © Scott Foresman Addison Wesley

1. Let $\vec{w}$ be the vector from (1, -1) to (-2, 5). Give the magnitude and direction of $\vec{w}$. Then find two nonzero vectors $\vec{u}$ and $\vec{v}$, such that $\vec{u} + \vec{v} = \vec{w}$, and $\vec{u}$ and $\vec{v}$ are neither parallel nor perpendicular to each other. Find the measure of the angle between $\vec{u}$ and $\vec{v}$.

Objectives A, B, D

☐ Is able to find the magnitude and direction of two-dimensional vectors.
☐ Is able to find sums of two-dimensional vectors.
☐ Is able to find the measure of the angle between two vectors.
☐ Gives the correct magnitude and direction for $\vec{w}$. (magnitude: $3\sqrt{5} \approx 6.7$; direction: $\approx 116.6°$)
☐ Identifies two appropriate vectors. (Sample: $\vec{u} = (-3, 4)$, $\vec{v} = (0, 2)$)
☐ Correctly identifies the measure of the angle. (Sample [for $\vec{u}$ and $\vec{v}$ given above]: $\approx 36.9°$)

2. Describe a situation that can be represented by the vectors in this figure. What do the components and the sum of the vectors represent in the situation? (Be specific.)

Objectives G, H

☐ Is able to use vectors in a plane to compose or decompose motion into x- and y-components.
☐ Can add vectors in a plane to solve problems.
☐ Describes an appropriate situation. (Sample: An airplane's instrument panel velocity is 160 mph on a heading 60° north of east. A steady wind of 40 mph is blowing from the west.)
☐ Gives a valid meaning for the components.
☐ Explains the sum. (Sample: The airplane's true velocity is ≈ 183.3 mph, $\approx 49.1°$ north of east.)

3. Give parametric equations for a line parallel to the vector $\vec{q} = (-2, 5)$. Use the theorem that describes parallel vectors to verify that the line you specified is parallel to $\vec{q}$.

Objectives F, L

☐ Is able to represent lines in a plane using parametric equations.
☐ Is able to identify parallel vectors.
☐ Gives correct equations for a line parallel to $\vec{q}$. (Sample: $x = 1 - 2t$, $y = 3 - 5t$)
☐ Gives a valid justification.

4. Give components of three 3-dimensional vectors $\vec{r}$, $\vec{s}$, and $\vec{t}$ so that each vector is orthogonal to the other two. Justify your answer.

Objectives C, F

☐ Is able to find dot products and cross products of vectors in 3-space.
☐ Is able to identify orthogonal vectors.
☐ Identifies three appropriate vectors. (Sample: $\vec{r} = (3, 1, -1)$, $\vec{s} = (-2, 3, -2)$, $\vec{t} = (1, 8, 11)$)
☐ Gives a logical explanation. (Sample: $\vec{r} \cdot \vec{s} = 0$, so $\vec{r} \perp \vec{s}$; $\vec{r} \times \vec{s} = \vec{t}$, so $\vec{r} \perp \vec{t}$ and $\vec{s} \perp \vec{t}$.)

5. Jameel says that the vector $\vec{j} = (-3, 6, 3)$ is perpendicular to the plane defined by the equation $x - 2y - z = -6$. Do you agree?

If you agree, explain. If you disagree, identify a vector $\vec{k}$ that *is* perpendicular to the plane, and justify your answer. Then sketch the plane and perpendicular vector on the axes at the right. Be sure to label the axes and all important points of your sketches.

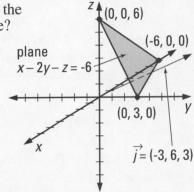

Objectives C, K, M

☐ Can represent planes in 3-space using coordinate equations.
☐ Can find scalar products of vectors in 3-space.
☐ Recognizes that Jameel's statement is correct.
☐ Gives a logical explanation. (Sample: By theorem, the plane is perpendicular to $\vec{v} = (1, -2, -1)$; $\vec{j}$ is a nonzero scalar multiple of $\vec{v}$ and, so it is parallel to $\vec{v}$ and perpendicular to the plane.)
☐ Makes a suitable sketch of the plane and of vector $\vec{j}$. (Sample: See figure.)

EVALUATION GUIDES

Teacher Notes

Objectives A, B, D, H, I, J

Concepts and Skills This activity requires students to:
- find the magnitude, direction, component representations, polar representation, and opposite of a two-dimensional vector.
- find sums, differences, and dot products of two-dimensional vectors.
- find the measure of the angle between two-dimensional vectors.
- use vectors to solve real-life problems.
- compile results to form a study guide.

Guiding Questions
- Does the order of the vectors matter when you compute a sum? a difference? a dot product?
- What types of real-life problems can be solved using vectors? [Samples: velocity, force]

Answers
a. Sample explanations are given. **i.** correct; Using a right-triangle diagram and the Pythagorean Theorem, the length of $\vec{v}$ is $\sqrt{6^2 + 8^2} = 10$. **ii.** incorrect; The angle θ between the positive x-axis and $\vec{v}$ is given by $\theta = \left(180° - \tan^{-1}\left(\frac{8}{6}\right)\right) \approx 126.9°$.

iii. incorrect; The translation from $(-1, -3)$ to $(-7, 5)$ is a translation of -6 units horizontally and 8 units vertically, so the standard position for $\vec{v}$ is drawn from the origin to the point $(-6, 8)$. **iv.** incorrect; Using the magnitude and direction calculated in **i** and **ii**, the polar representation is $\approx [10, 126.9°]$. **v.** incorrect; By theorem, the opposite of $\vec{v}$ is $(-(-6), -8) = (6, -8)$, or $\approx [10, 180° + 126.9°] = [10, 306.9°]$.

b. name: vector w; symbol: $\vec{w}$ or w; initial point: $(3, 2)$; end point: $(5, 2 + 2\sqrt{3}) \approx (5, 5.5)$; component representation: $\approx (2, 3.5)$; polar representation: $[4, 60°]$; magnitude: 4; direction: $60°$; opposite: $\approx (-2, -3.5)$, or $[4, 240°]$

c. $\vec{v} + \vec{w} \approx (-4, 11.5)$; Check students' diagrams.

d. i. $\vec{v} - \vec{w} \approx (-8, 4.5); \vec{w} - \vec{v} \approx (8, -4.5)$
ii. $\vec{v} \cdot \vec{w} \approx 16$ **iii.** The measure of the angle between $\vec{v}$ and $\vec{w}$ is $\approx 66.9°$.

e, f. Answers will vary. Check students' work.

Extension
Have students create a companion study guide called *A Tale of Two Vectors in 3-Space.*

Evaluation

Level	Standard to be achieved for performance at specified level
5	The student demonstrates an in-depth understanding of vectors in the plane. All calculations are accurate and complete. The student organizes a set of study guide pages that are crafted neatly and thoughtfully, and they may be presented imaginatively. The student may prepare one or more pages other than those required, such as pages that address parallel and perpendicular vectors.
4	The student demonstrates a clear understanding of vectors in the plane. The student utilizes appropriate methods in determining the required characteristics of the vectors, but may make minor errors in calculations. The study guide pages are well-organized and easy to read, but they may lack in some detail.
3	The student demonstrates a fundamental understanding of vectors in the plane. The student generally recognizes appropriate methods for determining the required characteristics of the vectors, but may make one or more major calculation errors, or may omit a major step of a process. The study guide pages are essentially complete, but they may be somewhat disorganized and lack focus.
2	The student demonstrates some understanding of vectors in the plane, but needs considerable assistance in responding to the given situation. Even with help, the student may make several major calculation errors, or may omit one or more major steps of a process. The student attempts to organize a set of study guide pages, but they are jumbled and incomplete.
1	The student demonstrates little if any understanding of vectors in the plane. Even with assistance, any attempts to determine the required characteristics of the given vectors are superfluous or irrelevant. Instead of writing and organizing a thoughtful set of study guide pages, the student may simply copy examples from the text.

EVALUATION GUIDES

1. Consider the function f with $f(x) = -x^2 + 144$ over the interval $[0, 12]$. Evaluate $\sum_{i=1}^{n} f(z_i)\Delta x$ for appropriate interpretations of n and z_i. Be sure to specify the meanings of n, z_i and Δx.

Objective A

☐ Is able to calculate values of Riemann sums over specified intervals.

☐ Correctly evaluates the expression for appropriate interpretations of n and z_i. (Sample: When $n = 6$ and z_i is the right endpoint of the ith subinterval, the value is 1000.)

☐ Gives correct meanings for n, z_i, and Δx.

2. Choose one property of definite integrals that you studied in Chapter 13.

  a. Describe the property in your own words.

  b. Give a formal statement of the property.

  c. Give an example to illustrate the property.

Objective C

☐ Is able to apply properties of definite integrals.

☐ Gives an accurate description of the meaning of one property.

☐ Gives a correct formal statement of the chosen property.

☐ Gives an appropriate example.

---

3. Kami said, "The graph at the right shows *without calculation* that $\int_0^6 10x\,dx > \int_0^6 x^2\,dx$."

  a. Explain why Kami's statement is true.

  b. Perform the calculations that support the statement.

  c. Find a value of n for which $\int_0^n 10x\,dx < \int_0^n x^2\,dx$ and justify your answer.

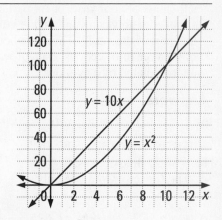

Objectives B, G

☐ Is able to express area in integral notation.

☐ Is able to evaluate definite integrals.

☐ Logically explains why Kami's statement is true. (Sample: On the interval 0 to 6, the area between the graph of $y = 10x$ and the x-axis is greater than the area between the graph of $y = x^2$ and the x-axis.)

☐ Correctly evaluates the given integrals. (180 and 72)

☐ Gives and appropriate value of n. (any integer n such that $n \geq 16$)

☐ Gives a logical explanation for the choice of n.

---

4. The equation below gives the velocity of $v(t)$ of a car in feet per second as a function of the time t in seconds, from $t = 0$ to $t = 8$. State as many facts as you can about the situation.

$$v(t) = -.875(t - 8)^2 + 56$$

Objective D

☐ Is able to find the distance traveled by a moving object, given its rate.

☐ States several significant facts, such as
  The car's initial velocity was 0 ft/s.
  At 8 seconds, the car's velocity was 56 ft/s.
  In this time period, the car accelerated.
  In this time period, the car traveled $298\frac{2}{3}$ feet.

5. Your friend was absent from class one day and now finds it hard to understand how the plane figure at the right could be related to volumes and integrals. Explain how.

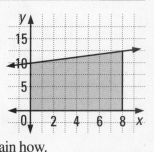

Objective I

☐ Is able to find volumes of solids.

☐ Gives a logical explanation. (Sample: Revolving the region about the x-axis generates a solid whose volume can be calculated using integrals.)

EVALUATION GUIDES

Teacher Notes

Objectives B, C, E, I

Concepts and Skills This activity requires students to:
- read information from text and graphics.
- evaluate and apply properties of definite integrals.
- use the definite integral to find volumes of solids.
- apply the definite integral to a real-life situation.
- summarize results.

Guiding Questions
- How many fluid ounces are equivalent to one gallon? How many cubic inches are occupied by one fluid ounce? [128; ≈ 1.805]
- If you don't have an equation for the silhouette of your vase, or for part of the silhouette, how can you find the volume for that part of the vase? [Think of slicing that part of the vase into sections, each of which can be approximated by a cylinder.]

Answers
a. $\int_0^8 \pi(\sqrt{x})^2\, dx = \pi\int_0^8 x\, dx = \frac{8^2}{2}\pi = 32\pi$;
   The volume is 32π cubic inches.
b. ≈ 55.71 fluid ounces.
c. The capacity would be only ≈ 13.93 fluid ounces.
d. $\int_0^8 \pi(-.5x + 2)^2\, dx = \pi\int_0^2 (.25x^2 - 2x + 4)\, dx$
   $= \pi\left[.25 \cdot \frac{2^3}{3} - 2 \cdot \frac{2^2}{2} + 4 \cdot 2\right] = \frac{14}{3}\pi$;
   The volume is $\frac{14}{3}\pi$ cubic inches.
e. $\int_0^8 \pi(.5x)^2\, dx - \int_0^2 \pi(.5x)^2\, dx =$
   $\pi\int_0^8 (.25x^2)\, dx - \pi\int_0^2 (.25x^2)\, dx =$
   $\pi\left[.25 \cdot \frac{8^3}{3}\right] - \pi\left[.25 \cdot \frac{2^3}{3}\right] = 42\pi$;
   The volume is 42π cubic inches.
f. $\frac{140}{3}\pi$ cubic inches.
g. ≈ 81.24 fluid ounces.
h. Answers will vary. Check students' work.

Extension
Give students the following theorem: If $a > 0$ and $n \neq -1$, then $\int_0^a x^n\, dx = \frac{x^{n+1}}{n+1}$. Then have them design a vase for which the silhouette, or part of the silhouette, is a quadratic or cubic equation. Have them use integrals to find the capacity of the vase.

Evaluation

Level	Standard to be achieved for performance at specified level
5	The student demonstrates an in-depth understanding of integrals and their application to the given situation. All calculations and graphs are accurate and complete. The student carefully plans the original designs, one or more of which may be quite complex. The letter is well-organized, thorough, and easy to read.
4	The student demonstrates a clear understanding of integrals and their application to the given situation. The student is able to perform appropriate calculations and draw suitable graphs, but they may contain minor errors. The original designs are well-planned, and the letter is thoughtful, but one or both may lack in some detail.
3	The student demonstrates a fundamental understanding of integrals, but may need some assistance in applying the concept to the given situation. There may be one or more major errors or omissions in the student's calculations or graphs. The student's original designs are suitable, but they may not be carefully planned. The letter is essentially complete, but may be somewhat disorganized.
2	The student demonstrates some understanding of integrals but needs considerable assistance in applying the concept to the given situation. Even with help, the student may make several major errors in performing calculations or drawing graphs, or may omit major steps of a process. The student attempts to create original designs and write a letter, but the designs are jumbled, and the letter lacks focus.
1	The student demonstrates little if any understanding of integrals and their application to the given situation. Even with assistance, any attempts to perform calculations or draw graphs are trivial or irrelevant. Instead of creating original designs, the student may simply copy the given sketches.

EVALUATION GUIDES